B.S.U.C. - LIBRARY
00212344

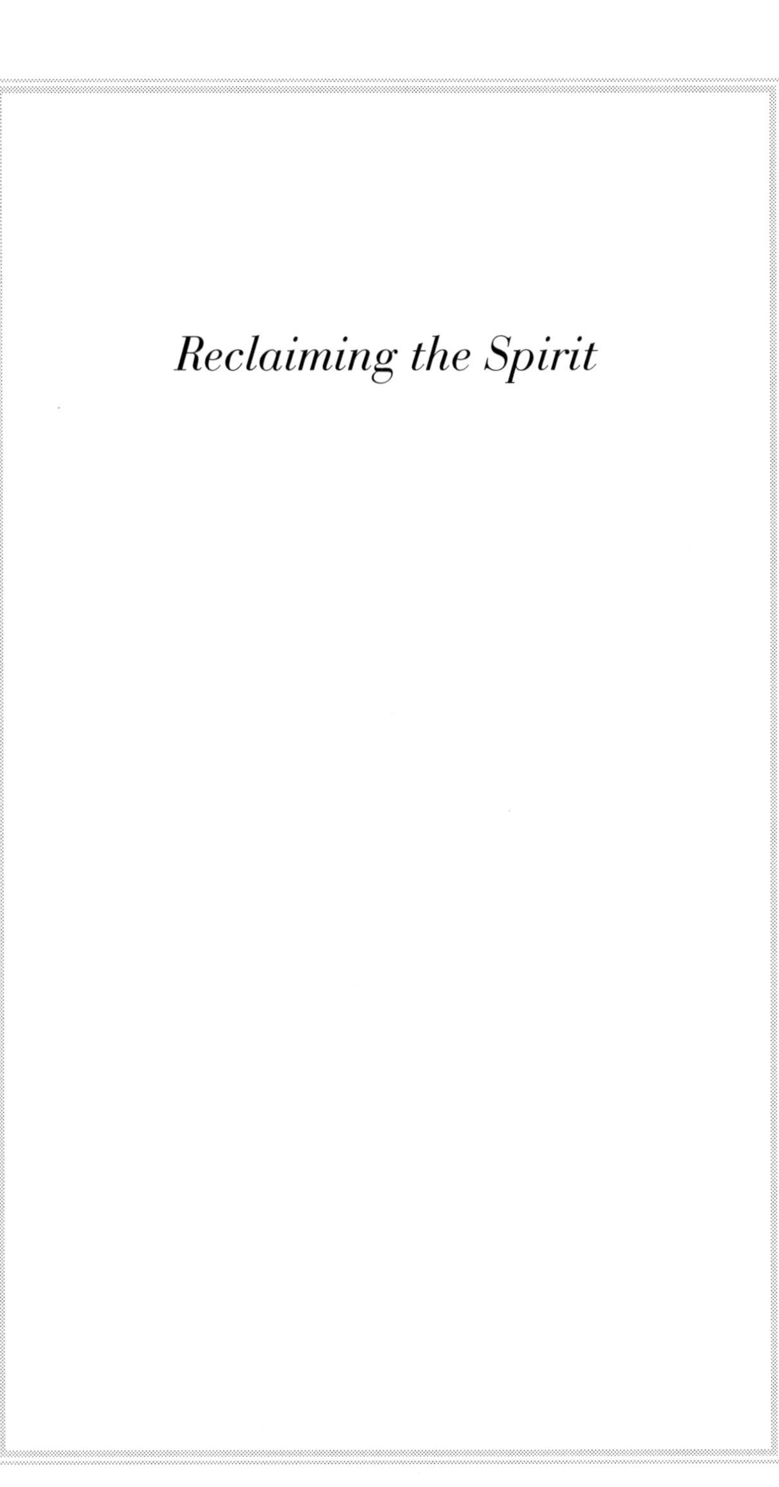

Reclaiming the Spirit

DAVID SHALLENBERGER

RECLAIMING THE SPIRIT

Gay Men and Lesbians Come to Terms with Religion

Rutgers University Press

NEW BRUNSWICK, NEW JERSEY, AND LONDON

Library of Congress Cataloging-in-Publication Data

Shallenberger, David, 1950–
Reclaiming the spirit : gay men and lesbians come to terms with religion / David Shallenberger.
p. cm.
Includes bibliographical references.
ISBN 0-8135-2488-1 (cloth : alk. paper)
1. Gays—Religious life. 2. Gays—Interviews. 3. Homosexuality—Religious aspects. I. Title.
BL65.H64S53 1998
200'.86'64—DC21 *97-24856*
CIP

British Cataloging-in-Publication data for this book is available from the British Library

Manufactured in the United States of America

This book is dedicated to those who are struggling to find their place at the table.

CONTENTS

Part Four Developing a Ministry

PREFACE AND ACKNOWLEDGMENTS

THE work leading up to this book took more than four years to complete from the original design of the study. Dozens of interviews led to many hundreds of pages of transcripts, which turned into a handful of articles and the book you are reading. Many, many people were involved, directly and close by or indirectly and at a distance.

Most central, of course, are the contributors whose stories you are about to read, as well as the more than sixty others who do not show up as explicitly in these pages. In early 1992 seventy-five gay men and lesbian women filled out a survey that asked about the highlights of their spiritual journeys; of that number, twenty-six met with me—often over two or three two-hour sessions—and graciously shared their stories in rich detail. Twelve of those are found in this book, but all of the twenty-six are reflected herein in one way or another. The twelve I chose to include here share many of the same questions, concerns, struggles, and joys as did those that I did not incorporate into the book. I am profoundly grateful to all who participated.

Before any of this work ever started, I was, of course, on my own spiritual journey. That path took a significant turn as I came to know and love my life partner, Harvey. He supported me deeply at a time when my world was crumbling under the combined weight of the loss, through AIDS, of virtually every close friend I had. My struggles continued after we met when, with a period of a few months, my father and two intimate friends, Grant and Bill, died. Harvey's generosity of spirit, patience, and love have carried me through.

Many others have played a role in the birthing of this book: friends, colleagues, people I know well, and others whom I have never even met. I thank DePaul University for underwriting some of the costs of the research; Doug Hoekstra, for being a conscious, thoughtful, and accurate transcriber; my coworkers at the School for New Learning, for offering suggestions, support, and ideas; Hal and Betsy Edwards and Brian Hastings, for acting as spiritual mentors and guides; and many gay men and lesbian women, for sharing their lives with me at retreats, in articles and books, in meetings, and on the telephone. Finally, I owe much of my inspiration to people who have never met me but who I have come to know through their writings; Madeleine L'Engle and Henri Nouwen lead the list. I am in your debt.

Reclaiming the Spirit

Introduction

IT was a very painful time. Over the previous six years or so, I had lived very intimately with AIDS—not in my body but in the lives and deaths of too many friends. The losses seemed innumerable, yet every one hurt in a particular way. Life partners, lovers, my deepest friendships, all felt taken from me. Walking through downtown Chicago, my body and heart dragging from too much death, I happened to pass the Chicago Temple (First United Methodist Church). I was drawn inside—nothing else was helping me deal with this burden—and I looked up and to the left at the stained glass and said, quite audibly: "I can't handle this anymore. I need your help."

It had been more than fifteen years since I had been in church. In my youth the First Methodist Church of Palo Alto had been a safe place to hide, even though I wasn't all that clear about what I was hiding from. All I knew was that I felt awkward in the world of my peers and here I was accepted. The feelings of separateness and loneliness in the world continued, and by the time I was in high school, I was considering entering the ministry. However, the pull of civil rights and Vietnam War protests, the inevitable confusion of adolescence, and the resurgence of other interests took me away from any sense of "call." College and marriage followed, as if I were acting out a well-integrated script of what a middle-class man's life was to be.

Then at the age of twenty-five the pattern was broken by the discovery that I was gay; I could no longer deny a swelling sense arising out of a lifetime of confusion. As I came to acknowledge my sexuality, first bit by bit and then in a flood, scattered pieces from my childhood fell quickly into place: memories of being sexually attracted to other boys, a recurring sense of not fitting in, boredom and anxiety around expectations about "the opposite sex." I burst through the closet door—a closet I hadn't even known existed a few months before—and became rapidly involved with everything gay: coming out in the graduate school newspaper I coedited, speaking in public settings about what it meant to be gay, joining a gay men's support group, and doing research on antigay discrimination in the workplace.

Divorce followed, and this new self-awareness only confirmed my need to remain distant from the church of my childhood, actually from any church. Institutional religion spoke, after all, with the loudest voice against the person I was finding myself to be. Coming to acknowledge my sexual orientation did not obliterate my spiritual appetite, however—if anything, it strengthened my need to find answers to the kinds of ambiguous questions that have brought women and men to faith of one sort or another for millennia. I turned to meditation and Buddhism, as did many others who found themselves alienated from or angered by their traditions. This path allowed me to meet others who would accept me as a gay person and gave me a way to connect deeply with an inner wisdom and tranquillity.

So it was rather strange to find myself in a Methodist church that day, some fifteen years after I had come out and left that institution. And yet there was something familiar and comfortable in the awesomeness I felt. That desperate prayer was the beginning of a reclaiming experience that has substantially changed my sense of who I am. In the months and years that followed, I entered into a primary relationship that was significantly grounded in a mutual valuing of our faith journeys, began spiritual direction, and—together with my partner—went "church shopping" for a congregation that would nurture us and our covenant. I enrolled in (and subsequently completed) a two-year ecumenical training program of spiritual companionship to learn how to help others move through their spiritual passages, went on retreats to intensify and focus my spiritual work, and transformed my earlier regimen of meditation into one that emphasized a more contemplative form of prayer.

The stories shared in this book are an outgrowth of this reclaiming experience and the personal reflection it spawned. A social scientist by vocation and a researcher at heart, I wondered if others had experienced similar moments in their lives. I had done substantial work on how gay men and lesbian women made sense of key aspects of their lives as part of my scholarship interests in graduate school and in my career as a professor at DePaul University, yet I had not directly explored spirituality. I felt compelled to move in this direction by the intriguing thought (to me) that some people (myself included) define themselves *primarily* in spiritual terms, a seeming contradiction in a society that finds homosexuality inherently incompatible with religious teaching. I decided that not only could this research help develop the scholarly understanding of what it meant to be gay at the end of the twentieth century, but that it could also inform and enrich my own journey.

The men and women I interviewed for this book grew up, as did I, during a time of powerful change. When they were young children, there were no positive role models, no gay rights movement, and no affirming messages about growing up to be gay or lesbian. However, lesbian and gay identity began to come into its own following the Stonewall riots of 1969. Now, in this highly politicized historical moment, it goes without saying that homosexuality is controversial, especially within the context of spiritual and religious dialogue. At about the same time as the interviews that formed the basis for the book were conducted, the Gallup organization released a poll in which 57 percent of the population sampled responded that homosexuality "should not be considered an acceptable alternative lifestyle." In many of our more conservative churches, synagogues, and mosques, homosexuality has long been seen as an "abomination" that keeps a person from spiritual fulfillment and blinds him or her to the discernment of God's desires. Homosexuality has been blamed from the pulpit for many of the evils of our society, from AIDS to the degradation of family values. Yet at the same time—over the last twenty years or so—a few of these institutions have broken with the homophobic trend and stated publicly that homosexual persons are welcome as full and participating members. Biblical scholarship that presents a more gay-affirming view has developed over the same time period, offering sophisticated interpretations of scripture that incorporate historical, linguistic, and theological insights not available earlier. Simultaneously, the gay and lesbian communities have matured, demanding understanding and acceptance and undoubtedly contributing to, if not effecting, many of these changes.

Those whose stories you are about to read were well socialized as children into a homophobic view of their lives—and have also seen these more liberating perspectives emerge. Virtually all of them were raised in families that could name some sort of religious affiliation—if only nominally so in some cases. Even though negative messages about homosexuality may not have always been explicit, these persons knew that being gay was "wrong." More often than not, they felt both hatred and self-doubt even before they were courageous enough to ask core questions about their sexual identities.

As the years passed and they matured and came out, a sense of other possible interpretations for their lives grew. At some point they began to reject the values and norms they had been given and to forge a sense of meaning and purpose that was more positive and affirming. One significant arena for this reformulating was religion, the source and buttress of much of their earlier foundational beliefs. The rejection of the stereotypes was not easy—for most people, it was, and may continue to be, a difficult struggle.

A path often characterized by deep and sometimes painful questioning, the building of new relationships, and the reclaiming of a spiritual self followed: I say *re*claiming because these individuals chose to assert their right to a self-as-spiritual that was being denied them by much of the traditional religious establishment only because many were gay or lesbian. As apparently heterosexual children, they had found welcome and refuge in the church. But now they rejected the homophobic thinking of the institutions, saying, in effect, "I have a right to my spirit." In this time of redefining and reclaiming, some of them chose to return to childhood traditions, empowered by this sense of rightfulness; others moved away, choosing another path that embraced them and their experience.

The purpose of this book is to allow a few of those stories to be heard and to reflect on what they have to tell us about how gay men and lesbian women address the significant spiritual questions of their lives. Here we can read the very intimate contemplations of people who are working to interpret their experience in a way that explicitly considers faith, spirit, and the divine at the same time that the larger culture in which they live questions their right and ability to claim that approach. Their honesty and deep reflection are powerful mirrors for us as we ponder our own lives.

The chapters that form the core of this book are in the words of a dozen of the twenty-six individuals I came to know through many hours of interviews and pages of reflection (more detailed information about the methodology can be found in the Appendix). Each story is unique and adds an important new perspective. The lives shared here richly illustrate the key directions within the spiritual journeys that gay men and lesbian women may take. Not every story is told, but each of the twenty-six lives is reflected in some way in this book; I hope many more will see themselves in some of these pages and understand better their own spiritual journey.

Making Meaning

At the heart of this work is the spiritual meaning that these dozen gay men and lesbian women make of the ebbs and flows of their lives. A primary goal here is to give full voice to people who have been silenced and made invisible. Here we can find a depth of reflection that can only enrich our understanding of human experience. That the interviews are in the participants' own words is important, for their language can best honor and reflect how they see their lives. The actual interview transcripts have been edited to allow their most significant messages to stand out, free of the stops and starts that naturally occur as people reflect on the substantial and complex issues of their lives.

The balance of this chapter is a summary of the major steps contained within these life stories: deep and challenging questioning, discovery and creation of community; exploration of wholly new directions and alternatives, and claiming of a ministry within one's tradition. These steps are presented as an opening framework for the reader to aid in her or his own meaning-making. Before we proceed to a discussion of the milestones revealed in these lives, however, some introductory comments about coming out are in order, for every individual I spoke with identified this process as central to their spiritual identity.

Coming Out

Self-identifying as gay, lesbian, or bisexual does not come easily within our society. Seemingly all of us, in this culture at least, have been born into a world that is very judgmental regarding homosexuality. Homophobic messages can be virulent and hateful, or they can be subtle, but they are still there, and most gay and lesbian people can cite numerous examples. In the 1950s and 1960s—the decades during which many of the participants in this study grew up—the devaluing of homosexuality was often expressed through silence. As the gay and lesbian communities have matured, and as gay and lesbian activists have become more vocal, the volume of the discussion has been turned up. Political debates, church sermons, and broadcast talk shows have tackled the topic head-on. Through and from all of this, from silence to shouting, gay and lesbian people—and youths who are coming to their sexual identity—are learning that it is not always safe to be gay or lesbian.

Coming out is, in effect, defined by the stigma created by the homophobia in society. That stigma, however, plays itself out differently in individual lives. For women or people of color, a layer of prejudice coming from at least one other aspect of their identity will shape the experience powerfully. Those living in different parts of the country with distinct norms and attitudes regarding homosexuality will face the issue in different ways; many rural gay and lesbian people migrate to the city in the hope that they will find an affirming community that they cannot find at home. Religious and cultural socialization will partially drive the direction and choices a person takes. And, of course, individual personality characteristics and family dynamics will play an important role.

Nevertheless, there seem to be some clear similarities in the overall process of gay/lesbian identity formation and in the theories that describe that process. Most authors put forward developmental models, many of which are included in the Bibliography. These theorists assume that identity takes a fairly predictable, but not totally fixed, course. Significant markers in this journey are

- A deep and often difficult self-questioning
- Growing self-acceptance as gay in the face of one's own internalized homophobia
- Disclosure, gradual or not, to significant friends and family
- Movement into the gay/lesbian community, including the development of important relationships with others and the adoption of the frames of reference and values of that culture (or a part of it)
- Integration of one's gay/lesbian identity into a larger sense of self

Through coming out, a gay or lesbian individual comes to replace society's (and the family's) norms—including spiritual beliefs—with a value system that is congruent with her or his evolving self-image. At the beginning a person generally adopts the more visible norms of the lesbian and gay communities as a substitute for those rejected. In the process of developing a firmer sense of self, she or he moves toward a more balanced self-definition. Not fully reached by everyone, the culmination of this stage is a self-identity in which being lesbian or gay is an important but not uniquely significant aspect of a larger sense of self: "I am David—who is gay—and a teacher, Harvey's life partner, and one for whom spirituality is central. I am at home with my gayness, and I know it is just part of who I am."

Coming out is never complete. Given the homophobic socialization so present in our society, self-acceptance takes time to develop and mature. Just as an individual begins to feel comfortable with his or her sexual orientation, something may challenge that acceptance. Looking for a job or moving into a new community, for example, may tempt a previously open man or woman back into the closet. Every time he or she meets someone new, the decision has to be faced: do I tell them? The opposite can be true as well. Taking a job in an organization that is notably gay affirming, moving to a gay-friendly city, or entering into a relationship with someone who is relatively more out may quickly propel a person in the direction of greater openness. All in all, there seems to be a human desire, innate or socialized, for greater openness, intimacy, and congruence in life, and so coming out is like a spiral with an overall forward direction. It is perhaps not as linear as the models presented in the literature suggest, but we can build on these models in helpful ways.

Given the diversity of the gay and lesbian communities, coming out is frequently the one experience that links all who claim this sexual orientation; in fact, for many it is the pivotal or defining homosexual experience. It is easy to see that coming out has spiritual dimensions when it is a process not only of accepting the self, but also of establishing relationships to whatever is beyond the self: personal relationships, the larger society, God. For many, institutionalized religion has defined precisely what it is that is beyond the self, yet this clerical arbiter is frequently hostile and homophobic, and so members of the gay and lesbian communities are typically estranged from the most visible religious institutions and forced to create their own spiritual visions or, alternatively, to reject this dimension entirely. We come back, then, to our initial question: how does someone who is defining her or his self within this excluding context handle the tensions between these religious communities and the self she or he is constructing? This is the framework within which I present the narratives included in the following chapters.

The Evolution of Self and Spirit

In the following discussion I put before you three stages of spiritual experience centered on the events of coming out—a sort of before, during, and after model. It is difficult, if not impossible, to understand the present and future without a sense of the past that led us here. To that end, I asked the people whose stories you will read to tell me about their families and their lives before they realized they were gay, whatever they felt related to their sense of an evolving spirituality. We then went on to explore the connections they saw in the flow from one transitional moment to the next, leading us to the present and speculations about where they see themselves going.

Before Coming Out. The men and women you are about to meet come from a range of family backgrounds. As children, they grew up in the Northeast, Midwest, South, or West Coast of this country, as well as in Asia, the Caribbean, Europe, or Australia. Their home communities were urban, suburban, or rural. Some lived in the same town throughout their growing-up years, whereas others moved around a great deal, within the local region, across the country, or even from one country to another. Family constellations were typically fairly traditional, though a few experienced the divorce of their parents and lived in single-parent households during at least part of their childhood. Some were only children, others had one or two siblings, and one came from a family of seven brothers and sisters.

Childhood religious traditions were varied as well, both in their denominations (Catholic, Protestant, and Jewish) and in the intensity of the families' identification and orthodoxy. All, however, expressed some sort of religious identification, even if their families rarely, if ever, attended services. Those who grew up in homes with the most tenuous religious connections expressed sentiments such as Harry's: growing up in the rural Midwest, he said his family saw religion and God as "life insurance," protection just in case what the churches were saying was right. Another, Dan, liked to go to church to sing, but his family did not particularly encourage him.

Others experienced a stronger connection to a religious institution. Their families typically attended services, the children went to Sunday school, there was some discussion of religious values, and there was a clear sense of identity as a Christian or Jew of a particular denomination. Approximately one-third grew up in families that were deeply committed to a particular faith. Two women, Mary and Ann, were the daughters of missionaries and lived for a time outside of the country in religious communities. One man, Rafael, was the son of a Methodist minister: typical of this group, he shares: "I was raised in the kind of household where the gospel was not only heard but lived out. . . . For me, attending church on Sunday mornings was as natural as breathing or eating." Still others lived in nonclerical, yet deeply religious families for which their faith was the center of their lives.

A recurring theme among these women and men was the sense of a particular religious institution as a sort of "refuge" from the pressures of the world. Feeling "different" among their peers, they could find comfort in these places and escape from the isolation of a childhood that compelled them to be other than they wanted to be. It was a haven where the harsh rules of life—how to be an "appropriate" boy or girl—and the costs for not following those rules did not apply. Harry, the man whose parents believed in God as life insurance, found church for a time to be a place "free of masculine pressure." Vincent, who defined his parents as "rigorously Catholic," has always had a close sense of God in his life, and at a young age he left home to go to a seminary and become a priest; in his life before the seminary, he had felt alone and sad, feelings that turned around when he found himself now in a more supportive environment. And John, whose best friend was the son of a Congregational minister, saw church as a place to escape from the discomfort of a dysfunctional family.

Eventually, virtually every one of the participants pulled away—slightly or significantly, for a moment or forever—from the churches and synagogues of their childhood. For some, this development was seemingly unconnected with their growing sense of themselves as gay or lesbian; instead, it came from an emerging discomfort with institutions they increasingly saw as hypocritical, irrelevant, or otherwise flawed. Sandra, for example, felt that she could not participate in a church that placed her father in a leadership position at the same time that he was abusing her at home. Others were angered at priests who did not seem to be faithful to their vows or institutions that seemed to be more concerned with money than souls.

As we will explore in the pages that follow, there were many who remained connected to their churches and synagogues until their awakening sense of themselves as gay/lesbian conflicted with institutional teachings. Even those who left because of reasons not directly related to being gay typically moved themselves even further away when they came out.

Coming Out as a Spiritual Turning Point. It should not be surprising that we would see a radical transformation in our sense of self (that is, coming out) as a moment of spiritual import. A lesbian spiritual counselor said it eloquently: "I think the first level of coming out to yourself is that level of facing the truth of who I am before myself and before God. And then I think the next piece would be, Now what? If I really live this, if I really live out of my own inner truth, what price will I have to pay?"

All of the people in this book identified coming out as one of their transitional moments. They often spoke of this step as a deepening and acceptance of their identities, a movement toward fuller integrity. Two comments from individuals whose full stories are not included in the following chapters add to our understanding and express this sense more clearly. John, thirty-nine, makes the following remark, couched in religious metaphors: "It's a step toward greater self-integrity to say, 'This is what I am, and I accept that and embrace that.' In some ways—this has been a later realization—I can almost see it as connected with the experiences the disciples might have had by becoming disciples of Christ: that to follow a path that you believe has most integrity for yourself sometimes puts you very much at odds with the prevailing society." George, a Unitarian Universalist minister who was raised as a Baptist, compares coming out to being born again: "When I was born again, it was a real experience. And the second time I was born again is when I came out at thirty-two, and it was a very similar experience. Except it was even more intense."

These are times of both struggle and joy, though the balance between these emotions is an individual one. For some, it is acutely painful; for others, it is profoundly ecstatic. Mark expresses a very positive recollection of reading a book shortly after he came out: "At that time it just hit about being gay—that it's very powerful and good and honest and real. . . . And I remember just sitting in my room like nothing else mattered in the world. . . . This was it; this was the true essence of what it was about. . . . Few experiences in my life will match that moment. . . . Everything I viewed was totally changed."

For others, the experience of coming to accept themselves as gay or lesbian was very difficult. In the case of these individuals, the internal struggle was particularly painful when compounded by an intense religious commitment. Rafael, the son of a Methodist minister, talks about his feelings during this time: "I remember sitting on [my sister's] porch feeling very, very guilty, feeling dissatisfied. Why can't I put this together? There was a lot of self-bashing in that coming-out process." And Gerald, whose religious background was both Methodist and fundamentalist, reflects on his feelings after his first homosexual experience: "I realized, somewhere down inside me, 'This is what I am; this is what I want.' And that began the struggle. All my Christian upbringing told me that because of what I'd just done, I was going to burn in hell forever. If I stayed this way, it was nothing but death for me." Later, after his wife divorced him, "I'd go around the townhouse yelling at God, saying: 'You were supposed to heal me of this. You were supposed to deliver me of this. I'm not supposed to be gay . . . so either you don't care, or you don't exist.'" All of these individuals have moved beyond this place, evidence that growth toward integration is possible.

After Coming Out: The Journey Toward Integration

Virtually all of the people who participated in this study reported going through a transition from an earlier inherited (and virtually never gay-affirming) religious tradition to a self-forged, responsible spirituality that incorporates their sexuality in a more positive light. In a sense, many gay men and lesbian women are forced to make this move by the judgments of the religious institutions that were a part of their lives. Mary describes this dilemma well: "The way I grew up [within a conservative Christian household] . . . left me no place to be as a lesbian. . . . How do you sustain a belief in something that says you're not? . . . It's kind of strange."

Finding themselves at odds with the childhood religions they may have been associated with at younger ages, they had no choice but to look elsewhere for a belief system that made sense to them. It was clear to many that they could not merely adopt the tradition that had been handed down to them, for in most cases it rejected a core aspect of who they were: their homosexuality and, for women, their gender, as we'll see in several of the stories.

There are many ways this journey of reclaiming and integrating can play itself out. Some pulled away from religion in any form and never adopted a stance they would define as spiritual, feeling so hurt by institutionalized religion; since they would have rated spirituality as an unimportant element in their lives, those who had chosen this path were not part of this study. Others identified new spiritual directions far outside of the belief systems they had been taught as children; these directions met their needs either temporarily or permanently. Some returned to the tradition of their childhood, perhaps after some time away.

Given the variety of trajectories these journeys took, identification of meaningful commonalities may seem an impossible task. Yet there were a handful of identifiable stages that a significant number, if not all, described: periods of distancing from long-held assumptions and of deep and reflective questioning, finding of spiritual communities in which they could feel fulfilled and "at home," exploration of nonmainstream alternatives to traditional religious expression, return to childhood traditions in a new way, and, possibly, defining of a ministry and sense of purpose. Not all of these individuals experienced all of these events; indeed, each journey was unique and is still in progress. Many experienced all of these stages in a repeated, circular, and ever-deepening fashion: thrust into questioning soon after they came out, they found a community—spiritual or otherwise—that met their needs at that point; later, after maturing in their sense of who they were as gay or lesbian, they reentered another period of questioning and again searching for community, but in a different place than before. These stages were neither finite nor fixed, yet they were representative of significant passages for many. My hope here is to share both the similarities and the individuality of the twelve journeys included in these pages.

Furthermore, I trust that readers will find in these stories ideas, experiences, and insights that will deepen their own spiritual journeys—whether or not they are gay or lesbian. Not only do the words shared here have value in their description of these individual lives; they also can be seen metaphorically as reflections of a broader human experience, one that embraces all of us.

PART ONE

DEEP QUESTIONING

FOR the individuals whose lives are documented in these pages, often the first step in forging a congruent spirituality was to reject the assumptions and affiliations, perhaps unquestioned, that they had lived with for many years. They therefore concretely and philosophically distanced themselves from the religious identification and creeds of their families. As described in the Introduction, these actions were sometimes a result of early discomfiture and disagreement or sometimes a response to the discovery that their familial religious traditions did not accept them fully as gay *and* Christian (or Jewish, or whatever the tradition was). What the men and women in this study described here was frequently an active distinguishing between the religion they had inherited and a broader, more inclusive understanding of spirituality: "Being ousted from my religious tradition doesn't mean I can't have a spiritual life." Mary, whom you will meet in the next section (Finding Community), describes her movement away from the God of her childhood as she came to reject her parent's patriarchal notion of women and the church:

> The farther I went with women's issues, the farther I went to the edge of the church. . . . I went through my "dark night of the soul," a kind of death-of-God experience. I can remember being in tears with one of my good friends on the phone, saying: "I don't know if I'm going to believe in God when this is over. Will you still love me?" . . . It was pretty clear to me that there was going to be no place for me in the world I knew if I ended up not believing in God. . . . I was on the outside of the church and God; I had gone from a paternal male God, a largely judging kind of Old Testament character, to paying more attention to the Jesus of the Gospels, . . . to something that was a more ethereal, disembodied, positive, joyful, creative spirit.

Others also spoke of similar movement made in the creation of a spirituality that was consistent with what they now knew of themselves. Ann, a thirty-three-year-old woman whose story is part of the section on defining ministry, was raised, like Mary, in a conservative religious household. In recent years she has come to see the world and God as bigger than they had been portrayed in her home. Now, many years after this process began, she is still estranged from her father.

Whatever places their spiritual journey took them, the people who participated in this research found themselves at a point at which they could no longer accept the beliefs that had been given to them, and they took a proactive role in discovering and defining a spirituality that fit. What is particularly impressive is the intention with which they took on this responsibility—they did not just drop spirituality out of their lives forever; they wrestled with it and in the struggle appropriated a spirituality that worked for them. All of the people interviewed considered this struggle to be a meaningful—if often painful—one that enriched their spiritual growth. They spoke of opening themselves to new experiences and understandings and of not being able to take the status quo for granted. In the end they felt stronger and more in touch with their own spirituality and sexuality. Three individuals, Rafael, Dan, and Denise, will highlight different aspects of this process of deep questioning. They are at very different parts of their journeys, yet all are asking themselves powerful questions. Indeed, their stories demonstrate how the questioning doesn't end, once and for all, shortly after a person comes out. What they show is that deep introspection can happen at any point.

Rafael's journey begins this part of the book. Now thirty-seven, he was born in Cuba and moved to this country with his family when he was five. His father is a now-retired Methodist minister, and Rafael's early upbringing was strongly religious. Coming out after graduating from college, he struggled for several years with his understanding of the Bible and with reconciling that understanding with who he was as a gay man. It is only in the last six years, through counseling and spiritual direction, that he has come to accept himself. Now he is finishing seminary and working with people who are HIV positive. He is out to his family, and his relationship with his father is consequently strained. He has come to an understanding that he and his minister father can have different beliefs about homosexuality: "I'm okay with him being where he is, and I have been able to make a kind of separation of 'This is who my father is, this is who I am, and this is who God is.' . . . I say, 'No, . . . you do make mistakes, and I disagree with you.'"

Dan, who is thirty-seven, lives in Chicago and has AIDS. He was born in the East, and his family moved to downstate Illinois right after he finished seventh grade. Talking about his childhood, he says, "We were not much of churchgoing people. About the only time I remember going to church when I was little was on holidays, like Easter and Christmas." Singing became a major draw to church for Dan, and later on in his life when he quit singing, he quit going to church. But his spirituality still remained: "I've always said my prayers before I go to bed at night. I still go to church during major holidays." After he was diagnosed HIV positive, he says, "HIV doubled my spirituality. . . . I say prayers more often and talk things out [with God] more often since I found out about my health situation than what I used to, in my prayers. . . . I feel guilty sometimes for asking God for strength to have faith in Him. Sometimes I don't get it." He is full of questions: "If there's a caring and loving God, why does He make us suffer this way? Like I said, the only thing that keeps me in line is that there is a God, that all these questions will be answered whenever I meet Him."

Denise is twenty-five. She grew up in the South and has only recently moved to Chicago. Raised in the Methodist church, which she characterizes as a "fashion show," Denise acknowledges her mother as the stronger of her two parents in terms of religious leadership. For a short time in her youth, Denise "was on fire for the Lord" after a powerful "born-again" experience, but soon she went away from home to a performing arts high school, and her spiritual life fell away from her. In her early twenties she started going to a Science of Mind church and found that somewhat satisfying but has lately returned to the United Methodist church. When first interviewed, she said she wasn't sure what she believed in and characterized herself as a "fair-weather Christian." She has only recently begun to take a clearer stand about her belief in God. She has had relationships with men and women and has just moved in with her lover, Kathy.

Rafael: Loving and Living in the Questions

Rafael lives in the Midwest and works in an interfaith agency doing ministry with HIV-affected persons. He spent much of his childhood in the church. At eleven he entered into an incestuous relationship with an older male cousin, which was all the more powerful in its frightening repercussions because of the secrecy it entailed—and the message he internalized from that secrecy. It was not until he had graduated from college that he came out.

He has come a long way since those days, and the nature of his questioning is quite different from either Denise's or Dan's. After years of therapy, spiritual direction, and seminar study, Rafael has come to value the ambiguity that arises from asking the most difficult questions. Most profound in his testimony here is his honest reflection on the move from a childhood faith in a religious household to a faith that allows a flow between clarity and deep questioning. What Rafael has to say about how he grew up helps us to appreciate the foundational understanding and experience of a man strongly grounded in his religious tradition.

I was raised in the kind of household where the gospel was not only heard, but lived out; where my parents truly attempted to integrate their beliefs. What it means, for them, to be charitable and Christlike was interwoven into our familial experience. I don't really know how to say it more fully, as it's all compressed in my thinking. Family devotions were a pretty regular thing during my earlier years. It became more optional for me at about junior high school and high school. But I vividly remember family vacations when we would stop to spend the night at a motel and getting up in the morning and either immediately before breakfast or just after breakfast having a family devotion, usually a reading from "The Upper Room"—a little quarterly devotional—and a Bible reading and some prayer. And the funny thing about it is that other Latino clergy families that we knew were also doing the same thing; I remember staying at their houses, and they'd have devotions in much the same way as we did.

A lot of people have very negative and reactionary sorts of responses to their church experience. Mine is just kind of ordinary. For me, attending church on Sunday mornings was as natural as breathing or eating—if it wasn't spoken, it was expected of us. Yet it wasn't just the expectation that kept me there—being always present and visible in the church was something that I enjoyed. I enjoyed singing in the choir; I enjoyed running the projector on Sunday nights if we had a film or running the sound system. I always have been good with electrical equipment, projectors, and that kind of stuff. If I were to look back at why I was involved, it is my own enjoyment of it. And perhaps some recognition that here was Rafael taking care of something that needed to be done and doing it well and people relied on me to do that, to do it well.

Rafael and his family moved to the United States when he was five. Right from the beginning he knew he was "special." The following stories reflect some of that feeling, in his place and role within the family and in how his sisters and parents treated him at key points in his early life, such as when they were about to leave Cuba or when Rafael was sick.

I was the long-awaited child. I was like the little darling. I've often described my family and growing up experience as not having just one mother, but having four mothers. I have three older sisters, the youngest of whom is eight years older than I am. And then they are two years apart. Even the youngest sister was old enough to babysit at eight years old and even changed my diapers and stuff, so I had a lot of feminine and female presence in my household. In addition to that, though, when we lived in Cuba my parents founded a student home for Christian students throughout Cuba who wanted to study at the University of Havana and wanted to live in a Christian environment. So this home, which housed roughly twenty-three or twenty-five students, became an extended family for me.

On top of all of this, I was born on the National Holiday, which in Cuba is the birthday of José Martí. Martí, who was a philosopher and poet and who wrote the popular lyrics to "Guantanamera," led the Cuban people against the Spanish, freeing Cuba from being a Spanish colony. So on his day, there was a lot of celebration. I was one of just a few kids that were born on that day, and my family received toys and a bassinet and sheets and clothing and everything they would need to have a kid, from the government. I was special right from the beginning. It was just really strange.

The process of leaving Cuba was one in which I played a big part. To some extent the reason we left was, in essence, to protect our family. Part of the indoctrination and the propaganda process by which Castro took over was that he took over the television and radio stations and also the telephone company. If you were to pick up the phone and wanted to make a call, you wouldn't hear a dial tone. What you would hear would be a thirty-second announcement, a pitch about the revolution. So I was picking up all of those slogans and the jargon about the revolution. We left partly because of how the revolution was affecting our family already and the fear that it could be bloody.

Once we were here in the States, I became very sick. In the hospital I remember people giving me synthetic pillowcases because, I found out then, I was allergic to down pillows and animal products. I think my parents spiritualized that experience: "God has reached down and saved your life. Here was a completely hopeless, no-way-to-go-on thing, and God was doing something special to you, Rafael." I sensed that there was something very special about me because that's what I had been taught. I think that was internalized at a very early age.

As the child of a pastor growing up in a religious family, Rafael encountered the shadow of judgment early on as he was becoming sexual.

From time to time my father would ask me, "How is your walk with the Lord?" I guess he probably asked me seven to ten times in my entire life. I experienced the question as intrusive—probably because I sensed there was something wrong in the secret of my sexual experiences with my cousin—and yet I didn't want to confess those or talk about them with my father. This would have been the opportunity for me to do that, to say, "This is going on, and it is really upsetting me." But I felt like I needed to keep it a secret. I think part of the impact of that early sexual experience was that it was just very out of the ordinary, different from any experience that I had had with any person, male or female. It was primarily that and the fact that it was happening when my parents weren't around. So the implied message was, "This can't happen when they're around. This can only happen in secrecy. This was our secret." In general, we really didn't talk that much about sex in my house. The one chat that my father and I had, he gave me a book, that sort of thing. I don't know if I had received any explicit teaching about homosexuality.

Rafael did not come out until much later, after college. For some time he struggled with his newfound awareness, which was in direct conflict with what he had been taught, directly or obliquely, as a child.

Up until my senior year in college, I dated women. I had fantasies about men, but other than my experience with my cousin, I can't really think of other experiences. There were other kinds of male bonding that I was doing with other guys, but they weren't sexual. It was the summer after I graduated college, when I visited my sister in Connecticut, who was breaking up from a lover relationship with another woman, when I really began to come out. I had been out to Provincetown the previous winter, during my senior year, because my sister had suggested this wonderful bed-and-breakfast place, and I had taken a bunch of college friends with me. I didn't really know Provincetown as being a gay place at that time; well, at some level, perhaps, I knew that it was, but I hadn't had any experiences, enough to piece it all together.

During the two weeks I spent in Provincetown, I began to have conversations with other gay men about their sexual orientation and my sexual orientation. It was more of an exploratory time, for me to ask questions. What was it like for them? I think that that was the watershed experience. In a sense there was an internal switch that went on that said, "This is who I am." Ever since that time I have self-identified that way—as a gay person.

And there has been, and continues to be, a process. For several years I struggled with conflicts between my sense of myself as gay and what I thought the Bible said. After college I moved to Virginia and was close enough to Washington, D.C., that I would go into the city and not get back to my sister's until four or six o'clock in the morning. And I remember sitting on her porch feeling very, very guilty, feeling dissatisfied. Why can't I put this together? There was a lot of self-bashing in that coming-out process.

I really think that any kind of resolving has only occurred in the last six years. Before that time I continued to operate under an old, polarized model. What I realized later was that the kind of theology that informed my sense of who I was, from my upbringing, was one that caused me to be very polarized into a good little boy who observes the rules and does everything by the books and pleases the parents and a dirty, nasty boy who likes to have sex in dangerous places, and the twain of those could not meet. Perhaps those two are rather extreme examples, but in reality they are two very real and polarized places.

The relationship that I was in for those eight years was with a person who in many ways reminded me of my father. And in many ways he set up for himself a very kind of polarized experience, and that's one of the reasons why I needed to move from that, because I felt like that wasn't where I was. He's still very AIDS-phobic and very homophobic, and successful as he might be in his business, he's still very disconnected from community, especially any kind of identity with the gay community.

The reconciliation of Rafael's sexuality and spirituality has come only in the last several years, as a result of inner work.

After those eight or nine years I reached a point where I said, "Now it's time to work on this." I entered into spiritual direction and therapy because of several things, some of which had to do with the relationship that I was ending and some of which had to do with a sense of my seeking further integration of myself. And I've been moving towards more of an integrated and centered place, where I see that those two polarized selves are both true. Part of this movement is self-protecting because I realized that my own sexuality was not something that was bad; it was something that was wonderful and creative and beautiful. How that expressed itself in some unhealthy ways was what concerned me. I felt as if I was setting up this kind of very polar existence, that in fact I would be swinging back and forth between these two extremes and would find myself in life-threatening sorts of situations and putting myself at risk—especially around HIV. So I decided I needed to do something about that. And that really has changed a lot in my life.

It was about that same time that I started seminary, which also allowed me to look at the whole theological system and come up with my own beliefs and my own answers to the question "Where do I fit?" Engaging that academic, historical research has been a point of liberation for myself. Last December I made a commitment to finish my master's in theological studies. And at that time I had a thesis topic in mind: the uses of New Testament paradigms on homosexuality and pastoral psychotherapy. It was, of course, too large a topic, and so, working with my colloquy and my adviser, it was narrowed down to much more of a hermeneutical task: a New Testament study, specifically in this case, of Romans 1:26–27 ["For this reason, God gave them up to degrading passions. Their women exchanged natural intercourse for unnatural, and in the same way also the men, giving up natural intercourse with women, were consumed with passion for one another. Men committed shameless acts with men and received in their own persons the due penalty for their error"], which I find to be the most challenging of the New Testament texts to gay liberation and most challenging to those of us in the gay community who want to turn the tide of oppression. People from the other camp who are scripturally against homosexuality can say, "Well, this is clear that this is a man with a man." Some people go so far as to say that this text is also about a woman with a woman, where lesbianism supposedly is mentioned, which I disagree with. I don't think lesbianism is involved. For me, doing this research has fairly well satisfied my questions about what that text is about.

The seminary I attended is United Methodist, even though I'm now in the Episcopal church. The seminary connection began before I became an

Episcopalian. I made the switch from Methodist to Episcopalian for several reasons. I think, behind it all, was a step away from the mold that I had created for myself or that had been created for me by my family. There was an assumption I would be in the Methodist church because my father was a Methodist minister. And in this way I was able to make some changes, to differentiate myself from my family.

Also, I had been working in a Methodist church and attending there. I had the sense that I couldn't work and worship in the same space because I would come into church on Sunday mornings and I would always be asked, "Did you pay this bill? Did you receive this money? Have you done this? Have you done that?" There was never a sense of this was just a worship experience. It was a work experience on Sunday mornings. I didn't like that.

At the same time, I was looking for a denomination that I felt at least was dealing aboveboard with its issues around sexual orientation and ordination within the denomination. And I felt at that time that the Episcopal church was much further along than the Methodist church. And there's some truth to that. Not always—you can always find churches that are very individual parishes that are further advanced than others and others that are in the dark ages, just like you would in any other denomination. In any case, the stance of the Methodist church was important enough to get me to switch.

There was yet one other memory that contributed to this move. I remember gathering at the chapel in an Episcopal school with about fifteen other students from that community to celebrate and to be with the priest, of course, at their Eucharist. I had a very romanticized notion of the sacraments, and it spoke to me. And the sacraments continue to speak to me very strongly. There's something very special or different about how we practice the Eucharist in the Episcopal church, a whole reverence for it that's different than the Methodist church. That's my experience, and that's why, I think, I ultimately ended up in the Episcopal church.

Rafael's process of coming out has included his family, though until recently he had not disclosed fully to his father. In the last few months, how-

ever—as a result of the work he has been doing in seminary and therapy—he made a significant step.

I first came out to my family twelve or thirteen years ago. It was shortly after Steven and I got together that I had spent the night at his apartment; at this point I was living in Florida, for two to three years. My roommate stopped me as I was dropping off my laundry because I had done my laundry at Steven's apartment. And he said, "Rafael, we have to talk." And I said, "Not now, Marlon, I'm on my way to work." "No, Rafael, we have to talk right now." And again I insisted not, and he followed me out the door and down into Steven's car, and he said, "Rafael, if we don't talk right now, I'm going to call your parents, and I'm going to tell them that I suspect that you're a homosexual." And I said, "Marlon, you do what you need to do." That's exactly what I told him. So I went off to work, and that weekend I was visiting my parents at their house. And, in fact, Marlon had called, and my father called me into his study and asked me if it was true. I said that, in fact, I wasn't dating anyone—which was a lie because I was really crazy in love with Steven—but that, yes, I had had those thoughts and those desires, and that was as far as it had gone. It sort of seemed to have put his mind at rest for awhile. But then the next weekend I was visiting them again, and my father came into the room where I was watching television and with tears in his eyes, Bible in hand, said, "But you must repent, but you must repent." An excruciatingly painful memory. And I don't remember what conversation we had afterwards, but I guess I must have assured him that I was taking care of myself because I don't think we'd ever come back to that discussion until very recently. I've also had the discussion with other family members, and two of my sisters feel very much the way he does. For many years it really had not been dealt with in my family at all. I didn't bring it up, and they didn't bring it up, and that's that. I guess only once one sister brought it up about four years ago, and I told her that I was starting to see somebody, and she said something about God's plan and that I could change, but that had been it (that happened about four years ago) until very recently.

What happened was, in the process of working with the biblical texts for my thesis, I came out most fully, completely, to my father and my family, about my sexual orientation. This has been met, I wouldn't even say with mixed results, but with a lot of resistance—not hostility, but resistance. And I've come to understand that my father, who is the core of my family at this point relative to my siblings (because my mom died last year), is not going to be budged from his position. He's seventy-four, now, seventy-five, something like that.

Last night I decided to call him and share with him that I had been tested for the HIV antibodies and that my results had come back negative, and he just didn't get it. It was like, "Well, sure, it would have been a real tragedy if you had been infected." And then he said, "I never did receive the letter you said you were going to write," a letter that I was going to write in response to one of his. I had written a letter but had decided not to send it, went on vacation, and since then I've rewritten it—have written, essentially, a different letter—which I will send to him this coming weekend after I've had time to talk about it and process it in therapy. And to that he said, "Well, homosexuality is a sin, and it's still morally wrong," and he doesn't know of any birth or child that has ever come forth from a homosexual union and that clearly means that homosexuality is wrong. So he comes at it from a natural law kind of perspective, around procreation. So I listened to him. After he was through speaking, I allowed there to be about fifteen seconds worth of silence, which can sometimes seem more than that. But I was careful that I didn't want it to seem too long—it was also my phone bill—but I wanted there to be silence, for him to punctuate and say, "Rafael is not responding to me." I wanted him to say that. And then I said, "Well, it was nice talking to you, I hope you're doing well, and I'll talk with you soon." And that was the end.

I decided that my intervention at this point was not for me to share myself because I've shared all of what I need and want to share and he just shared all that he needs to share. And he is still hoping that through his continual putting out of his message that I will change. And I decided that my intervention instead was to hear it and remain silent and then to go on. So it's a whole new tack for me.

It's been a difficult last three months, in coming out to him, seeing him face to face, and discussing the thesis, talking about the impact of homophobia, that it has not just societal impact, but that it has a personal impact on me. I even went so far as to tell him about how I had been feeling that kind of polarity and that I feel immobilized: I have this pious side, and then I have this dirty sexual side, and the two never come together, and it's been a healing process of me to really be able to hold the two at once. I told him that anything less than that, for me, was suicide. So I have been able to just get out all of that anger—and I was very angry—that was weighing on my chest.

But this time I engaged only by listening, and my process, when I began talking with him, is that I said, "I'm not asking for your approval. I'm not asking for your acceptance. I'm only asking that you listen and hear." And I've since come to realize that he cannot hear. He does not have ears to hear. So I have to let him off the hook on that, too. But that's okay. I'm okay with him being where he is, and I have been able to make a kind of separation of "This is who my father is, this is who I am, and this is who God is." I have begun to take apart that piece from childhood where I see parents as God. I say, "No, you are family, you do make mistakes, and I disagree with you. With God, I don't see it that way."

Let's turn to the changing way in which he has seen, and sees, God, for these few paragraphs are like a slice of a hologram: they reflect the whole of the journey. In it we see a deep transformation from a child's traditional view to a more expansive sense that transcends gender and physical characteristics.

As a young child my sense of God was twofold. At first, I guess, my most vivid image would be God as Jesus. I remember vividly the Bible stories that describe Jesus as rescuing the lost sheep, those kind of pretty Bible stories with wonderful color pictures. And at the same time, I had a sense of God as someone who looks like Father Time, on a big chair on a throne somewhere, with a big long beard and perhaps an image of Justice sitting at one side, weighing the scales, and a New Year's baby on another side, a triune kind of thing: Father Time and New Year's Baby and Justice.

Gradually, gradually over the years, my image of God has changed. And I guess that I would say it developed more consciously than intentionally, through therapy and spiritual direction, to where my sense of God is now less shaped to a person and more to qualities of transcendence and immanence. It is more of God as other-worldly and yet at the same time extremely personal—as within myself and within the other person. It is visible in all kinds of acts, of kindness and mercy and those sorts of things, and, perhaps, invisible in acts of violence and acts of injustice.

I don't know that I can really give God a face or a gender. As a matter of fact, whenever people ask me, I try to pick out what their bias is with gender, and I always try to turn it around on them. So if they use "He" quite a bit, I always say, "She." And I mean it quite seriously. I used to joke about it. But now if they say, "She" a lot, I always go back to "He." I always try to do that for them.

I try to get them to expand their concept of God. I have this concept of God that I think, in many ways, goes against our social understanding of God. As a society we construe God as what my spiritual director calls the wm-wm God. The wm-wm God is white, male, wealthy, and married. And, for me, my sense of God could include white, male, wealthy, and married, but it also includes poor, black, and unmarried.

I currently see three clients. One of them comes from more of a Swedish fundamentalist perspective and now has left all of that and is very much more New Age and cosmic with his spirituality. Another is an African-American Roman Catholic man. And the third is a Muslim. And in no way do I feel that it is my role to impose on them my middle-class Episcopalian belief system, and yet in each of these three cases we have a very significant connection. I guess what it comes down to for me in my work with them is, "Does your faith work for you? Does my faith work for me?" It makes a lot of sense for me. But I know that for other people it doesn't. Does it mean that I throw away God? Yeah, some days I do and other days, no; most often I cling to knowing that God is a part of everything.

Rafael speaks of living with the questions, with the grays, in his work at the agency and his life in general. These questions are the kind that have no black-and-white answers, and he allows their ambiguity to be there and allows himself to appreciate it.

Working here at the agency is completely tied to my spiritual journey, first because this is a ministry setting and because we are about pastoral care and we're about religion and faith and belief—and we are interfaith, that is, we don't identify with any particular religion, faith, or belief. As far as our clients are concerned, they're all over the board in terms of their faith experiences. And at the same time, many of us—staff, volunteers, and clients—are gay or lesbian, yet this is not a gay or lesbian organization. So what the agency has become for me is a very safe place, and it's been an instrumental place for me just to be, a place that supports both my spiritual and religious side and my sexual orientation side in a way that I find is very beneficial. It comes together for me here.

The experience of many Christians that I talk with is not quite like mine at all. As a matter of fact, if I talk to people within the church, they're easy and quick to bash the gay community. If I talk to my gay friends, they feel like it's very easy to bash the church community. So why is it that I've been able to incorporate this experience, both being within the church and being a gay person? I guess I never felt as marginalized, and my experience of the church was never such that I felt that persecuted or marginalized by the church. And at the points where I felt they were speaking against me as a homosexual, I felt they were misguided. And that's all it comes down to: I think they're wrong. I feel like they're entitled to their position, just as much as I'm entitled to mine, and frankly, when it comes to issues of scripture and text, analysis and exegesis and hermeneutics and all of that, I can do it virtually as well they can. As far as I'm concerned, I think they're wrong if I'm talking about my experience. If I'm working with a church, I'm not usually quite so upfront. I try to bring them along; I try to create bridges; I try to create understanding. I wouldn't just say, "Well, you're just plain old wrong."

I think that in some ways I have always felt that clear about it. Existence is akin to an onion, and on most days, through most layers of the onion, I am very clear. I still have a resonance that says, "But are you really sure about this?" It's like when I work with people who are dying. On most days, I'm okay about that, but occasionally I meet a Latino gay male who's cute and happens to be my age and somehow his story strikes me at a different level, at a different core place, and I want to cry my eyes out, or I want to flee from the situation as quickly as I can. I don't know that there's ever a sense of complete resolution with anything. As a matter of fact, that's kind of how I'm built. I operate a lot in the grays and in the ambiguities, as opposed to the solid foundation.

I think that a new question has popped into my head recently: how do I integrate my mother's death into my spirituality? What's the meaning of it? Good people are left to die, you know, and good people do die. What's this all about? So there's questions around what's the purpose of faith? What's the purpose of life? At a whole new level of the onion perhaps.

Having these questions is very comfortable. I am not reaching any resolution, and I choose not to, at this point. Instead, the quote that comes to mind is, "Love the question, and someday you'll live yourself into the answer."

These kinds of difficult questions are present in the work I do as well. My own tack is to sit with the individual who is asking that question, to support them as they ask the question, to tell them that they're okay to ask those kinds of questions. I allow them to explore the questions for themselves. I don't enter into those conversations lightly. I'm always very cautious to not present answers unless they want to know what I think. Then I'll share my experience, but most often I will just tell them it's okay, support them in their process.

I think I need to hold two things simultaneously at one time, and one side of it is there are no rules. We create our own path, our own rules. What you perceive as priorities and truths may be different from my priorities and truths. And there is no absolute kind of structure. The other side of it is, of course, there *are* rules. If there are no rules, there are no outcomes; there is no way for me to gauge if I've succeeded or I've failed, there is no way to progress, to have any movement, if there are no rules. So that's what I mean about ambiguity. I think for a good part of my faith journey I've been focusing on not having the rules, not buying into another person's rules and appropriating them as mine. So I've been in this gray period, which was, I think, a reaction to too much structure—too much structure that was imposed. And where I'm coming out, through all of this, is that I have also found that that gray area is not a very productive area. It's a lot of fascination and imaginings, but it doesn't seem to be very productive. So what I'm trying to do is strike a balance. Having too many structures, too many rules, inevitably squelches creativity—my creativity and another person's creativity—and perhaps their and my humanness. And so having too much was the first step. After that I'd gone through the extreme of not having any, and now I'm finally saying, "Okay, we need to have some rules; we need to have a way of somehow predicting how each of us is going to be with each other."

I think that balance is very important here at the agency, working within a network that is interfaith. I can do my work with clients who have a very different perspective from mine partly because I have gone through this journey of abandoning my own rules; saying, "Okay, this is what fits for me"; and having the kind of tolerance for other people in which I choose to embrace their experience.

As Rafael brings this conversation to a close, he shares a dream that has been a powerful expression of his journey.

My spiritual journey is in some ways an ever new and unfolding kind of reality. I have a dream, and I feel I should share it with you. The dream occurred this first weekend of October when I was in Washington, D.C., for the National Skills-Building Conference and the International Display of the Quilt. In my dream I'm assisting someone in the installation of three air-conditioning compressors, the kind of things that normally sit outside of a house, on the ground, for central air-conditioning in the house. And someone in the dream suggested that the air-conditioning compressors ought to be placed in a closet. And I explained that, no, they need to go outside. So I suggest that we go up into an upper attic, and this is the kind of house that has two different roof lines and two different attics, an upper attic and a lower attic. And we go up into the upper attic to see if we can look out through a window and see if the air-conditioning compressors could be placed on the roof of the lower attic. As we get ready to ascend and go up in this narrow stairwell, I have a kind of premonition or sense that whatever is up in this upper attic is kind of spooky and perhaps the attic is haunted—I remembered that the person that lived in this house had died a violent death, but I decided to go up in the attic anyway. As I climbed up the steps, I realized that the steps were carpeted, and they were plush. It was clean, not what I would expect, going up into an attic. When I got up to the attic, it was empty. And it was completely clean. The floor was painted. There was a finished room. And again, not what I expected. I expected trunks and boxes and a lot of books and dust and all that kind of stuff, but not at all what I expected. I went to a low window where the ceiling met the roof. I went to a low window and opened up the venetian blind and looked out, and sure enough, the roof of the lower attic would be a good place to position two of these compressors.

As I stood up and turned, there appeared in front of me a tall woodsmanlike man made of mud. And I was startled, and I said, "Who are you?" And he mumbled some words. And I couldn't understand the words, so I asked him, "What was that again?" And he said, "I am the spirit of everlasting goodness in man." At that time I remembered that I was with this air-conditioning person. And I turned around to see if he was observing my talking to this spirit. And when I came back to the spirit, he was gone.

In the next sequence to my dream I'm walking through some woods, a very lush and kind of North American kind of forest. And, from out of a rock, a large kind of rock, there appeared the head, neck, and shoulders of this man, this woodsman, mudman. And I said, "Who are you?" And again he mumbled some words, and I said, "What?" And he said, "I am the spirit of everlasting goodness in man." I said, "Oh, yeah, yeah, I remember." And then he said, "Stick around and you'll see more of us," or "Stick around and you'll see more of me," or something like that. So that was my dream. And as I come to tell the dream, you can probably tell I've told the dream a few times; I wrote it down immediately. I think that this spirit made of mud, not just dirty with mud, but actually like a mudman, a caricature of mudman, is in some ways related to my spiritual journey. So you ask, "Where am I going spiritually? Where is that journey going?" I'm exploring whether the mudman is really in transition, in other words, like a caterpillar becomes a butterfly, sheds his mud, or perhaps there's just a kind of truth about life in the mudman. Because not only is he made of things that we're made of, soil and elements and water and very common sorts of things, but he also identifies and says he's the spirit of everlasting goodness in man. There's a kind of dual nature in one there already. So I'm asking this mudman, in my being, "Who are you? Where are you taking me? What are you about?" He's a strong person; he's a powerful person who really is able to have a metamorphosis of sorts, coming out of a rock, and yet appearing from out of nowhere the first time and then coming out of a rock. So if you were going to ask, "Where's spirit taking me, or where am I going?" I would say, "Exploring more along what the mudman means to me." It's a very central question for me at this point in my life.

Often I haven't really known where I was going. Most often. And I still don't really know where I'm going in any kind of final sense. I just kind of know where my very next step is—and being true to myself is a very important part of what that next step is.

Take coming out. Being gay, I don't know; that to me is a mystery. But the coming out process and saying this is my truth and I know that it will offend some and draw some has been a very rewarding experience. Just taking a stand has been important. This is who I am. I begin here. I end here. You begin there. You end there. It's a liberating experience because in other times when I was less clear about that, I became you; you became me; your opinion about me was much more important. Or another person's opinion about me was much more important than my opinion about myself. And when I had lots of people telling me who I am, boy, was I confused. It's not to say that my father's opinion is not important. His opinion is important. Your opinion is important. Someone else's opinion is important. But it's been my task to decide what of that is my stuff and what of that is their stuff.

I think that one of the connections between my coming out process and my spiritual journey that I see is that in one sense I am more sure of myself. In another sense I am less sure of spiritual laws or God's intention for us. I'm more sure about who I am. My lesbian sister, twelve years my elder, said to me relative to my father finding out, "Well, did you ever think he might be right?" Yeah, in fact, I do consider that he might be right, about how he interprets scripture, that there is some kind of spiritual mandate, you know, against homosexuality. Sure I do. And in the back of my mind that is still a very present spiritual dimension or even reality. But I don't think—and this is where the big *but* is—I don't think I'm willing to engage that. He can still have his stuff. And he may very well be right. But I don't see the proof, for myself, as that clear-cut. When I look at the scriptures, I don't see it that clearly. So I'm not seeing that I have stepped into "the light," that I know all truth and I can say, "You are absolutely wrong." I won't say that. I'm willing to own that I make mistakes, and I'm willing to say to my father, "Hopefully, you're willing to own your own mistakes." That's the best that I can do with what I know about myself right now. And so I welcome his prayers. In the letter that I wrote him, in response to his letter about my homosexuality being quote "a problem," I said, "My sexual orientation is not a problem to me unless someone else makes it a problem." And what came to mind was the scripture when Jesus says to Peter, "On you my rock, I will build my church and your hands will have the keys to the kingdom of heaven. If you bind it on earth, it will be bound in heaven. If you set it free on earth, it will be set free in heaven" [Matt. 16:18–19]. And that's what it comes down to for me. If you call my sexual orientation a sin, to you it is sin. But if you call my sexual orientation a gift, to you it will be a gift. And it will be a gift here, and it will be a gift in heaven. So it's kind of up to me and up to him and other people to decide where that is and what that is. And I think that for me—I also wrote this in my letter to my father—salvation is something that is worked out with quote "fear and trembling" and not something that happens externally or magically. So we have a responsibility to ourselves and to other people because I'm your salvation; I'm your damnation. Your damnation can impact on my salvation, and I don't mean that in cosmic terms; I mean that in primarily immediate terms. So that's been a whole new growth; that's been a whole new edge for me in the last couple weeks, that's just coming out.

We end with some final thoughts about Rafael's spiritual "cutting edge."

Sometimes I feel like I hide behind my spirituality. I just spent a weekend on a grief and healing retreat, and that came up between one person and me. And I needed to hear that because I wonder if that's not true or maybe if it is true, how much of it is true. But my intention has been to become less spiritual and more human, through my participation in church or whatever, more of a humanizing element than a transcending element.

The first time I encountered this notion was when I was doing a workshop around making some distinctions around spirituality, religion, and faith. And this one very tough-looking punk, in the cultural sense, said, “Well, you know for me, spirituality is about embracing my situation, embracing as fully as possible, the reality of AIDS, the reality of losses, NOT transcending them. Not avoiding them to get to the other side. One way of getting to the other side is by embracing and passing through them, and that's been a lot more of my model.” I mean, he was not a learned person; he was not a theologian. I think you would have expected something profound like that from someone like a Karl Barth or a Paul Tillich. That's been the humanizing element, embracing my reality. And whatever happens in the transformation is the transcendent. Before, I had come from the belief that God'll fix it. Well, let's pray right now, and the answer is on its way. More of a heaven by-and-by, you know, on the other side you'll be healed. Well, no, I don't think so. I think that even with AIDS, healing happens now. In many ways. We may not have the cure, but healing does happen now. It's an oppressive stance on the part of those who are in control: “You have to suffer now because your reward will happen later on.” Sorry, I don't buy it.

Dan: "HIV Doubled My Spirituality"

Dan lived in Ohio until the end of seventh grade, when he and his parents moved to the Midwest. His older brother and sister had already moved out of the house by then. Although his family was not overtly religious, he did develop a sense of God and prayer as a child, and when, after high school, he went into the service and moved to Germany, he joined the Catholic church on base because he enjoyed the liturgy and wanted to be in the choir. After returning to the United States, he went to cosmetology school and had a short-lived career in that field prior to becoming a sales representative in suburban Chicago, a job he has been doing for seven years.

He lives in a garden apartment in one of Chicago's nicer sections. He is part of a support group of men who are HIV positive, yet otherwise has few friends. In the survey he completed before the interviews captured here, he identified contacting AIDS as a key stepping stone in his journey. As he relates here, the year prior to the interviews was a hard one for him: his father died only a few months after Dan had disclosed his sexual orientation to him, and Dan came out to his mother and sister about both his sexuality and his HIV status.

The day of our first meeting would have been his father's seventy-first birthday; it was the eve of Dan's thirty-eighth. On meeting him, one gets the impression that all of Dan's life pales in comparison to the last few years when he has been living with AIDS. Nevertheless, the roots of his spirituality can be found in his childhood and family. Let's ground ourselves in the stories he tells from this time, beginning with the way in which Dan sees his family.

I'm very close with my mother. I have always considered her my friend, I guess, before I considered her my mother. A lot of it has to do with the fact that growing up there were lots of times when I didn't have a lot of friends; I was a lot different from my siblings in this respect. "Not fitting in" is too strong, but I always knew there was something different about me. And my father used to drink. And although he never hit my mother, he was sometimes quite verbally abusive to her. But he was a very good man. He always made sure that us kids had food and clothing; he just had a problem with drinking. It upset my mother so much, and I always felt very sorry for her, so I always made plans to do something with her—a movie or something like that—and later on, when I got older and got my driver's license, I remember driving her around, trying to find my father, to see what bar he was at that night. She always suspected that he was seeing other women, which we never found that out. I guess I was her confidant, and I still am today. So my relationship with her is very, very strong. And I have an awful lot of respect for her, for what her life has been and what she's been through all the while working very hard at making the best of what she could for me and my brother and my sister.

And my father was like that, too. He always worked very hard, and it was always very physical labor, and he didn't have much to show for it. And he had three kids to raise. I can see where alcohol would be an out for him, but I never understood him treating my mother that way. I know he didn't mean to do it, and he'd always come back and apologize to her, but I always remember her life being that way until I left. When I left, I think he quit drinking. And things completely changed because after that his health deteriorated. He was always a very heavy smoker. It just seems like both of them have just always worked really hard with not much to show for it. I have an enormous amount of respect for both of them, regardless of the way their life went or the choices that they made.

When we moved here, my father was the one that transferred. My mother was working for a factory back there. It's a very small town, probably now about twelve thousand people. But she was working for that company, and she had gotten laid off, and then my father was going to lose his job at the factory if he didn't transfer to one of their new plants. And they agreed to move him, and the furniture and everything else, if he was willing to do that. So that's what we did. He had come out to Illinois for awhile prior to my mother and I coming out because he wanted me to finish seventh grade before we came out, and then my mother and I came out on the train and joined him.

I remember going hunting with my dad once. He took me out and I shot a squirrel, and we came back and we cleaned it, and my mother cooked it for dinner; I sat at the table and cried because I had shot it. So he never took me hunting again. I just bonded more with my mother than my father, but I never neglected him. I never have not talked to him. There was love there, unspoken. I never felt once that he didn't love me. And I guess I really didn't start telling either one of them that I loved them until, I would say, when I came back from Europe, when I was in the service, 'cause I had missed them so much. The word *love* just was never thrown around a lot whenever I was little.

I used to be very close with my sister. My mother was basically never there during the day in my preschool days, so my sister pretty much was my mother. Both of my parents would get home late after I was in bed. Sometimes my father would have to drive two hours to work—this is before expressways—he'd be eight hours at work and two hours back in the evening.

I don't remember my brother being home much, even when he was in grade school and high school. He was always out with his friends. What is in my mind a lot about my brother as we were growing up is no matter what, he would always protect me or he'd always stand up for me—regardless of whether or not he knew the full story. His relationship with my father was much different from mine.

I think the values I grew up with in my family were, basically, traditional things like not lying to your parents. That was very hard to do; when I found out I was HIV positive, I kept my health status away from my mother and my father for so long. But it was for protection; I didn't want to hurt them. I never wanted to have to have them go through dealing with my death. I've always thought that for a mother or father there could be no worse pain and grief than the loss of their child.

I was always a good boy. I always did what they told me to do, and I never got in trouble. My brother was always getting in trouble, my sister would try and get away with things, but I was just always the good boy. I remember getting spankings, but they were usually for sassing my mother. I felt so close with her, but she would do or say something that would irritate me as her friend, and it would just come out before I realized this is your mother, too. My father made me realize that because he was usually the one to give me the spanking. So I think I learned, basically, regular values that most people are taught: to have respect for everyone and to get that respect back from them.

I've learned that you have to tell people how you feel while they're here; you can't do it after they're gone. My grandmother, my father's mother, who I was very close with, died when I was here, and I couldn't make it home. This is when I was between jobs and I didn't have a lot of money. I've always regretted not going back to say good-bye, to tell her that I loved her one more time.

There was always a thread of spirituality in Dan's life, though it was not based in strong formal religious training. Instead, it was present in the more private tradition of saying prayers at night and in the formative experience of seeing his grandfather in a casket.

We were not much of churchgoing people. About the only time I remember going to church when I was little was on holidays, like Easter and Christmas. The church that we belonged to was so far away, and it was difficult to get there, especially with my father doing all the driving during the week that he had to.

When I started first becoming spiritually aware of my life, I guess, was when my grandfather died. That was 1962, I believe, and I was only eight years old at the time. That's the first time any one of our family had died. And I guess, even at that early age, I felt that there's gotta be something more to just your mortal life; there's got to be something afterwards. I think that at age eight, realizing that was a major stepping stone for me, a beginning to understand what praying and going to church really are all about. It didn't really click until my grandfather died. I remember still being quite small or short at that time, and my father picking me up at the end—this was before they closed the coffin—and they took my grandfather's glasses off and stuck them in his breast pocket; I remember that vividly. And my grandmother, although he had his ring on in the casket, she removed that from his finger. It's like it was yesterday. That was very profound for me.

As I became a little bit older, I became interested in vocal groups, choirs. So when I was in grade school and high school, I belonged to church groups for choir. After I went in the service, that continued on. After I got out of the service, I quit singing, and I quit going to church. But spirituality still remained. I've always said my prayers before I go to bed at night. I still go to church during major holidays. I've always felt that as long as I kept a relationship in my own personal way with God, or the higher being, or the creator, that I wasn't going to be chastised for not going to church. You know, everyone has their own feelings about what life is about; I believe that whenever I talk to God, it doesn't have to be in church. I don't think He's going to love me any less.

Perhaps Dan's first significant departure from his family's norms was in coming out. He can trace his self-awareness of being gay to puberty, though earlier his experience was one of feeling different.

I didn't receive any messages about homosexuality when I was growing up, nothing like that at all. Looking back on it now, after we moved to Illinois, I think I based a lot of my friendships on guys that I was sexually attracted to, probably exclusively. But I never pushed myself; I never approached them sexually. And I remember being eight and nine years old and going to the local swimming pool, where I'd be fascinated by changing and noticing older men. I didn't have the same feelings about women. I didn't understand; I thought it was bad, but I never really discussed it with anyone. I just knew something was different. Understanding came later on after I admitted what was going on with myself.

I didn't know what it was then, but I date my coming out to when I was about eleven or twelve. I knew the word *puberty,* but I always thought of a pimple or something. I didn't know that other things would happen to my body; you know you're going to get body hair whenever you grow up, but you just don't sit down and talk to people about it. Things just started happening. I remember lying on the floor watching TV, with my hands over my head, and I felt this tickling underneath both of my arms. And I went into the bathroom, and that's when I noticed I was starting to get body hair. I'd explored different areas of my body that had started developing differently. My legs became stronger, and my metabolism and the physical part of me just completely changed. I really changed my looks completely. It was amazing to me.

I had my first sexual experience with my best friend, who I went in the service with. We had had sexual encounters even before I went in the service with him. We're not friends anymore. He's married and has a couple children. I guess with him it was more of a phase than what it was with me. And he was brought up in a strict Catholic environment, where they were taught that they were going to go to hell if they were gay, and I think that played a big part with him. I, on the other hand, felt that God was not going to punish me, and I was not going to go to hell for loving another human being, regardless of whether it was female or male. I had no control over my thoughts. I had no interest in women sexually. There were two times when I had to have a date when I was in school, in my junior and senior years. And I knew who I wanted to be with, but I had no interest in these girls sexually. I was a class officer those two years, and I probably wouldn't have gone to the prom if I didn't have to be there. But if I had to be there, I wanted to be with a girl that I felt was attractive. I guess it was only for aesthetic values because I certainly had no interest either time. And I would have rather spent the evening with my guy friend.

Of course, that was not expected or allowed. I just feel it wasn't a phase with me. It's hard to describe; you just know that something's different, but you can't pinpoint what it is. And like I said, I was always brought up that God is not going to discriminate against who you love. I think my friend, the one I went in the service with, was brought up under different circumstances, so after a year of being in the service he didn't want to have anything to do with me. And he started dating girls, which upset me, and he didn't want to be around me 'cause he knew what was going on with me. And I think I realized, too. So we've not talked since.

I was never ashamed of what I was. I've never considered my lifestyle as being something bad in God's eyes. And that goes back to what I told you: that I don't think you're going to be condemned over something that you really have no control over. Even when I was as young as eight, I knew there was something different that I had no control over. I just didn't know what it was at the time. Now a lot of people make their own mistake, thinking they're heterosexual and finding out that they weren't happy, that they were doing it to appease other people. They think it wasn't "correct" socially to be involved with someone of the same sex. I never felt that way. I always felt it was my decision.

While I was still in college, when I'd come home, I'd be asked if I had met any girls yet. Finally, I just told my parents that "the grandchildren you have right now, that my brother and sister have, are all you're gonna have." I mean, "Accept it." I didn't come out and say I was gay, but I said that I wasn't going to get married and that they weren't going to have any grandchildren from me, and that's it. And that was my way of telling them, and it was dropped and never said again. They knew what it meant. They just wanted, they wanted to hear it from me. I didn't come out and say that I was gay, and the word was never even mentioned 'til years after. But they knew; they understood.

The prime focus of Dan's life for the last few years has been HIV. It has propelled him on a new phase of his spiritual journey, replete with questions, anger, and confusion. In the rest of this chapter we are able to see Dan's progression as he struggles with these feelings.

When I was thirty-four, I tested HIV positive. When I first found out, I just felt invincible, that it couldn't happen to me. I was probably infected way before it was even known what caused it. That's what bothered me most when I first found out. I remember asking the question, If I was to get this disease, why wasn't I given at least the knowledge to not come in contact with it? I always thought it was unfair. I still think it's unfair that I didn't have the knowledge to protect myself. And, of course, why me?

These are the kinds of conversations that I would have with God after I found out. Of course, you never know the answer to those questions.

If you're faced with a life-threatening disease, it really changes your mind; it makes you think 180 degrees different. Even something as simple as taking a walk and noticing how nice the stars look or going for a walk during the day and noticing how blue the sky is. Just simple things that you take for granted. Or losing someone. Realizing how fragile—you're here today and gone tomorrow, and that's the way it was for my father. I still can't believe it. That he's not here anymore. I guess you become sensitized that life is not going to go on forever and things are not going to remain the same from one day to the next or one week to the next. I've just become sensitive to everything.

I guess when you're faced with the fact that we're only here for a millisecond, when you're faced with the reality of dying, that you acquire new priorities on what makes you happy, and the things that you've taken for granted in the past, you don't take for granted anymore. I guess whenever you have no other recourse with something that's not controllable, you go back to something that is familiar. And I guess God has always been familiar to me. Even early, when I was looking at my grandfather when he died, lying in that casket. And I can see him there just like it was yesterday.

I just can't take the world for granted, so I live each day like it's my last 'cause it may be. I never used to think that way before. I felt invincible, that none of this stuff was going to happen to me and that my parents were going to live forever. Then I started finding out that life is not like that. And it's still hard facing that.

Has my spirituality changed? HIV doubled my spirituality, from realizing how fragile life and the line between life and death is and hoping there's something after my mortal life. I still sometimes feel that maybe this is it. I don't want to believe that; I feel guilty sometimes for asking God for strength to have faith in him. Sometimes I don't get it, and then I wonder, Why is it that I'm being made to go through this? This year has been pretty awful. I told my father last Christmas when I went home. At that time I didn't have an AIDS diagnosis, but I had always been afraid to go home, for fear that I'd have to go for some kind of medical treatment while I'm there. And that happened when I was at home. I have panic attacks, and in that particular area of the country back there where my parents live they don't know how to handle HIV and AIDS patients. Of course, I had to tell the emergency room of my status when I went in; the doctor came out with a big visor over his face and gloves. Anytime he went to touch me it was in a very distant and detached way; I mean, you're not going to get it. I couldn't believe it. And that's when reality kicks in. It's completely different seeing a doctor back there than one here, one who is used to it all the time.

I don't think my visual picture of God has changed. I've always pictured God as the same thing: long hair, beard, a very chiseled face, very strong, very fatherly. My father didn't have long hair or a beard, but he was always that feeling to me. He would always tell me not to worry, no matter how bad things were. I guess the thing that's changed as I've become older is being able to talk more freely to God. Talking like we're talking right now. I always felt before that prayer had to be in a prayer form, like, "Our Father who art in heaven"; it had to be something prepared or formal, or God wasn't going to listen to you. And I had so much to say to Him after I became sick that I couldn't put in prayer form. Then I realized, well, He's not looking for that.

On the other hand, sometimes I feel really sick or I'm not handling this mentally very well. And I wonder—I ask Him for help, and I don't get it. And then I think, maybe He isn't there; maybe this is it, which makes me even more upset. I've always felt I don't want to lose control mentally. That's always been a fear of mine. Anxiety attacks are a mind game, and that snowballs, and I think, maybe I have some kind of disease in my brain, where I'm going to be a vegetable, and I'm going to have to have people take care of me; I'm not going to know who anyone is. I've always thought that that would be an awful way to go.

I guess the saving grace is that I've always, always felt that God knows best and He never gives you more than what he thinks you can handle. I told my mom that when I told her I had AIDS and she was crying uncontrollably. She's the youngest one in her family, and her entire family died before her—all her siblings, her mother and her father, and her husband,

and probably her son—and she's really surprised a lot of us by not losing control. I knew my father was going to die someday, even though I also thought he was going to live forever. I dreaded his dying because I didn't want to see her go through that. But she handled it very well. And then, within two months after that, I had to tell her I had AIDS, and I thought, Why are we all being made to go through this? If there's a caring and loving God, why does He make us suffer this way? Like I said, the only thing that really keeps me in line is that there is a God, that all these questions will be answered whenever I meet Him. He doesn't give you more than what He thinks you can handle. If you think about what you've done through your life and the pain that you've gone through, how could it possibly be worse than being ridiculed and spat at and put on a cross and crucified? Can you compare this to that? The answer is no.

I have moments all the time when I doubt that there's a God—whenever I ask for help and I don't get it. I have a book called *The Color of Light;* it's spiritual passages, and that's been very helpful to me. Lots of times the message that's given for a specific day will be for me. I feel that it really does apply for that particular day, and lots of times I've thought that's been God's own words or his message getting through to me. Telling me that day. You know, you'd rather it would be, "God, if you really exist, make the lamp shake" or something physical like that. God telling you what to do can come from a friend doing something for you that wasn't expected. I like to think that's God doing that, working through that person to make you feel better, or getting a birthday card from your mother and you know that God planted the words that she says in that birthday card in her mind. That's how I like to think that God works. But it's not always like that. I still have doubts that there's something after life. I still sometimes fear that there's nothing more than our mortal life, that it's only what's here right now.

I still pray, though. I would say a lot of it is asking God for things. To give me strength to deal with what I have to deal with and if he's going to take me, to take me quickly and not let me suffer. Asking to give me the power to heal myself or make myself well. That's the kind of stuff I ask for. There are certain prayers that I will read out of the Bible. I never used to keep a Bible beside my bed. Now I've got a bookmark at the Lord's

Prayer, which I read. And the bookmark is a pamphlet that a nun gave me at Columbus Hospital. The head of the rectory department there, I believe her name was Sister Bernadine, came in one day. I was pretty much a basket case when I was in there. I had to have the catheter, and she just came in to be with me. We talked for awhile, not specifically about anything really. And then towards the end of our conversation, I told her that I was still concerned about my mother; she was dealing with my father's death, and now she's going to have to deal with me telling her that I have AIDS. She came back and she brought with her a pamphlet that has a lot of interesting stuff in it that would help my mother. And I thought that was awfully nice of her to do that. She also included a pamphlet that had a list of prayers on it. One is the serenity prayer. Another one is a prayer when you're in pain. Another one is prayer before surgery. And, of course, they had a rendition of the Lord's Prayer in there. They sound very nice. I know that a prayer is just conversation, that it doesn't have to be something that sounds nice, but I still feel it's nice for God to listen to something nice, too. And by saying those prayers to Him, it makes me feel better. Not only just for the dialogue, like you and I are having, but because these other prayers that are already written for me are sometimes prayers that end by discussions with Him.

Sometimes I get angry with God, on days where I don't particularly have a good attitude about what's going on. I get angry and I revert back to thinking, Why are You putting me through this? If You're going to take me, take me. And, then again, I've tried to make myself understand that it's God's way of being able to love other people more, of being more understanding with other people. A lesson or something along that line. Because the next day it might be a 180-degree turnaround and I feel great. And I handle it completely different. It's the roller-coaster ride, I guess, is what it is.

I've always said the Lord's Prayer before I go to bed at night. That's my upbringing, my mother staying there with me whenever she would take me to bed at night and tuck me in, saying my prayers. It was just instilled into us, whenever my parents were raising us, that you must always say your prayers. I say prayers more often and talk things out more often since I found out about my health situation than what I used to, in my prayers. Sometimes it's the only thing that's really kept me thinking reality or kept me from completely losing it mentally.

HIV changed the nature of his relationship with his family as well, perhaps even before the family had spoken about it. He told his brother first and then, sometime later, decided he needed to let his father know.

Right after Magic Johnson had went public with his HIV status, I thought it was time to tell my father. And I didn't know how much he knew about AIDS because we had never talked about it, but I decided I just couldn't carry that around on my shoulders anymore; someone else had to help me. And my father was always a rock; he had always handled things on an up note. He thought, what's gonna be is gonna be; there are things that you can change, and there are things that you can't. And he took it very well. He understood. But he agreed that mother shouldn't know until I get an AIDS diagnosis. So he would do things like, he'd read something in the paper on AIDS or AIDS benefits, and he'd cut them out. And then my mother would read the paper, open it up, and she'd see this big hole here in the paper, wanting to know what it was, what he was sending to me. And I like to cook, so he could always come up with something, like, there's a recipe for something. And she'd go, yeah, okay. He would do things like that, trying to show his concern and trying to be helpful, telling me that he prayed for me two or three times a day. He'd call me at least once a week at work, 'cause we have a WATTS line—we could get one phone call a week, and the company would pay for it. And he would always ask, "Is there anything you need?" I'd say, "Just a prayer." And he'd say, "You get two or three of those a day anyway." And he would always end the conversation by saying that he loved me.

He had told me when I was visiting about his problem. He had an aortic aneurysm, which is what his father died of; it ruptured before they found out what it was. He had it tested three years ago, and the doctor thought that there wasn't any need to have it corrected at that time—they would check it once every year. Well, the last year he went in was just before Christmas last year, and it had grown larger than what the doctor thought it would. So he said that he needed to have an operation, or he would only have one year to live. Keep in mind that my father was always a very heavy smoker. And for the past twelve years he'd had a very bad chronic back problem—there were no discs, basically, left in his back, so he always had neck pains and back pains. His days for the past twelve or fifteen years were spent lying on the sofa. Driving the car up the street two blocks to go to the post office. So his only exercise was from sofa to the car or from the sofa to the dining room table, where he would smoke cigarettes.

Well, he had told me that he was going in for the operation, and I was supposed to be there a week after that for my normal vacation in May. And I had asked him if he wanted me to come back to be there, it would be no problem. And he said, "No, the doctor says that the operation will go fine; we've caught it in time." But he neglected to tell me that they had him go in for lots of tests; they found out that his heart's pumping output was not as strong as it should be, and after they make the repair, it changes how strong your heart has to be. He never shared that with me. And he always told me not to worry, that everything would work out fine. He was always very positive that what's going to happen is going to happen. You just can't change a lot of things. And he knew that I was under an awful lot of pressure, carrying around my own health problem. He just didn't want to burden me, but I wish he would have. I would have liked to have been there. I didn't know that there could be complications unrelated to the aneurysm after the surgery. And if I would have known that, I would have wanted to be there. Well, the operation went well, but his heart wasn't strong enough because he got no exercise. So I always felt that if he would have gotten a little more exercise, his heart would have been stronger. After they sewed him back up, they couldn't get his blood pressure back up, and his heart just quit. So the last that I saw him was last Christmas, and he died in May just before I would have come out. The fact remained that he knew then of my HIV status, and now he was gone. So now I had all this weight back on my shoulders because he was going to help me with informing my sister and my mother, and it took so much off of my shoulders, telling him. Now he's gone.

He did come out to his mother shortly thereafter.

Let me tell you a little bit about my mother. Her life for the past twelve or fifteen years has consisted of taking care of my father—and not going on trips, not going to do something she wanted because she had to be home to fix my father's meals and make sure that he was comfortable. When my father died, although it was very painful for everyone, it just opened up a whole new world for my mother. Because now she's got all this time on her hands and nothing to do. She doesn't drive, and she lives in a village. There are no stores to get groceries, so now she has to rely on my sister to do all this for her. So I told her, "You're welcome to come out here anytime you want." Well, they did come out. That was in August, with my sister and my niece.

But right after my father died is when I got a diagnosis of CMV retinitis, which is an indicator of full-blown AIDS. I didn't want anyone out here at the time 'cause I was dealing with that. And they had to be told. Time was wasting, between July 13th, when I found out, and August 3rd, when they were going to come. My brother didn't want me telling my mother over the phone, and there wasn't enough time for him to make it from Williamsburg, Virginia, to set her down and talk to her and tell her face to face. And I didn't know what to do. So my mother had called me at work one day, and she said something about coming out, and I told her there was something we had to talk about. I said, "I really don't want to do it on the phone, but I don't know what to do." And she goes, "Well, what's wrong?" And I said, "We just need to talk." And there was silence. I had had three close friends die of AIDS since Christmas, and one of them was named Robert. Well, I don't know what made her say, "Does it have to do with Robert?" I said, "Well, yes." And she says, "Well, is that what's wrong with you?" She wouldn't say AIDS, and I still have not heard her say that. And I said, "Yes." She started crying, and I told her it's okay to cry. I could tell when father died that she wanted to keep these tears in, and I kept telling her: "You know, we've lost a father, and you've lost a husband. It's okay to cry. I've got AIDS; it's okay to cry. I cry about it all the time." So she said: "Well, it doesn't make any difference. I want to come out and see you now more than ever."

And then I called my sister, and she said that she's known. She was just waiting for me to tell her. I had sent her a snapshot that was taken a few years ago—I'd lost a lot of weight right after I found out about the test, and a lot of it was psychological. I think she knew something was up then. And I would always tell Mom and Dad when I would get some kind of infection. It used to be the infection of the week, an ear infection or an eye infection or something. And I think she just put two and two together and figured out what was really going on. But it didn't seem to faze her. They were all very anxious to come out, and at that time I had said, "I need you here now more than ever." So they came out, and they had a real nice time. They were here for about a week. And I was taking them back to the train station, and I kissed them good-bye, my sister and my niece, and then my mother, and I hugged her, and she wouldn't let me go. I know what she was thinking. She was thinking that was the last time she was going to see me alive. And she started crying. And I told her, "We've got a long ways to go with this. It's okay to cry. We have to take this one day at a time." And she finally relaxed, and I just left. And I think she was okay with that for awhile because she didn't discuss it with anyone. I thought she would have lots of questions for my brother. But she finally came around and started talking about it and told some of her friends. She seems to be doing all right with it now. We talk probably twice a week. She stills calls at work, and if she doesn't call me at home here sometime during the week, then I end up calling her.

Dan's family is the core of his support right now. Many of his best friends have died, and other than his family, his support group is the only real source of connection he has.

I live here by myself, and I don't have a lot of friends to talk to anymore. A lot of them are dead. It's just not fair that I've had to watch all my friends die before me. And it's difficult for me to go out and meet new friends.

That's why I really enjoy going to my support group 'cause you're there with someone that knows what you're feeling. The entire group doesn't show up all the time, but you get an update there on new treatments that individuals' doctors have used on each other, and you discuss that. And lots of times we don't even think about anything that's really AIDS related. Just the camaraderie of being with a people who you know are going through the same thing, mentally and physically, makes me feel good every time I leave the meetings. Lots of times I won't feel physically or mentally well enough to go to the meeting, and I'd rather just go home and go to bed. But I'll go to the meeting anyway, and every time I come out feeling like I was glad that I came. That's 'cause a lot of times if someone's feeling down, I might say something to lift their spirit, and that makes me feel good. If I've said something to make someone feel better about themselves or feel better about their treatment, then I'll leave the meeting feeling better. That goes back to what I said about God putting people on earth for a specific reason. I mean, if that happens just once, then it's worth it to me.

My best friend lives in the apartment upstairs with his lover. I've known him for probably pretty close to fifteen years now, well before he met his lover. He's sort of extended family. Michael really watches over me, and he's become very close with my mother, and I think it's a relief to my mother knowing that there is someone out here that watches over me and makes me feel comfortable.

A few months later I had an opportunity to speak with Dan again. What he has to say here reveals a new stage in his process.

I think when we talked last I was wondering why this is all happening to me; I had lost my father a few months before. I don't so much ask myself those questions now; it's more or less like a test of faith. If God gives you something to handle, He doesn't give you more than what He thinks you can handle. I like to think that I'm gaining some good stuff from all this bad stuff, like learning how to be more responsible or learning to care for other people like they're caring for me and learning that the love that I get from my mom and from my family and from my friends is unconditional. There's lots of things that can be said about the bad things that happen in someone's life, too. I don't think I was quite aware of that when I talked to you last time.

I also think I've become more patient with people. Whenever I ask for help—if I have a bad day or something and I ask for help spiritually—

then I generally feel like I get it. And that's what I wasn't doing before; I was asking the question of why this was happening instead of asking for help to deal with it. Instead of saying, "Make this go away," the question is, "What can I do to help myself?" Instead of asking for something all the time, I ask the question of what can I do to help myself? And I believe it's helping me get over not just the AIDS aspect, but also dealing with work and with other people. That's probably been the biggest major change in the last few months.

Denise: Moving Beyond the "Fashion Show"

Denise is originally from Alabama. Her mother was a showgirl before she got married, and Denise has followed in her footsteps in some ways by having studied theater and performance in high-school, college, and graduate school. Currently, she is actively involved in a local singing group. Her father, a career officer in the armed services, died when she was twelve, an event that had profound spiritual ramifications in her life.

Her story reflects a period in which she has been questioning and resolving some of those questions as she encounters new ones. Only recently fully out, Denise is encountering the tensions between a new relationship with someone who does not share her religious beliefs and commitments and a growing and more mature sense of herself as a Christian.

Denise's spiritual life has had many significant stages, from experiencing church as a fashion show where she just wanted to fit in, to a sense that religion was irrelevant, to moments of profound faith. The ebb and flow of this journey began early.

My mother raised me as a United Methodist, even though I'd been baptized at the air force base Presbyterian church. I always went to Sunday school, and I always sang in the choir. I was forbidden to speak to my father about religion because mother said that he didn't believe in things that we believed. Although he was raised by nuns in a parochial school, he was an agnostic by the time he reached his adulthood; every time I tried to talk to him about religion, he would say that he believed in God;

he just didn't know what to believe about it. He believed there was something out there.

The church we went to was pretty big—they prided themselves on calling themselves "the fastest growing United Methodist church in the Southeast"; they are building additions onto it almost everyday. It became like a fashion show, and I wanted to fit in so bad—I remember spending all week trying to pick out an outfit that might look halfway as nice as the little rich girls I went to Sunday school with. That's one of the reasons why my mother wanted us to go there: because the quality of those people's lives was much better than anything we'd experienced before. And they took us in and really loved us, especially when my father died.

When I was five or six years old, I was baptized. It made me feel like Jesus loved me. I thought of him as God's son. And God made him, and he looked just like God, and he was born at Christmas, and he went through his life telling everybody about God and that God loved us, and then people didn't believe him, and they thought he was crazy and killed him. But he did all that just so I would know now, a million years later, that God loves me and that when I die, I will go and live with God forever. [Long pause] And God was a man with white hair and a beard and mustache and sat on a big throne with his golden crown up in the clouds.

At ten years old I was confirmed, and I learned a lot about how to follow Jesus. But basically I believed it to please Mama. We'd already moved, and Mother was still dragging us across to the other side of the town to go to church. A confirmation class became available to take, and at this point I thought that church was a big drag, especially because there were no kids, really, of my age, in that church—there were just a bunch of really old folks, and the church was real old and it stank, and it was musty and rank and icky. So Mama got me into the class. I said, "Okay, I'll try" because I realized that it was the next step and Mother wanted me to do this; it's like you graduate from grade one, you go into grade two, and I knew it was the next thing. And so I learned all the stuff, my beatitudes and so on, and by the end of it there was such a mishmash of shit, I was just like fine, whatever. I remember the day I was confirmed; I woke up that morning, and I was like, "I don't want to go." But Mother threw a dress on me and drug me, and I remember standing there and being blessed, and I'm feeling like this is total and complete bullshit because I don't want this anymore and I'm still doin' it. Something's wrong here.

Yet a couple years later I accepted Christ. Looking back on all the stuff that I had, it's like going through a professional development seminar in a corporation when you're just a receptionist, and then you have an opening a year down the road as a client consultant and saying, "Damn, I'm glad I took that seminar 'cause it helped me get this job." So it's kind of like that; I was glad I knew the rules because now I knew how to act. The experience was a complete spiritual wash, and it could have been just a lot of great energy flowing through the room from the people and a lot of love and everything, but it also could have been a direct touch from a creative spirit in the clouds, or it could have been totally me, needing it, thinking, just a mind thing I did for myself. But it felt very genuine; I still remember the feeling, and I don't necessarily want that same feeling again unless it's an extreme time of need, which is what it was then.

Because my father died. I knew he was going to die, and I knew the day and the time, and I remember that the fact that I knew it, just hit me like a ton of bricks. So his death was not that much of a shock to me, even though no one told me he was going to die. He died of cancer. I can tell you in a nutshell what happened. He was down in Biloxi, Mississippi, at an air force base hospital. He was only in the hospital for a month with cancer, and he was transferred to Biloxi during the last week of his life. My mother went down there and was with him. We went down and visited, and I knew he was pretty sick, but no one ever said he was going to die. I was twelve, and my sister and I were staying across the street with neighbors. I came back and we were feeding the dogs. I stuck the key in the hole of the door, and I looked at my sister and said, "Sally, Daddy's going to die tonight," and she's like, "Oh, okay, I guess I know." She was about five. And I remember just, boom, the sun hit me; it was about five o'clock and it was the bright sun and I was standing on the porch and I knew it and no one told me. And then at about five fifty-five Daddy died, and at about six o'clock Mother called. Our neighbor answered the phone, and she looked at me and started to cry and then she said, "Okay, I'll get her," and I knew it was Mama telling me that Daddy died. I didn't cry then; in fact, I cried about a day later, just because I thought I needed to. I handled the funeral completely, while my mother went into shock, basically was a basket case. People came from all over the country; there were at least eighty cars in the funeral procession. I handled everything; I wrote the obituary, everything, at the age of twelve.

When my father was dying—my mother and my brothers had told me the exact same story—he said, "Move the door; move the door." And then, people say, he was saying it like it was the gate, heaven or something, and then he said, "Bernard, Bernard," and he was motioning off in the direction where my brother Sherwood Bernard was standing—but we never called him that; we called him Woody. And he came up there, and he said, "No, Dad, it's me, Woody." And he's like no and he had moved, and Daddy's still looking over there, going, "Bernard, Bernard," and then soon or thereafter peace just came over him and he died. Bernard was his Uncle Bernard, his best friend growing up, who, as they say in the family, went to the store for a loaf of bread and never came back, and that was my father's greatest loss. You've heard this story: your favorite person comes back and carries you to the life thereafter.

So when my father was dying, I had some pretty spiritual experiences, and my father did as well. It really made me believe that something else was out there and that I really need to hook into something beyond this life because that was what was going to give me the love and support I needed to get through the grief of my father's death. I had just moved to a new church, and so when I was grieving, the church was there.

Anyway, I went to a retreat in a hotel in Gatlinburg, led by an evangelist who was big in the South. The way it worked was that you paid a price and you heard preachers and special guests, like one of the singers from the rock group Kansas. You listened to testimonies and sang and had fellowship, you visited, and you had fun things to do, and that's essentially what it was. The evangelist asked people to come up and accept Christ as their savior, and that's when I went up and I did it, and I did feel something. I don't know if I really just wanted to feel it so bad, or something really did touch me. I have a feeling that something touched me. Somebody, something, I felt the power; I knew that there was something out there that had picked me to love. And it could have been my father; I don't know. There's no way I can ever know. I was taken in by it and really got into it for a long time. I became part of this Fishers of Men group, and I was caught up in the whole hoopla in the church. I kept being elected to positions of leadership. I was very sincere. I was into it.

Not long thereafter, however, Denise focused her energies in other places.

Not too long after that I moved to Birmingham, to a fine arts high school. I had done a summer show the summer after my tenth grade year, and the director said if I wanted to be an actress, I had to get the hell out of Montgomery and get some training. And so I went up to Birmingham to visit my brother. I brought home all the paperwork, and I said: "Mom, I'm auditioning. Just sign on the bottom line." She was just a little addled, she didn't know what was going on, but she signed something and then even drove me up. I remember her being there, and she didn't realize the impact it was going to have on my life, taking me away from home and everything; she thought it was just a whim, and I'd get homesick and come back home. Well, I stuck it out, and she, still to this day, says that I "aborted home" at that time, which hurts me. I think it had a lot to do with roles; I knew that I needed to do this, but I also knew that I could probably do a little something in Montgomery until I went to college anyway to get some training. But at that time my mother and I were not getting along at all—in fact, we have never really, truly gotten along. My mother and I are a lot alike; she's a little more histrionic than I am, which made my father tend to want to be around me a little more than her. So, no, we weren't getting along, and I needed to get away.

Anyway, when I went to the performing arts high school, I started falling away from church. I lived so much through talking over a beer with friends or taking a little drug and taking a long drive; how much more my mind was stimulated. Little things made me believe that "I'm such a sinner; I can't handle it," and I started getting into that deep valley, and then I almost gave up on the church. I went into psychotherapy, was majorly depressed for three or four years. By the time I was a freshman in college, I hadn't been in church for years, and I kept on pretending that I was going to go back.

I'd go home and go to Easter Sunday service and Christmas services with my family and say hi to everybody and make them think I was going to church in the places I was at, but it never came to pass. I remember one Easter Sunday when I stayed in Tuscaloosa and made my hungover friends get out of bed and go to church with me—it was a total, complete disaster. And not any fun. So seven years—I never really thought about it—is a long time to be floundering. I was going through many changes. Doing different scenes. I went for a whole year and a half without shaving or anything like that. I punked out and wore black constantly. I did the preppy scene with the little fraternity boys and I hung out with the lacrosse team. I threw myself into my work really hard—just different kind of things, just going through different changes, growing up.

Denise did, however, begin exploring new spiritual possibilities.

My friend Betty Jean is responsible for getting me into the Science of Mind church. She was in my graduate school class, she lives here in Chicago, and we're still good friends. She is one of my very dearest friends in that she is one of the few people who I know why she's in my life; I know. She's a mirror to me, she's totally opposite from me in many ways, but she calls me on my shit, and she's like a sister in that respect. She's taught me a lot about the zodiac and about tarot cards and spirituality and having faith in yourself, which I really needed to tap into when I was in graduate school. She taught me that the inner strength and the inner creative powers, all of that's within myself, and it's about choices. We've had endless hours of conversation about this kind of thing, endless; it's her favorite topic, and she really stirs me to think about things. She met her husband through the Science of Mind church there in Sarasota. We called it the happy church, and she was very devout and always carried her little devotional around with her. I just wanted to try it out, and she never pushed me, she never invited me, she just shared what she knew, and that's what made me say, "Great." I remember the first time I went—it was on Easter Sunday, and I had a great time. I went by myself, and people were nice to me; nobody bothered me with anything. I got a carnation. I believed what the man was saying about cycles and rebirth and going on to a different level when you die and everything, and I was just digging the whole thing. I went back a couple more times when I could, when I wasn't too tired on Sundays.

At the same time, my early beliefs that Jesus was God's only son kept creeping in, so I felt blasphemous, and Mama disapproved. It was mostly Mama and my sister. And then I moved, and the preacher that I liked so much got transferred, so I just stopped going and got into other things in my graduate program. We rehearsed all day on Sunday most of the time.

I did stay in Montgomery for a good while, and during that time I think I went to church maybe three or four times. My mom didn't bother me; she didn't make me get up out of bed because I got a job as a waitress, where I waited on tables ten o'clock on Sunday morning, so I didn't have to go to church. I waited until two in the morning on Saturday nights and had to get up early on Sunday morning to go back to work. She never bitched, so I was glad.

And then I moved to Chicago. I moved here alone, right after a terrible breakup with my boyfriend, Peter. Peter went to Italy for a visit, and then he was supposed to come back, and then we were supposed to move here. He's from St. Paul; he was flying back home where I was going to meet him, and then we were both going to be moving here from St. Paul. He came back from Italy saying—it was the day before I was to fly up to St. Paul—and he said: "I'm sorry; I have to go back. I fell in love with the country." I'm like, "Great, fine, go." I moved to Chicago on my own. He spent some time making some money and then went back to Italy. He came back a month and half ago. We had had a great relationship; we never fussed or fought.

Coming out, for Denise, happened over many years, and it wasn't until very recently that she came to name her sexual orientation.

Coming out was a slow process because I guess I always knew that homosexuality was about love. I was fortunate, I suppose, to be from the South—when people come out down South, they come out for a damn good reason, not to just get their rocks off. I had friends all through my years who were gay and came out to me first because I was open-minded about it and I knew that if you wanted something, you had to get it in your own way. I've always been of that belief. So I suppose I had my first experience with a little kiss when I was a senior in high school. And nothing ever really happened. I went to college my freshman year and had an affair with my vocal singing teacher, who was married and who had herpes, so I couldn't reciprocate. All these things are with women who were good friends—except one one-night stand that I tried to turn into something else, and she fell in love, and then I realized she was crazy. It was my one bad experience, just going with it because I thought maybe it was all purely physical with me. And it isn't. I'm the kind of person—I've always been this way—who believes that it's not the package; it's the person inside. So I had a few experiences, just with good friends, some good, some bad, a lot of sexual exploration, and a lot of rejection, I suppose. Just because I picked the wrong people to have feelings for. And it wasn't really heartbreaking; in fact, it just kind of made me say: "Well, there's probably someone out there for me. It's just going to be a matter of time before it's truly reciprocated, and then I'll know it's the right one."

Denise met her lover, Kathy, through the personals.

Meanwhile I dated guys, and it wasn't until mid-April that I decided to respond to a personal ad in the *New City* newspaper here in Chicago. I was sitting at home one night, on a Friday night, and I was feeling good about being alone. I said to myself: "Damn, my life is great: I've got this great job; I'm in a great show that just got Jeff-recommended; I just had everything in order. I had cleaned my apartment, spit-spot, I could lose a few pounds, but that's beside the point. Peter is not around me for the first time in my life, and by that time we had decided to date other people. I had dated a few guys, but none of them had turned me on at all. Hmmm. I didn't know why, but I just decided I didn't need these guys. Do I need anybody? No. So there I am sitting at home—and I'd had a couple beers, I admit, and it freed up my thinking and my inhibitions somewhat—and I was asking myself: "Well, what do I want? I would like to see if I could find a female companion who is really open-minded and would like to hang out with me." I'd always pass by the Closet [bar] and say to myself, "It would be really cool to go in there and meet some interesting women who weren't so fickle on men and stuff." And I thought, "Well, I can't go there alone, and I can't just go there with a guy;

maybe I could go there with a girl or something." I was looking for a friend. I answered the guys' ad of the week, and by the way, I went out with him, and it was a total stupid thing. I had lunch with him, and I was so anxious that lunch was over, and he asked me out again, and I just said, no. I was nice, though.

And I went through the women's section, and I had always just looked at it because I'd never seen such a thing as women seeking women. And there was this very, very reserved ad: "Single white female, twenty-seven and professional but fun, enjoys outdoors and romantic nights, seeks same, hope you're not allergic to cats." I said, "Kitty-cats!" (I'm a feline fanatic), and I called her up and listened to her voice mail, and there's this little-bitty voice that sounded really cute with kind of a southern kind of twang, just a little bit. And she just said, "I've never really done this, and I'm kind of new to the North Side here, and I just wanted someone to do something with, so if you want to leave your number, I'll call you back." And it was so laid-back and secure; you can tell when someone's got their shit together. So I called her right up, and I just said, "I've never done this either, and it's the truth, and I'm new to the area, and here's my number." And I never left my name. We played phone tag back and forth for weeks 'cause our hours are screwed up. And she kept saying, "Leave me your name," but I wasn't going to do that—I didn't know who she was. Finally, I took a chance and called her at eleven o'clock one night; she was just getting ready to go to bed, and we talked for two and a half hours about everything. I asked her to dinner, and when she walked up the stairs, I took one look at her, and I knew that something was going to happen. I never flirted with her because I knew she was going to be my friend; I knew she was a beautiful person before I saw her, but I didn't really want to bed her or anything like that. She was cute and everything, but it was like, sex was not what I wanted; I wanted a companion. And I got it. She's been in my bed every night since. And we're moving in together October 1st. I move into her apartment.

Denise's mother continues to be a strong influence in her life.

I suppose I came out to my mother around that time. I never volunteered any information to her other than I met a girl; we're good friends; I love her; she loves me. She wanted to know if she has a boyfriend, and I said, "No." And then she said, in a later conversation, "Is she a lesbian?" and I said, "Yes." And then she said, "I knew it; I knew it," and then it was fireworks from then on out.

When my mother and sister first got the gist, the key argument was that my being lesbian was what's breaking their heart. Well, my mother's being very selfish, thinking that she'll never have grandchildren, which is a big lie; I'm going to have children, and Kathy wants them, too—God willing, and the creek don't rise; we've only been together five months now—but we have big plans. My mother and my sister follow the Bible, point-blank, and if it's a sin, then I'm wrong; they keep saying, "All you have to do is turn back and ask God for forgiveness, and we'll never mention this again." But the more time passes, the more despondent they become.

Now my sister's different than my mother. My sister has never cried, to my knowledge at least, in front of me; if anything, she has seemed mad that I could be so stupid and do this: "You're just causing a scene, you're just being extremist, and you're doing this for attention." And then she pitied me, and now it's "I've got my own life to lead"; she could give a shit, and I'd almost prefer that.

This is a time of asking questions.

I'm at a place in my life where I'm clarifying and answering questions. I wish I knew of a religion that will fill in all the blanks for me—the things that I think I believe in right now, I wish they would help me concretize them. I would like to see it in writing, some kind of thing that I can study every day. Even if it's a little devotional guide or something. And I would like to see some of the blanks filled in for me and have complete congruity, have it all mesh together. It was such a world-rocking thing when I came out to my family and my friends. My friends were totally supportive, but it was an ordeal for me to tell some of them. None of them are upset or anything, but I would hate to say, "Okay, now I'm going to be a Buddhist" because they'd freak, and that would just cause more stress and trauma in my life, and I don't need it.

Denise (left) *and Kathy: "I want to share with her the one thing that I think that we need more in our relationship, and that's a spiritual communion together."*

The reaction of my mother and of other people is a really big issue now. And you know what it has a lot to do with? Kathy. I want to share with her the one thing that I think that we need more in our relationship, and that's a spiritual communion together, because we've got a lot of the other good stuff. I think she's open to it; she desires that, too. She off-handedly says, "Oh, it's just that I'm a person of science, I'm a doctor, and therefore I don't believe there's anything out there." And I throw up examples and make her admit the truth of what she believes, which is something's out there; I just don't know what. And I'm thinking if we can just get a grasp on something we can follow through on, then we can share that together.

We have a spiritual side; we just can't define it. We talk about it a lot, and she believes that I'm here for a reason. And I ask her, "Well, who or what orchestrated all this?" And she's like, "I don't know." So I go on to say, "Well, wouldn't it be nice to know?" We both recognize that it wasn't just by happenstance that we came together; it couldn't have just been two people with such a direct need, just like two little laser beams that found each other and became one energy. Who knows?

I feel the call to express my spirituality every day, on some level; however, I usually ignore it, unfortunately. When I wake up in the morning, I thank God that I'm lying next to this beautiful creature and I've been so blessed. And I think of what I have to do during the day, about how lucky I am to have my job and my friends and a purpose in my life, even if it's a superficial one, like getting through the day at work and going to an audition. And I have all these drives, all these creative things going on within me; I feel like I need to praise whoever gave this to me because it didn't just happen.

It could be just a bunch of energy bowling around in space; it could be that my soul's been reincarnated to this point, in this evolution, right now, so I don't even know if I believe in that. I have so many different little theories that could possibly be true, and I could go any way on many of them. Especially when something good happens to me, I just feel like, thank God—well, who's God to me? I'm a very introspective person these days because through all my therapy and everything I've found that's as aware as I can possibly be; that's as good as I'm going to be and as happy as I'm going to be. So I can stop and say, "What's going on with me right now?" even if what's going on is I want to be superficial; I don't want to talk to this person; I'll be cordial. It's a choice, and that's what I'm into right now. It's about choice because for a long time I didn't have any choices: I had to get through school, do this thing, be this way; now I'm living my life as my own choices. I don't want anyone to make them for me; I don't want to make them according to any set doctrine or anything like that other than my own personal happiness, whatever makes me happy in the moment. So sometimes, a lot of times, I ignore it, instead of saying, "Since my body is a temple, I shouldn't smoke this right now," I'll smoke it. I'll have a great time doing it, and then I think, "Omigod, I just cut ten years off my life." Fine, I'm happy right now. That's another thing that my sister is especially concerned about; she's like, "You're not happy; you're not happy." I'm like, "You should be happy; I'm happy." "But you're not happy; you're not happy." I'm like, "What are you talking about?" And then I realize that she's talking about instant gratification, and when it comes down to it, my soul will die 'cause I'm going to hell. So I don't stop and think about those things; I ignore those little things. When something bad happens, then I turn and say a little prayer to myself, and I think: "This is hypocritical bullshit. What the hell do you think you're doing?" I still do it. A lot of time I think I'm just talkin' to myself, but it helps.

Going to a traditional church, like the one of her childhood, has been a challenge to Denise.

When I go to church and have to sing, "He, praise Him," I have a problem with the language because who the hell said it was a him? Who the hell said it had genitals? And it kind of makes me think it's another one of those things that the patriarchal translators threw into the Good Book. And I'm just offended by it. That's another reason why I don't make it a point to go to church every Sunday. I tend to be a fair-weather Christian, the kind of person who might pray for reassurance or guidance or help in a time of need. And I realize that's very hypocritical and sucks and I need to do something about it. I also realize that every time I go out and party—and I party a lot; I like my alcohol, and I love cigarettes and things like that—I don't feel guilty about it anymore. It's part of my life;

it's who I am. So I know that maybe I should ask for forgiveness; I don't know if I'm a Christian right now. I know I was brought up as one, I call myself one, but truly, I don't know. I haven't been able to find anything that truly jives with what I believe. I know there's something else out there after death, and I have a strong desire to find a faith that I can concretize in my own life, where I can worship and pray and have faith and give and give and receive and receive. I don't know if it has anything to do with United Methodism, really, although that is what I feel most comfortable with, but that's conditioning.

The Science of Mind church seemed to be more apt to refer to God as a creative force or power that is within every living thing—God as me, God as you. And they don't believe in Jesus being the Son of God dying on the cross. They think Jesus was the Son of God, as we are the Children of God, and I tend to much more believe that than anything I've learned in the United Methodist church. But when I went to the Science of Mind church and felt really good about it, Mother and Sister shamed me and shamed me and said that I was going to hell. So for the next Easter I went to a Christian church, and I felt much more comfortable. Now all I know is that I tend to believe that Jesus was a prophet who had wonderful powers and probably could work miracles. I do believe that miracles can and do occur every day and did occur then. I think that the Bible is a bunch of blown-up bullshit that has essential truths in every little parable and probably all this stuff did happen, and it is wondrous, and we do need to study it, but I think it's been translated so much—I mean, what does it say in Leviticus? I was looking at it the other day—homosexuality is the most evil thing you could possibly commit. I say bullshit to that; God taught us to love. I'm not going to hell because I love. That's a simple truth; I know that. So I think it's more a creative force; I feel God pulsating within me whenever I'm at my most creative, especially being an actress and being on the stage. About a year ago when I was going through my severe breakup—I don't think that I was so heartbroken over this guy that that's what made me turn to lesbianism or anything like that—I'd made so many plans, and we couldn't stay together, and when the bottom fell out, I turned to God. And it was a great feeling to have that weight lifted off my shoulders and be carried by God, like the footsteps-in-the-sand poem. As soon as I adopted that positive attitude and was open to good things happening to me and coming to me, things happened left and right and they continue to do that. So I think that has something to do with it, too. The creative positive power within us: it could have all just been a mind trip I laid on myself; it could all lie within me. I prefer to believe that; that gives me more control over my destiny.

Denise has been searching for a church where she can feel comfortable.

When I moved here, I was alone and I wanted to find a church. I was doing all the things I wanted to do, finally. I made the choice to go the closest United Methodist church, but they were extremely cool. I made a lot of pretty superficial friends when I went, I joined the choir, and I noticed that I was in the choir with a bunch of lesbians and gays. And I was kind of freaked out. It was the Sunday after Christmas, after we had performed a lot of Christmas choir shows and stuff, when I found that a friend of mine who is gay was seeing another gay guy in the choir. A member of the congregation had attempted suicide on the altar on Christmas Eve. And I'm thinking, this is screwed up because my knowledge of United Methodism does not allow homosexuals in the congregation, but this place is very tolerant. I was asking myself, Are they just lackadaisical, or are they too weak to say, "Listen, our doctrine doesn't allow you in"?—and I got real confused. And then I was thinking, well, these poor souls are thinking they're getting something substantial and they're not, and no wonder they're trying to kill themselves. And I got the hell away; it scared me bad, and I only went back one more time, for Easter Sunday, with a Russian guy I had just met, who had never been to church like that. He had a wonderful time, and right after that, we walked out of the church and our car had been towed, so that was another bad experience. Since then Kathy and I have been to a PFLAG [Parents, Families and Friends of Lesbians and Gays] meeting, and I expressed my desire there to have a church that accepted me as a lesbian, and they told me about reconciling congregations [the United Methodist movement to affirm gay men and lesbian women in the church].

I really enjoyed the Easter service at another local reconciling Methodist church. I really loved it. Kathy was uncomfortable, so she won't go back. I thought it was wonderful. I was singing it at home, and Kathy was kind of upset, I don't know why she felt uncomfortable. I think it's basically the Jesus thing. I think that's what she can't deal with, and she doesn't believe me when I tell her that this church doesn't mind that you're gay or lesbian. I could tell one person was lesbian, and I don't even know for sure, but there was only one person there who came near to a stereotype. And I think that's what made Kathy freak. And I'm dressed to the nines in my little Easter coat and everything, and Kathy's wearing pants, and she had this jacket on, and she wouldn't take it off; she kept saying, "I would bet that there's maybe one gay person here; we don't belong here." And I'm going, "I don't know." I'm going to try and get her to come back, but you know what, Sunday's the only day we have together—that is not an excuse, it's a reason, and it's the only one I can think of to give myself when I look at the card from the church or when we get something in the mail; it makes me say I really want to go. Sunday is the only day we sleep in. And it's so precious because rolling over and finally being able to look at each other and wake up together and say hi is a luxury.

I'm content. It would be a luxury if we'd be able to go to church together, which is what I really want. I have my own peace of mind, and I don't hunger for that spiritual knowledge or fellowship. No, I don't need the community. It scares me because it reminds me too much of what I've been through before, with fellowship and witnessing and everyone's in it all together, collectively judging. I would just rather work on my own self and try to become the best person I can be. In my old church situation it was very catty and it was very gossipy and it was very fashion-showish; it was a social club. It didn't have anything to do with what I sense as important, and so I tried another church. I kind of happened on it in Sarasota with the Science of Mind people, but I don't think I can go anywhere that tells me that Jesus is not the Son of God. That's the only thing that I was taught as a kid that I don't know to be true, but I cannot dispute it. And so that's the thing that I have the childlike faith about. Everything else to me is a given: do unto others as you would have them do unto you, all those parables. I guess they're so ingrained in me that I take them for granted. I catch myself judging; do you know what I mean?

I know when I'm doing bad. But the other things that churches teach about sin I do not believe. So I don't need it.

Her experience since coming to Chicago has been a significant change from what she has known and lived before. I asked Denise if she thinks of herself as lesbian or bi.

I do not define myself. If someone had to do it technically, on a completely scientific level, I don't have a problem with that. I suppose I am bisexual, but I've never been able to look at a man and think in sexual terms since I've met Kathy. And I've tried—I talk to men who, six months ago, I would have just fallen over and panted after; so I don't know. I just got her a ring for our six-month anniversary. I've had this rare green garnet forever, and I just had it set in a deco setting.

Something Kathy always asks me is, if it doesn't work out between me and her, am I going to go back to another guy? How the hell am I supposed to know? Who knows? I could get married to a guy and have ten children and look back on this as just a phase I went though. But I don't think so. I want more than anything in the world for it to work out with her. I can see a very, very happy life with her.

At different points in my life in the past I've thought, I see a wonderful future with this person, but never, during all those times, did I know that I could, if I wanted to, imagine this kind of life. And now that it's happening and everything is going so well, I have a chance to apply all the positive things I've learned. I deserve this. And when Kathy and I look at each other and say, "Why are we in each other's lives?" I can praise the fact that something has got us through all this bad shit to this point. We are being rewarded; we are being blessed by having the chance to sit back and enjoy the peace. You know what I'm saying?

Being lesbian made me damned scared because during the time that my mom was saying, "Omigod" I could hear the heartbreak in her voice. She and my sister really believe that they'll never see me once I die, you know. And I was always raised to believe that we'll see each other in heaven, I'll see my daddy in heaven again, and if they think that I'm going to die and go to hell, I'll never see my dad again. And it just chokes me up, still, because it could be true. But I still believe that essential truth:

that I know I'm not going to go to hell for loving someone as wonderful as Kathy. Forget about it; we'll go to hell together. Kathy and I laugh about it because during those times, during the tears and everything, she just puts her arms around me and says: "You're not going to be alone; you're going to be with me. We'll both go to hell." It's nice to know she's there with me every step of the way.

In a meeting a few months later Denise shares how some of her questions have changed, particularly around her sense of herself as Christian and lesbian.

When I was a kid, I used to freak myself out wondering if I wasn't here, then I'd be someplace else, and if I wasn't there, I'd be someplace else, and if I wasn't there, I'd be someplace else, and I would just get into a frenzy saying that over and over, and then there's nothingness and that's it, and then I might as well just run out in front of that car right now. Life is meaningless. It's terrifying. It's absolutely terrifying. It will wake me up in the middle of the night. I will cry and cry. But I can control it now when I stop and say: "No, this is not arbitrary. All this great energy is not arbitrary." As long as I know I'm here for a purpose—and that's to learn whatever it is and to grow and to experience and, above all, to love—I know that no matter what the hell happens, I'm going to come out on top.

I do know I'm a Christian; now I do know that. I've finally asked myself that enough times, and, now, as an open lesbian for over a year now, I know that love is it, and I still believe that Jesus is the Son of God and I'm his daughter as well. I am a Christian; I believe that that is true. I think maybe back then I was struggling with it, when I said a few months ago that I didn't know because I still had those preconceived images of what Christian is. I still had the Pat Robertson idea of Christian. And now I know that Christianity, to me, is whether or not you believe the things that are inherent in the essence of the Bible.

I've noticed that every time I tell a fellow gay person that I'm a Christian—and this has only been the past nine months—they are usually astounded or shocked, and then I see a twinkle, a longing in their eyes. I see that love in their eyes. I mean, I only tell the people that love me as much as I love them. I don't tell everybody off the cuff. I tell them in deep spiritual conversations, and almost all of them that I'm getting in this conversation with haven't made the correlation that it was sinful to be gay. Truly. I speak primarily of my "southern brothers." They were brought up in good Christian families—and I use that term loosely—and went to church and learned the elemental things that they live their lives by. But Christianity and going to church, especially with the one they love, is taboo. They want more than anything to go to church with Mama, with their lover. They want to get married in that church they grew up in, and I use marriage loosely. Maybe not in the same way, but I know that they want it. And no one has asked me anything about it; they just kind of think that it's a habit, that I was always Christian, so now I'm a Christian. They don't understand that transformation, the assimilation I've had to make to stick with it and stay on it and explore where I'm at; I was able to make the transition of coming out, being gay, and bringing Jesus with me.

Coming out as lesbian and Christian is sacred to me. It's not something I'm going to say in a bar or something. A lot of people at my workplace, and some friends of mine, pretty much know, but I've never told them. But whenever they talk about who I'm going somewhere with, "Oh, is Kathy coming?" They've asked enough questions that I've answered correctly, so I don't have to tell them, but we don't talk about it because it would probably make them feel uncomfortable. I don't need to come out to them. They know; I know; it's fine. A couple days ago I was talking to a friend of mine at work, and I ordered a music box from her—and it was of the Virgin Mary, little angels, and the Christ child, and it played "Ave Maria." And she was astounded that I got that. She was looking at me like: "Why did you get this? You're gay; you can't believe in Christmas." And I said, "Well, I'm Christian, and I like this. It's a beautiful thing." And that was all. She just couldn't make the assimilation; maybe she thinks I'm straight or a very confused lesbian.

My mother still does not believe that it is possible to be lesbian and Christian. But she does believe a real straight girl can come out and be very, very happy 'cause I've shown her that. She believes it. And she believes that this whole thing has brought us closer; I know that. She believes that I love her. She believes that I care. She believes that no matter what, nothing's gonna pull us apart. Nothing's gonna pull the family apart. She believes that Kathy won't intentionally hurt me. Finally, she believes that Kathy's not out to hurt me, in other words, and she's not playing with me. Kathy's not messing with her daughter.

My family and my support system are two different things. I have my family in the sense of the people I consider my family, and I have my clan or my chosen family or my support system. I think truly and honest, my own support system is within myself. It's not that I can't count on people; it's just not possible for one person to be there for me all the time. It depends on what it is, who I'm hanging with, what's going on, how long it's been; I have friends all over this world, and there's always someone there if I need them, a couple people, but at different times. My grandma taught me that.

And I'm not independent. I'm more codependent than independent, but that's a totally different ball game; that's relationships. But I know I was born alone, I'm going to die alone, and it's between me and God as to what's going to happen. And it's up to me to just give over and do what I want to do, which is hopefully what He wants, which is what I have to pray for during my life, between the time I'm born and dead.

I can imagine it's going to be hard for me to come out to a couple people. Like at work, there are friends of mine, and we don't talk about it. They would have to say something. I couldn't. Even with the people that know me, if they're friends of mine and they find out I'm gay, to watch their lives transform and their hearts open up is a wonderful, wonderful thing. One of my dearest friends is my very first boyfriend. We met in the church; our relationship happened in the church, over and over again, for like four or five years, on and off. And he gave me my first teddy bear, in eighth grade or something. Well, he's really happy for me. He's a lovely man, very kind, gentle, open, always has been. But it's so funny to watch him come out in the way straight people have to come out in dealing with their own fear of homosexuality. One of the pivotal moments was when I asked him if he would support me if I joined the air force. And he said he would. And I said: "But I'm gay. Do you think I'd make a good soldier?" And he's like, "Oh, yeah, you'd be fantastic." And I said, "But I'm gay."

And he said, "Oh, you'd be great." And I said, "Well, how do you feel about gays in the military?" "Oh, no, I don't know." And I said, "Can you actually let me in and not let my gay brothers in and my other gay sisters in?" And he's just kind of, I could hear him falling through the ground. He just stopped and said, "No, I can't do that, can I?" I said, "No, you have nothing to be afraid of." So that was neat.

PART TWO

FINDING COMMUNITY

ALTHOUGH each individual must come to some resolution of his or her own spiritual struggle, it is typically not done alone. Many of the men and women who speak in these pages have moved toward an identification as a member of a community, similar to or different from the religious institutions they knew earlier in their lives. Yet even before they chose these particular affiliations, individuals and groups played influential roles in their spiritual development.

Several could identify someone along the way who was a role model or mentor. Some were distant—authors of important books, for example. Gerald, who felt very alone in his struggle to reconcile his very conservative Christian beliefs with his growing acceptance of himself as a gay man, turned to the writings of Sylvia Pennington, a heterosexual woman who said that it was fine to be gay and Christian. The book *The Impersonal Life,* by Joseph Benner, was key to Mark's coming out. And another participant, Sylvia, found Edgar Cayce readings powerful. These three individuals share their stories in Parts 3 and 4 of the book.

Others identified as a pivotal catalyst or support key individuals with whom they were very close. Several participants mentioned friends who took them to an accepting church for the first time. Many described persons who had already demonstrated in their own lives that one could be gay and spiritual: pastors, chaplains, teachers, and spiritual directors were singled out in the interviews.

As participants progressed through their coming out, finding a larger community with others who shared some aspects of their spiritual journey was crucial. That goal has led many to look for a group of likeminded individuals. This quintessentially interior process (the development of one's spiritual life) evolves, then, within the context of others. The directions that these men and women took were affected by the people they met, knew, or read and further framed by a larger, homophobic society.

Two women reflect the importance for many of finding a spiritual "home." One, Sandra, has found community; the other, Mary, is searching for it. Sandra, a thirty-one-year-old African-American woman, was born, and has spent most of her life, in the Chicago area. She grew up in a Baptist family; her parents went to different churches, and she went to both, splitting her time between them. Her father, a leader in his church, sexually abused her as a child; her intense struggle with this painful experience and with the hypocrisy she found in a church that could honor her father led her to attempt suicide at age thirteen. Feeling distant from her childhood church, she went on to explore other possibilities. When she was away at college, she discovered the women's spirituality movement at about the same time that she was becoming aware of her sexual feelings for other women. She eventually became part of a women's spirituality group, "something like a coven," but she soon found herself disagreeing with other members of the group over important values and life questions, and so she left. She later entered into a relationship and after a period of struggle, separation, and eventual reconciliation joined a Metropolitan Community Church and celebrated a Holy Union ceremony with her lover. She found a spiritual home where her values came together within the institution, and she has been in MCC ever since.

Mary, thirty-six, is a professor in California. She grew up in a missionary family in the Philippines, where she lived until she came to the United States for college. Her family was very religious, and she carries strong ties to that background, although she has clearly moved on. A growing consciousness of herself as a feminist, and later as a lesbian, led her to a "dark night of the soul" in which, she writes, she felt the "death of God as [she] had been taught God." It became very clear that she could not continue on the path she had been following as a child. These experiences have taken her outside the church, yet with an intense personal commitment to spiritual values. She misses a faith community now, but there doesn't seem to be a place where she is completely at home. She talks about the Quakers as a possibility: "In every way I can identify, in every way I can point to, I believe the same things. But for some reason I'm not a Quaker." And so the search continues.

Sandra: A Roller-Coaster Ride

Sandra has lived in the Chicago metropolitan area all her life except for four years of college, which she spent in Minnesota. She comes from an African-American Baptist family, and her parents were divorced when she was fourteen. She moved away from her childhood church out of anger at its hypocrisy. Later, coming out at college, Sandra pulled away from her family, as it did from her. She used the energy of her anger at her family to connect with other lesbian and gay people and to reexamine her values and beliefs.

She returned to Chicago and joined a women's spirituality group. Here she explored the neopagan philosophy and practices of Wicca, participating in rituals and celebrations with the women in the group. She separated from them over significant differences in the interpretation of a dream that she had and over the direction her life was taking her. Eventually, she found her way back to Christianity, this time through a Metropolitan Community Church. She and her partner began to attend the church as a condition of its agreeing to do a Holy Union ceremony for them. Her draw to MCC grew as she found that her spiritual needs—beyond just the ceremony—were met here, and she has stayed in MCC; now she practices a "more balanced" Christianity that incorporates what she learned from Wicca as well as more traditionally Christian teachings.

Most noteworthy, perhaps, in her words are the themes of challenge and choice; she has demonstrated in her life that she can face the obstacles that life presents her by figuring out what she believes is right and by making active choices. Significantly, for the focus of this study, are the choices she made to leave her tradition, explore alternative paths (including Wicca), and then return to a Christianity that accepts and honors her.

We begin with Sandra's discussion, retrospectively, of her journey and what it says about being gay or lesbian and spiritual. It's a wonderful statement about a lifetime of challenges and choices.

I think being lesbian, or being gay, or being anything that's "out of whatever norm," means that your spiritual journey may be a little bit more trying. And I don't know—maybe other people will agree with me—maybe, in the end, it is more enlightening, more satisfying than if the journey had been, let's say, streamlined. And when this journey has come to be at the pace that you're comfortable with, I think it's an even better feeling because then you get more of a sense of home. I think you go through a lot of ups and downs and hills and valleys to get there, but it's more satisfying in the end, and I think you're more secure in it once you come to the point where you have a stronger foundation. And I've seen that in other people who are very spiritual; there is a gentleman at the church that I attend, who—just by his presence in the room—you know he has a very good foundation. He has had some trying times, too. He's just like everyone else; he's human.

I think being lesbian or gay gives you a little edge, which is good, because we have such a hard time. It's helpful, once you have developed your spiritual base, in dealing with the roughness you have to deal with in the world. I definitely believe that. Once a lesbian or gay man attains their spiritual level, it's a lot easier for them to go with the things that they have to go through. 'Cause we still have a lot to go through. It's harder to get there, but once you get there, it's a smoother journey.

It's like riding on a roller-coaster ride, one of those roller-coaster rides where you're standing up with your hands up and you really feel every motion; once you come to the part where your spirituality's in base, instead of standing up and holding on, it's like you get to sit in the seat with the seat belt, and it's a little easier ride. Not to say that you still don't have it rough, but it's an easier ride; it's not as bad as it was when you were hanging up there.

Sandra's telling of her childhood before she left home to go to college is particularly powerful, for in it we discover what led to her more mature choices.

I come from a—I won't say highly-developed—Baptist background, kind of in between Southern Baptist and American Baptist. It was not extreme Southern Baptist, but it wasn't as liberal as American Baptist. As children we were to go to church regularly, every week, once a week, at least until we turned the age of fourteen; then I didn't have to go every week if I didn't want to.

In the beginning, when I was very, very, very young—we're talking like the early primary grade years—from what I can remember, church was just something you did. It was just like going to school; you know that you go to school five days a week, and you know you go to Sunday school on Sundays. It was part of the routine. I couldn't tell you much about the religious lessons; we learned the basics, to know the names of all of the chapters of the Bible, a few verses and so on, but as far as any of that really sticking, none of it did. It was very vague—I just kind of knew God was. I guess it was just like going to school. It was something that people had told you, and of course, since people told you, then it must be. But as far as really feeling it in yourself, I didn't really feel it. It was something like, when everybody says you go to school, so you go; I'm like, okay, well, everybody says so, then it must be. But I didn't really have the feeling inside.

Toward the preteen years, about nine, ten, or eleven—I think I was baptized at age nine—it took on a little more significance. I guess that was the start of some type of religious awakening; it wasn't just something I did because it was part of the routine. I'd go to Sunday school, and I'd feel better about the world; I'd feel better about myself, all those kinds of good things. At that age I couldn't put words onto it, just that it was something I enjoyed going to because I felt good about going and then I felt good when I left. A shot in the arm, I'd say, from nine to eleven or twelve.

And then a time of a lot of pain and confusion began in Sandra's life. Angry at the church and at her father, she cried out for help by swallowing a bottle of aspirin.

Between the ages of eleven and fourteen, I was confused. That's the time when I was becoming awakened to my own personal identity, my sexual identity, and all those kinds of things, and so it was very much a confusing stage.

I think that it was fourteen when I attempted suicide. Thirteen or fourteen, it was somewhere around in that age. Part of attempting suicide was a result of sexual abuse for two and a half years by my father. I couldn't understand how my father could say one thing and do another and be a very devout, well-respected member of the church. To me, it was like, this is really a joke—you just don't know the other side. I couldn't understand, if you're supposed to be so religious, so devout, how can you be doing things that to me seem so contrary from what you're saying? You could say, "Love one another, blah blah blah," yet you could harm people. So I thought, maybe church is just something people feel they have to do because they have to do it, but that it does nothing for your own human spirit. It didn't seem like it was doing anybody any good. I'm like, well, you can go to church, but then I'd think that you'd act with the humane principles that you're supposed to be learning in church. I didn't see that, and I'm like, so then what's the need to be going to church?

My personal belief at that time—that's when I'm starting to make that separation from family and all that stuff—is that they can be hypocritical, but that doesn't mean I have to be hypocritical. Being older now, I can think if I didn't like what they were doing, well, you're human, and you're going to have some problems, and so on. Then I was thinking that they would at least try to be consistent.

Anyway, at that time I was trying to sort out exactly what was what. I think I'd come to a really low, low point where I wasn't feeling good about myself, really not feeling good about much of anything at that time. And I attempted suicide—unsuccessfully, of course, 'cause I'm here, and I didn't really mean it; it was more one of those cry for help things. I swallowed a bottle of aspirin, and it made me sick to my stomach. I remember I went and gave my mother a little note that I did this, so, of course, she came downstairs and asked me what I did, and I had to drink mustard water. Uckk! I was so sick, and I threw it all up. She didn't understand what was going on then; after I did that, she said, "Well, you need to make some goals in your life since you really don't seem like you're happy."

That's when I had the choice of going to church or not. I don't think that she knew that was kind of helpful, to sort things out, but at that time I could think things through and try to figure out what I wanted to do. Looking back at how everything worked out from that moment, I ended up with an inner feeling that there was a higher power. People did reach out, and things did kind of work out better—my mother and father separated, which was both plus and minus, but things were kind of making a turn for the better, and it was nothing of any individual person's doing, so I had the feeling there had to be somebody up there that took care of this. I definitely couldn't have done any of this, and things were kind of working in their own way, so it gave me a gut feeling that there was a higher power, that there was something that takes care of things that we have no control of and directs things in the way they can be directed.

Something I guess I kept all the way through was that I always prayed. I knew there was somebody to talk to. [Laughs] Even if there was nobody else there, I always felt good about the sense of prayer, so I always prayed. I may not have always been sure exactly to who-what-where I was praying, but I felt better, so I felt it must be doing some good.

Gradually, Sandra began exploring new religious avenues.

One of my goals at that time, after I attempted suicide, was to think about what I did believe regarding religion: that I didn't have to go to church; I don't believe people are doing what they're informed to in church. I decided if I felt the need for it, then I'd go, and if I didn't feel the need for it, I didn't have to go. I did a lot of reading, and I went to different friends' churches. During those teen years, and especially when I first started in college at sixteen, I went to a Catholic church, and I knew some people who were from a Judaic faith, so I had a chance to really start to get into what other religions had to offer—what their basic concept was—and I always still had the feeling that God was there. I really didn't understand how you got to it, but I still believed that there definitely was a higher power. I didn't at that time agree that using the Baptist route was exactly the right route to go. I guess I based that on the hypocrisy I saw. Maybe that wasn't really the right way to get there, but there was still belief in the spirit, and I could feel that the spirit can be healed as well. So I'd say that from sixteen to eighteen I was checking out different places, going to different types of churches, reading a few things here and there, along with day-to-day living.

I did my first year of college at Lincoln College in Minnesota. I was there for one year. And it felt too competitive for me at the time. So the next year, I went to Bart College, which is also in Minnesota.

While she was away at college, she came out.

One of the big things from staying in Minnesota was realizing I was a lesbian. After I had identified it, I inadvertently informed my mother. I was going to school in Minnesota at that time, and for the summer I helped my mother with their move from Park Forest to Hartford and tried to help her get on her feet. She came across some writings that I had written, and what could I do—it was in black and white? So I informed my mother that I was a lesbian at that time, although I hadn't been a "practicing" lesbian. I said, "Yes, well, I identify that I've had these feelings, blah blah, but I haven't been with anyone yet, but . . . but I know it's there; I just know it's there." And I guess, for my mother, it went fairly well—understanding my mother, who knew that was it: I was going to hell; I could have no more contact with the kids, with my brothers and sisters. She thought it was something contagious, that I was going to infect my brothers and sisters, and they were all going to become gay. I don't think it works like that. [Laughs] I don't think so. We were in Hartford at that time, and my mother was not working; I was the sole supporter of our whole family at that time, so I hung in there for three months until my mother was able to get permanent work, so that she could take care of the family. She found a place for her and the rest of my brothers and sisters, and then I took off to Minnesota, and that was that.

And when I went back to school, I vowed I was going to stay there. I was in Minnesota for the next four and a half years.

So I lived in Minnesota, I found an apartment off campus, and I just basically stayed there for the next few years. I figured it was better for her, and better for me, and since she informed me not to have any contact with my brothers or sisters, better for everyone involved. It was not bad. I got to connect with the gay community there, which was a really fun-loving community. All of us who had been disowned and warned off, killed off by our families, we had a good group of people.

Around seventeen or eighteen I came across some readings on female spirituality. I guess Mary Daly was the first one; that's the first name I remember. There were also a few other writings on including the feminine in spirituality. I thought, it sounds like a good idea; I could understand it. Thinking back now, at that time I had always felt a strong love for nature: I liked plants, I liked bugs, and I could understand the nurturing thing, the whole environmental thing that's becoming really big now. I could understand taking care of yourself and also having a responsibility to the environment. And using your spiritual connection with the earth and with yourself, tying them all in together really good. That's one of the basic principles I live with: do what you need to do as long as you're not harming anyone else in the process. And I'm like okay, this is very simple, very easy to understand, and very easy to carry into day-to-day living. So I thought I'd run with it.

I finished college, and I came back to Chicago, reluctantly. I didn't want to come back; I wanted to stay, but I couldn't find a job in Minnesota. My father still lived in Chicago at the time, so I stayed with him and my stepmother—my father remarried one year after he divorced my mother, and I had a little sister, maybe a year after that. I stayed with them for six months, found a job, found my first apartment, and tried to adjust to Chicago and to suburban gay life, which is different.

It was at this time that Sandra joined a women's spirituality group and began studying and practicing Wicca.

There was a program, offered through the YWCA, for rape/incest counselors, and I thought that would be good to work with. And it was awful good in helping me, as well as doing some good. One of the women who was presenting that program was also known as a spiritually involved woman, and later, after this course—maybe within a year later—she presented a women's spirituality group, something like a coven. The group was strictly women, but it was mixed, gay and straight. She went through some of the basic practices and ideas of Wicca, and so that's how I met her and other people who were interested in women's spirituality. We would contact her, and she'd let us know when she was starting this group. And we came to her house once every month and did various different types of practices, such as pulling down the moon and other little things. We'd do some—how do you say it?—far-reaching thinking, things to get into the spirituality. This went on for about a year.

Toward the end of the year, before I left the group, I had an intriguing dream. The way the dream came about was, you do some types of deep relaxation things, and you think through your "soul": about what's important to you. I guess it had to do with my subconscious or unconscious, a thought that I wanted to have a baby. It was one of those dreams where you feel like, I think I want to do this. And we had a disagreement as to what the dream meant. They just didn't agree with my perception of what I dreamed.

What I did later—'cause I have a five-year-old, so I must have done something—is that I decided to go on my instincts, on what I felt I should do regarding the dream that I had. And I did it fairly quickly, too. The time was just right for me to get pregnant. It was one time; it was very easy; it was very quick. Later I came back to the group, and other group members' perceptions on how I chose to handle what I felt was right for me became a little uncomfortable. And so I felt at that time that it was probably best to leave this group, which was not becoming a support group. Most of the women in the group, except for our presenter, didn't have any kids, and I didn't know that was an issue.

I felt uncomfortable about the group feeling uncomfortable about me, and that's definitely not the situation I wanted to be in, so I considered it a mutual parting of the ways, an agreement that it was best not to be in this group. I felt that I learned more about women's spirituality being in the group, and I appreciated that, but it was time to leave. And then it was time for me to sort out my thinking about the women's spirituality issue as a whole. If we were not being all encompassing, was it really what I was interested in? Not all encompassing in the sense that it was totally focused on women without any male input, which up until that time wasn't a concern for me, but later did become a concern for me. Not all encompassing as far as feeling that there was only one—maybe just really that particular group's—right way to do things; I don't get into things that are only one right way. I'm like, everybody is different, and when you start thinking that there's only one right way to do this, this may not be right 'cause people are just too different. It's too hard to have everybody thinking along the same lines. There has to be some allowance for variance, as long as you have some basic things in common.

Sandra's term for her major movements over the next few years was "firming up." This was a time of pulling strands together and building "a solid foundation"—another term she uses later.

In the next three years Mary was born; we had a house, lost a house, had a job, changed jobs, did reorganization. What else was going on in my head at that time? My partner was at that time a practicing alcoholic, and we had some difficulty with that issue and were definitely putting a lot of faith in spirituality. The fact that she'd come home every night was amazing, that the car didn't get any more totaled than it did, that the baby didn't get hurt, all those kinds of issues. Two years later she went in for treatment. We decided to temporarily part ways for awhile, while she went through treatment. That was a very good decision, as I think back now. I was kind of making it on my own again without a partner for a little while. That was a time of more soul-searching and firming up my identity issues, firming up career issues; there was a lot of firming up of issues at that time.

After my partner had been in treatment for about a year or a year and a half, we started talking on a more regular basis—we'd always been talking, but before we had just decided to kind of distance ourselves for a while. Career things improved; we were working out the day-to-day things, getting older I guess—that's the basic thing—getting older and maturing into what's really important and what's not really important, where your focus can be. My daughter was becoming older, and after going through the terrible twos, pulling my hair out, we were mellowing out a little more, and we were able to talk and try to firm up exactly what it was that we wanted, exactly what I wanted, exactly what she wanted, exactly what we thought would be good for our daughter. We decided that we would have a Holy Union.

For the Holy Union, they turned to a local Metropolitan Community Church, where she "ended up with a little more than [she had] bargained for."

I had been to an MCC church before, when I was twenty. I went there once, and it was okay, but nothing that would stand out. So I had no qualms about going back, going to MCC in the Chicago area, seeing how it was strictly for the purpose of the union. I wasn't really changing my mind-set since I still believed in God; I didn't have any firm beliefs such as, "What I believe is God going through Christ, or blah blah." I still believed in God, and I wasn't making a total pull away from nature, the importance of rituals, et cetera, from Wicca; I didn't throw all that away when I first went to the MCC church. The ideas were still there, and we went strictly for the process of the union. But part of the process of going through the union was that you needed to attend a few services there, an understandable request. The minister there was very good in his descriptive language about situations and things that happened in the Bible in the past and how they related to everyday things that we deal with now, especially with gays and lesbians. And it was intriguing. That was truly not the purpose of going, but I ended up with a little more than I bargained for, so to speak. I enjoyed the services. I learned so much more about religion and spirituality at this time than I had in all the time before, and that's a long time. Also, the minister, as part of the ritual, was able to connect the importance of day-to-day dealings, the importance of your environment, the importance of other people, and the importance of you. And it finally seemed to me like everything tied together, as if now all these little pieces that I've picked up on the way all came together.

There was no question. It was like the bell went on: okay, this is it; male and female are both important; there is no one over the other; nobody needs to be putting anybody down at all; everybody works together.

Of course, you can't be so totally into yourself that you have no concern for other people in your environment—including outdoor things, such as plants, as well as the environment of people. So it all clicked.

I also didn't see anything that was presented in any kind of hypocritical fashion, which was a really big thing for me. Now, from getting older, I think that you should do your best not to intend to be hypocritical. Sometimes you end up yourself being hypocritical, and you don't mean to, but you are trying your best; once you've been informed and made aware of your own hypocrisy around something, you should try to take care of it. Now I know that you get to the little gray areas; if you're made aware of it, you can do your best not to be like that.

I still get the good feeling, in fact an even better feeling, than I used to have when I was nine, ten, or more, a feeling at peace with myself. For me, I think that spirituality is not something that always just comes to you; you have to work at it. Some people may have to do less work than others, other people have to do more work—everybody's level of work is different—but I don't think that you can do it alone. I believe that you can be very spiritual, but you still need to have contact with people. That helps. It reminds you—when you've gotten high on the horse, as you say, and forgotten about taking care, or about being concerned about others, or you're considering that your way is the exact right way—how everything is kind of important in the scheme of everyone, that it's important to have a connection to other people. In your day-to-day life, you affect people, and you need to be concerned about the way you affect people. We're all connected. Like the movie that comes every winter, *It's a Wonderful Life,* where George is gone. What happens if you weren't here, George? As old as that movie is, everybody watches it, every year. But it does make sense that everybody affects everybody's life and that you need to be the best that you can be. No matter what you do, you still are connected with people, unless you're off on a desert island and there's no contact, but then you're interconnected with animals and stuff.

We return to where we began, with Sandra providing perspective on the challenges she's faced. As she says, "It's a hard, rough journey, but when you get to the end, it's worth it."

Spirituality has always been part of my life. I think that without the spirituality—and I guess this is just personally for me—it takes the heart out of everything. It's always been important. I've always done prayer, it gives me a sense of peace, and it gives me—some things it's hard to find words for, it's like there has to be better words for it—a sense of comfort. I've always considered spirituality a day-to-day thing, and I still feel that now, even when for a year and a half I was focused on Wicca spirituality. There was still a focus on major Wiccan celebrations, holy days, when I always made sure that I put in a little more focus for that day.

That's one of the things I like about the people who practice Judaism because their spirituality's more intertwined with the day to day, whereas I think that for some Christians—I say some, not all, Christians—spirituality has not become more of a day-to-day thing. That's not to say that you're practicing it constantly, but that it's in your mind, with what you do on a daily basis. It doesn't mean that you need to talk about it constantly, but that it's part of your day-to-day thinking. When you're doing something, you may think, "Oh, yeah, maybe I should do *this*." I know a few people like that, who may not attend any churches or anything, but their spirituality is focused on their day-to-day concerns. You know when you see it in their doings and things that it's part of who they are. I think that's the best way to say it: it's part of who they are; it comes out through their day-to-day living.

I had a time when my faith was really low when I was twenty-seven. I won't say I gave up, but I probably came pretty close. It was a time when things were not going well for me personally. Financially, emotionally, everything was an absolute wreck, and I didn't know which way to turn. It was definitely trying on my faith; it truly was. I won't say that I totally gave up, but I got real close. I didn't know what to do. I didn't know where to go. I didn't know who to talk to. I was just going to have to go through it blindly. I knew that there was a reason for this, but I didn't know what it was—and you could probably see it, too—that I was on my truly last leg. I felt like I just had to keep doing something and eventually something would work out. I have had some of those times where you felt so low, and nothing was going right and you didn't know where to turn, and you didn't know what the next minute would bring. It was, it was a rough, rough time. But I always had a base, a faith that something's going to happen, something. . . .

How has being lesbian affected my journey? Of course, you have to think of the timing: if this was twenty-something years ago, it would've been so hard to even find Wicca to start off with, if I would've had this feeling. You wouldn't have had any of that basis to come with; you would've truly only had negative witches and potions and evil demons and all that stuff that you would have thought of. I guess, in that respect, being lesbian has given some more opportunities in examining spirituality, plus I think that my spirituality as a whole became a little more balanced. Nowadays most religions—well not most, but a few more, religions—are becoming less inherently dictatorial than they have been. Most religions have been affected by women's participation.

Someone said this somewhere, in a book or something—the author is gay—that being lesbian, that being gay, gave you the option to challenge. In the fact of being who you are, you're already challenging. For me, it gave me the fact that I could challenge because being who I am was very challenging; I had the opportunity to say, "Well, you know, this may not be right for me because . . . " I was growing up being what everybody wanted me to be, and then all of sudden I became outcast for challenging, "I really don't have to believe this either. I don't have to believe any of this. I can go through and figure out really what I feel is right." So being lesbian has had an effect in that I had the opportunity to really challenge and I guess really to search out my faith and to have some trying times.

Spirituality now, in the lesbian community, is becoming a big thing. Being a minority and lesbian, spirituality is becoming a big thing for people who want to still stick with the mainstream churches. Being black and lesbian, definitely, in a mainstream church is more challenging, than being black and gay in a mainstream church. Black gay men have been part of mainstream churches for awhile; it's accepted. But to have black lesbians as part of the church, it's an uproar.

Sandra ends her comments by reflecting on her future and what it means spiritually to be lesbian.

I think at this time now I best can say that I'll probably be staying with the MCC church. I'm very comfortable with the church, and I'm very comfortable with the atmosphere. If I felt that there was a mainstream church that gave me the same comfortability, the same basic acceptance—'cause I don't know what this world will have twenty, thirty years from now—if that were the case, then I would see no problem with going to a mainstream church. But for right now I'm very comfortable at MCC, and I could see myself being with MCC for awhile.

I'm glad that we have MCCs because there are a lot of people who are going through that journey period. And I came across my church inadvertently. I truly didn't intend on it—it was a nice side benefit, for sure—but I'm glad that we do have MCCs because the journey is so hard because of the times we live in. I can't imagine what people did twenty, thirty years ago, before there were any MCCs, when there was nowhere to come to where they could feel comfortable. I cannot imagine what a time they had going through that.

I'm glad that people like you are doing surveys like this, so they know there's people like us out here who are very comfortable with themselves, and I hope that for gays and lesbians whose spirituality may be locked up in a bottle or a pill or something else that really doesn't give them their peace that information like this would be available for them. We have so many, one out of three that's locked in somewhere else. I guess that's the basic thing: I'm glad things like this are going on and that we have places like MCC for people to go. There are just so many other people who are into other things that do more damage to their body. A lot of it is that their own spirituality of peace is buried so deep, you know, that it makes the roads that they ride even harder. But I'm not going to end on a dark dreary note like that. It's worth it. It's a hard, rough journey, but when you get to the end, it's worth it; it's definitely worth it. I feel everything's come together, and it'll get rough again, too, but I think the foundation's there. I think the foundation's there.

Mary: In Some Intangible, Strange Relationship to the Church Universal

Mary, an educator in southern California, grew up in a strongly Christian family and spent much of her youth at an ecumenical missionary school in the Philippines. She has now moved a great distance from her roots, though she maintains a deep spiritual base linked in some ways to her upbringing.

She reflects powerfully on her experience and her journey in the pages that follow: the struggles of a woman and a lesbian trying to find her place in the "church universal." In her story she takes us from the Philippines to Colorado and California; her spiritual travels have been equally long. Mary and her life-partner, Brenda, asked that I use their real names as well as the names of the institutions of which Mary was a part.

To understand Mary's spiritual journey, it is essential to know something about the very strong and conservative roots she came from, for they both give a sense of how far she has moved in her understanding and, paradoxically perhaps, remain reflected in some profound ways. In the following pages she describes what her journey has been like, giving an orienting perspective that can serve to frame the subsequent discussion about her childhood and family.

There is not and has never been any conflict, for me, between being a lesbian and being spiritual. I am a spiritual person. And at the same time there is almost no connection, for me, between being a lesbian and being in the church. So I just have to let that be and sustain relationships and conversations that nurture the spiritual journey without the church. On some level that remains a loss. I never would have guessed my life would look like this.

I am slowly building a sense of a spiritual community, I think, outside of the church. It's probably taken five or ten years to untangle those things, to unbraid my understanding of spirituality and faith from religion. For a long time I was just delinquent from the church. And about once a year I'd meet with my family, and the conversations would have an interesting twist. They're all fundamentalists and evangelicals. And from their perspective my experience completely follows in the line of what happens to people when they lose their moorings: you drift to a place where everything seems right to you, and so you reorient yourself by some less absolute kind of standard and change how you define things. And they just see me drifting off. I had quite a passionate conversation with my father about spending a good part of the last ten years seriously working on another way to understand spiritual and religious issues because I need another way to understand them. As a lesbian, how do you sustain a belief in something that says you're *not?*

I'm really more clear about asserting myself on my own path than drifting. And I think there probably have been several years that might have been like drifting. But I'm a spiritual person, and what I experience on the inside, in terms of faith and purpose, is really important to me. I need to be identifying the people around me who also care about those things. I'm really reclaiming something. Which is really hard. Gosh, it takes a long time to work your way out from under, from under being the sinner. Maybe that's a life task; I don't know.

I keep feeling like I've made headway, but it's really just headway up out of a hole. I envy people describing a more New Age, lighter sense of spirituality. Because the hole I've been crawling out of, in terms of what's religious and what's spiritual, has been so dark, and it's so heavy, and the reclaiming of myself is so at essence; it's so central. There's not a whole lot that's just really light. I don't know; in some weird way maybe it's like reclaiming your body after a rape. It's basic and central and essential and healing, but it's still not very light. The early woundedness is just so profound. Maybe my experience would be different if I was just more angry—but I've been angry, and I feel like I'm just slowly making steps.

"I am slowly building a sense of a spiritual community, I think, outside of the church."

I'm more aware of how much I've shifted when I'm with my family than with anyone else because I can see where I started. When I'm talking with someone like my friend Michael or my life-partner, Brenda, I'm less aware of what's happened to my thoughts and my experience over time. I had a conversation about feminism this summer with my brother that just kind of stunned me. He made this offhanded comment—I told him I thought myself and his new wife were quite different, and he laughed, and he said, "You epitomize everything she hates." I went, "You're kidding?" And he said, "Yeah, all that feminist stuff." And I went like I would with a freshman and said, "Now wait a minute. Isn't the labor of women valuable? Isn't what women contribute to the world important? Don't you want your daughter to be able to choose her vocation, her occupation? Don't you want her to have the opportunity to develop her skills and talents? Don't you want her to be able to live in the workplace as fear-free as possible?" I went through this whole list of things, and I said, "That's what most feminists value." The fact that men won't share power has made this a really difficult issue; it's really hard to give up privilege. And I think he heard me on that topic for the first time. And so something's shifting. I'm far enough away that I can go back and have some of the conversations. It's pretty clear to me that all of the issues aren't about me, that each of these people is having their own experience of the world and of the church and of spirituality and of their place in the world.

Maybe from a place of great pain and anger, everything feels like a barb. I am seeing more of other people's struggles, difficult in their own ways, and we all have this incredible tangle. All of this goes to my essential understanding of life. The first line of the textbook about life is about struggle, and that is right at the core of how I understand human experience. And, even on really good days, when I'm in a really good place, I have more internal stuff to engage a struggle with. I don't think about the good days as being the recess; something about meaning and forging purpose and sustaining it are right at the core of how I understand spirituality. And I probably have few experiences of sheer joy.

One of the disputes between Brenda and me is that at my very core I believe life is well and I'm well. So there's this struggle, but there's not any despair connected to it. She doesn't have that. At the core she's more despairing, though she's lighter on the surface. In that sense we're real opposites; the deeper I go, there's goodness there, and the universe is good, which is a great context for struggle, as opposed to a kind of struggle in the face of despair. Her struggle is different from mine, and her life tasks are different from mine, and she also comes out of a fundamentalist background. She even went to a Christian college, so all this stuff is incredibly similar. Our dads are similar. But by personality she's melancholy; underneath it she's not sure things are well. I think the way we experience the world and ourselves and spirituality is different.

It would seem arrogant or presumptive for me to take the description of my struggle and my sense of reclaiming myself as a spiritual person in the world and seem to be describing everyone's struggle. I think my best understanding of oppression comes out of being a lesbian, not from being a woman. And I can now extrapolate from that experience somewhat generally to the experience of women. When I hear other people talk generally about gender struggle, it makes more sense to me. I think my sense about what it means to be a minority is to have a set of values that are invisible, to have a whole life that can be invisible, just because it's not in the same vein as most others. That sense of being a cultural minority, I understand, as a lesbian. It is really strong in the teaching that I do in multicultural issues; my value that people need to be respected comes out of the sense of the experience of what it's like to be invisible. I don't know how you come close to those issues until you have an experience that sharpens it all. It's possible to come close to them intellectually, but I think if I were living only as a white woman of privilege, I wouldn't be who I am now.

I had a real powerful moment in a class last fall where I had to come out. I typically don't make an issue of sexuality. I was in a multicultural issues class, and I had a gay male describing experiences in the workplace, and in the course of the conversation that he was engaging the class with another student, a woman, identified herself as a lesbian that hadn't identified herself in the class session prior to that point. And the class was surprised that she identified herself. And I needed to. And to join with them and address the issue of passing, and that the ring I wear symbolized commitment, not heterosexuality, and I can look like a white woman of privilege real easy. What was important in that whole exchange was the description of issues of being gay and lesbian in the workplace and what it means to be invisible and have all the things about our lives peripheral. It was important to not be the neutral facilitator at the front of the room. I had several comments from students afterwards about my coming out giving them some context for me: they heard the understanding in my voice, but previously they couldn't peg it or see it in my life experience. And I had one other experience, with an Afro-American faculty member, after a blowup here last year and civil unrest. We were talking about what does it mean to not be able to see excessive violence, excessive force. And I said to her that it seemed really clear to me that if white people had been watching a white man beaten by the LAPD, they would have risen up. None of those women want their sons beaten by the LAPD. But because the person was black, they couldn't see excessive force. And she got this real funny look on her face, and she said, "I hear what you're saying, but I don't understand how you see it." And I said, "I can see it because I'm a lesbian." Well, there wasn't anything in her understanding of just general white folk for understanding what it's like to be marginalized. So I feel like I wouldn't change who I am for anything. I understand more.

Let's look back now at where Mary came from, both literally and metaphorically.

As a child I lived in a missionary community. My folks were teaching at Faith Academy, which is a school for American kids overseas in Manila, Philippines. It's the largest missionary kids' school in the world, with five hundred students. You can imagine that five hundred kids represent an awful lot of families. About half of those families had their kids commuting and lived in an urban area of Manila. For seven years while I was in school my parents were house parents; they lived in residence and took care of high school boys.

Faith Academy is a cooperative effort of sixty different religious organizations. So I had this experience as a kid of being involved in a successful ecumenical project. What I didn't know at the time was that all of those people only got along because they were overseas. They worked together to create Faith Academy because the education of their kids was important. In the U.S., they act like other groups aren't Christian, but overseas—at the level of desperation they felt about the need for their kids to be educated—they began working together, and they had a cooperative board representing twelve different organizations. What irritated me as a kid was realizing that the people who were the most conservative had the most power because they have less range. So when there was an agreement on a behavioral code in the group, the conservative people won. There was just less that they could agree with. So as a whole community we had a behavioral code for school that was no drinking, no dancing, no smoking, a particular kind of skirt length. It was clear to me as a kid that the conservatives had power.

Theologically, my dad would place himself in the middle. My mother would identify herself as a fundamentalist. So there was that kind of division even in our family. Dad would drink a beer and enjoy it. Mom thought it was morally wrong. So I watched that play out in our family: because my mom felt like everything was a moral issue, in that regard she had power. Dad didn't believe it was a moral issue—why make it a moral issue? it isn't one—so he'd give in, which meant she could define the moral code. But what was also a powerful model to me was that the ecumenical community was in many ways successful. It was very powerful to me. I think it probably fueled a lifelong interest in community, which I carry regarding what it takes to sustain connection across difference.

I have two siblings: I'm the oldest. There are ten years between myself and the youngest. We used to sit around at night—I started drinking coffee when I was in high school because Mom and Dad would sit at the supper table and talk after dinner, and so I started drinking coffee to sit and talk after dinner about all kinds of things, what was going on in the world, great political, current-event kinds of discussions. I'd come home before supper and read the paper from cover to cover. I enjoyed it very much, and I grew up knowing we could talk about anything. What I didn't get until later was that the free currency was ideas: we could talk about any idea, but we didn't talk about feelings. And I had a book of poetry and a journal that I wrote at, late at night while I was in high school, expressing all the things that I was experiencing, that weren't finding their way into any of those open, incredible conversations. I had this sense that I could talk about anything except feelings.

One of the most painful things between my dad and me, in the course of my growing up, has been that there seems to be more and more taboo kinds of subjects; not only are the conversations about feelings hard, but there are fewer and fewer topics he's really willing to get into. Once it became apparent that I was coming to different positions, he was less willing to get into the conversations. It never occurred to me that my coming out in the same place was one of the prerequisites for good conversations, that we only had good political conversations because we were both political conservatives. I didn't have that pegged at all. He never challenged where I came out; he would just say, "Okay, tell me how you got there." So I would say, "Well, I thought this, and then I thought this, and then I came out here."

He was very interested in my learning how to think. I don't think it ever seriously occurred to him I wouldn't think like he did. That's gotta be one of the great pains of his life. That the more I learned, the farther away I went. I don't know how an educator resolves that. Especially conservative educators. My brother's an archconservative. He has no place in his life for me as a lesbian, as a Christian committed to social justice, or for my partnership with Brenda. We will send his family gifts, and he sends back a thank-you note addressed to me. He's very closed. He's a career military intelligence person, you know. It's a pretty strange family.

Brenda and I just were in Florida, where I was presenting a paper. Dad was away on a trip, and we got to have several really long conversations with my mother, more authentic conversations than we've had in a long time, where we could really acknowledge how difficult our life is for her. She could express to us that she doesn't have anywhere to put us, and we had a great conversation about what it means to be a moral person, what it means to be a moralizing person, how one loves without judging. We talked for hours and hours. I have had more of that conversation with her as an adult. I've had good conversations with Dad, growing up, but the authentic conversations now are happening with my mother. And I have very few memories of her in my childhood. She was almost invisible in my childhood. I don't know what made the switch happen. It may be that the part of her that's connected to day-to-day reality will find a way to stay connected to me because she loves me. She wants to call me on the phone. The way she makes contact is real, tangible. That may help. One summer my dad got depressed when I disappointed the family hope of becoming his colleague, and she was the one that talked to me. He couldn't talk to me all summer. She was the one that talked to me about how I was going to move my stuff to California, and ultimately they helped me with that move. As a kid I had no time for my mom. I had nothing in common with her, I didn't understand her, and I didn't want to understand her. Dad was the dominant, colorful personality. It's very interesting that it has come to be my mother that I'm in a relationship with in the family. I never would have expected that. Even when I was in graduate school and I was reading all this stuff about mothers and daughters, I just thought, "What is this? I don't even have a relationship with my mother."

Mary speaks of the central role religion had in her family and the path that took her away from these beginnings.

My family was centrally religious. We're talking the kind of family where people studied the Bible together, where people studied the Bible individually and told each other what they studied, and where they talked about what the Lord's telling them. And there was incredible value placed on spiritual learning distilled from Bible study and prayer. There was—and still is—higher value placed on an individual's experience of God than on one's church experience. That's a classic fundamentalist view. I had conversations with my mother when I was in college, when it was real clear to me that if I came home and used certain kinds of words, she would relax. She waited to hear a certain kind of language from me. If I said, "You won't believe what I learned." It came up again and again and again, all right, so I finally have this lesson; I think one of my life's lessons is she wouldn't pay any attention to it unless it were cast in religious terms. I asked her at that point, "Are you so riveted to the language that the language is more important than how I am? I can use all these words, and then you'll relax. But what you need to know is that I'm not experiencing my life in religious language. It just seems like I'm required to put it into religious language for you to hear it." There was a part of her that wanted to be able to hear it the way it was meaningful to me. But it was translating. I really needed to put my experience, if it was at all possible, into words she could understand. And at some point that began feeling hypocritical to me, that it was not paraphrasing. And I've done that less and less.

I went to Oral Roberts as a freshman. In July 1974 I didn't know who Oral Roberts was, but I knew I was supposed to go to school there. My dad didn't really know what to do with me earlier that year: I'm the kind of person that has a clear plan for everything, and I didn't have any picture of where to go to school. I was on tour that summer with a vocal group, and I met a distant cousin in New York who was going to ORU and having a great experience, and just like that, the fog lifted; I was clear that I was going to go there. And so I wrote a letter to the school and said I want to come here next year and this is my name. And they wrote back and said, no, we're full, and I wrote back and said, no, I know I'm supposed to be here next year. So I went to ORU my freshman year. And transferred my sophomore Christmas to the University of Tennessee, where I subsequently finished with a B.A. in human services in '78.

As she moves ahead in her exploration, she says, "The further I went, the less in that world I fit."

Between '78 and '80 I got real involved with organizational staff issues at an interdenominational Christian organization called International Students, Incorporated. We had women on staff from very conservative backgrounds who didn't believe they should assert any kind of leadership if there were males present. They were missionaries, full-time Christian workers. It was pretty clear to me that if they had a gift or leading in their life about being vocationally religious, that they needed to have enough spiritual authority to assert that leadership. Being a missionary and not able to lead a Bible study if there was a male student in the room just seemed really limiting to me. So I began to study everything I'd been taught about the rules for women in the church. I remember where I was standing when I said to my dad, "This is a very important study for me because what I'm finding out are not the things I was taught, and I'm going to be somewhere else when I end this study." And he said, "Well, keep track of what you study, and let me know where you end up." I said, "It's already clear to me that women being silent is a conservative warp on scripture. This is really powerful stuff—women have been seriously limited in the church for what is not a rational, nor even an accurate, interpretation of scripture." I was just stunned. And the further I went, the less in that world I fit. When I started graduate school, I began a serious study of feminist theology with a group of women who were in graduate school at the same time, and the further I went, the more clear it was that I wasn't an evangelical anymore and I didn't belong in the church or Christian organizations as I knew them. And I couldn't tolerate a limitation on women that couldn't be defended by scripture. At that time I was still accepting biblical authority. I knew I couldn't go back to this organization, so I resigned.

The summer of '82 when I started job hunting outside Christian organizations, my Dad went into a depression. It turned out that one of his dreams had been that we would work together. I had a hard time finding an interview; I kind of floundered for a while. I ended up accepting a position at a Lutheran school, Cal. Lutheran University, as director of counseling.

While she was at Cal. Lutheran, Mary ran growth groups, one of which was for women on issues of spirituality and female development. Describing her work there, she says, "I had these fascinating conversations with them about where hope comes from and what allows you to believe that your life can go the way you want it to go, what empowers you and pulls you into the future." She was at Cal. Lutheran for two and a half years and left when she was ready to begin doctoral work.

The farther I went with women's issues, the farther I went to the edge of the church. In 1985 when I was leaving Cal. Lutheran, I went through my "dark night of the soul," a kind of death-of-God experience. I can remember being in tears with one of my good friends on the phone, saying: "I don't know if I'm going to believe in God when this is over. Will you still love me?" My family was grounded in a common belief, and it was pretty clear to me that there was going to be no place for me in the world I knew if I ended up not believing in God. It was bad enough to not be in church anymore; to genuinely no longer believe in God would have been completely inconceivable in the whole world I had grown up in and with my family. And she said—she comes from the same background—"You're more important to me than what you believe." That was the right answer at the time. I had to work out what I was experiencing and its relationship to what I believed and what made sense to me. It was clear to me that I was on the outside of the church and God; I had gone from a paternal male God, a largely judging kind of Old Testament character, to paying more attention to the Jesus of the Gospels. And to spirituality, to something that was more an ethereal, disembodied, positive, joyful creative spirit. For about three years I had tried to let go of my embodied male images. It made sense to me that someone cared about the planet, that there was some positive power in the world.

At the same time, I was working on what it meant for humans to have power inside. I came from a conservative religious tradition in which all power was external. There is no theory of change in conservative religion. That's why my mother prays for miracles because she can't act. I was processing what does it mean for people to be agents? It was real clear to me I was an intentional actor in my life. And there was something inside me; this wasn't all coming from the outside, even though I sustained this idea that there is something powerful outside.

There are different literatures for this perspective. Some of them describe the Holy Spirit as indwelling people, and that's what gives us hope and power and capacity to act. And in the New Age literatures they're talking about the god within, and some of them use God with a big *G* and some use god, little *g*. It's real clear to me that I'm an agent, and I choose, and hope comes from somewhere down inside of me. Hope isn't like socks I put on in the morning. It's an internal kind of strength. So the notion of external power has diminished. I have less tolerance for people who use it as refuge: I want to say, "Get a grip." You have to begin identifying how you take action, even if it's a small step, so it's believable to you, so you can move.

Reading Matthew Fox in '85 was a complete reframing experience for me to think about humanity having been originally blessed instead of originally cursed. It went down deep in me somewhere, a kind of healing salve. I just looked at old stuff about having been born and cursed in the same day just drop off. It was time to replace it with something else—everywhere, my own experience collided with what I'd been taught, and it was clear to me that I was going to have to drop that next piece away because it wasn't fitting. The less what I'd been taught matched reality, the less useful it was to me. It is only useful if it allows me to problem-solve and imagine how to move into the future. If not, if it doesn't relate in any way to my life experience, it doesn't have a place. But the past has never been sacred to me. Meaning is sacred to me. So when the teaching isn't meaningful, it's not sacred. I'm in this very strange place. I deeply value what I'm experiencing in the world, and I have a deep commitment to the issues of justice and equity and the power of education and critical thinking. To empowering. My own willingness to study has completely changed my life.

After leaving Cal. Lutheran, she took a job in Residential Life at Chapman University, where she was hired "as a straight person that could help mediate the issues between gay and heterosexual members of Residence Life staff." Shortly after she got there, she met Brenda, who would become her life-partner.

Six months after I got to Chapman, I was involved with the first woman I had ever been involved with in my life. Happier than I'd ever been in my life—and in deep conflict. I was in all the identity conflicts around experiencing myself to be truly in love for probably the first time in my life and it being with a woman. I was wondering how someone who had done as much self-assessment and reflection as I had done could completely miss this. It clearly wasn't environmentally encouraged. Whatever I was experiencing was coming from deep within me. I had gotten within four days of being married once before, but there just hadn't been enough in my relationships with men to make them permanent. There was not much to it. I couldn't imagine being like this for another fifty years. On the other hand, I wanted to do anything I could do to form a life with Brenda.

As a teenager I had a very strong sense of being different, of making different assessments, of evaluating things differently, of fundamentally valuing different things. And I've never known where I would end up. I've always just seen myself on a path away from what was familiar, which has had, as its accompanying feeling, a strange kind of isolation. I know when I was at Chapman, and when I was first involved with Brenda, the deep loss of my life was the certainty that I could never go back, that I had lost a world. I had gone as far as I could go to the edge. Identifying myself as a lesbian wasn't just having an experience with a woman, but embracing it. See, I could have had the experience and repented of it, and then, okay. But to embrace my life had very much the feeling of costing me a whole different other world, and I didn't have any idea how to build a new one. All the people I had known in graduate school, at the master's level, prided themselves on being liberal thinkers but weren't out there very far, in any regard, themselves. I'd really moved out of any world I knew.

On our first date Brenda took me to a lesbian bookstore. I'd never been in a lesbian bookstore before. I stood on one aisle and pulled down the spines of the books that were in my library at home. Three-quarters of the books on the shelf were in my personal library. I had clearly been moving in that direction, but I just didn't have a language for it; I didn't have a community. I was stunned. I had never been in a bookstore in my life that had my collection. I didn't even know what kind of books I was looking for. I was stunned, and then I was angry. There was a name for this that I hadn't found out about. Other people looking at my collection for years had identified something about me that I didn't have a language for—I hate not being the person in the know about myself. It turned out that four of my friends were lesbians. And we had never talked about it. And one of them said, "If I had to listen to another story about a messed-up relationship with a male, I was going to shake you." They were just watching me on my own path.

Mary speaks of wanting to find a spiritual community that has integrity for her, with deep and authentic ties based on shared values.

I never went out to see anybody else for answers. That's part of my MO; I'm willing to listen and talk and read, but I don't go out; I don't believe in any experts. And I'm more of an experiential learner than I knew. It isn't real until I have my experience. I understand that other people have experiences, but my own learning waits for my own experience. I'm a late bloomer. It took me about two months to identify that I was in love with Brenda and it was going to change my life and that was it. No looking back. It just kind of clicks like a kaleidoscope into a pattern. And I've no idea what it is until it clicks into a pattern. It wasn't difficult at all to accept it on the inside of me.

I remain in some intangible, strange relationship to the church. I'm outside it in every imaginable way. By church, I mean a kind of church universal, the church of all people who believe something about God. On some levels I resonate with the way Cornell West described his background in *Breaking Bread* because I understand what I believe only comes out of a prophetic Christian tradition: that liberation is possible and it's essential. And that liberation of individuals is part of social change, that the gospel was about being aligned with the poor and the elimination of basic kinds of human needs. And I think what I believe about social justice is grounded very much in something that went down deep in me about the Gospels, which the church is no longer largely about. So I don't feel like I belong, but the gospel is powerful to me. Liberation theology is powerful to me.

The difficulty has been trying to resolve whether or not there was any meaningful way I could be in relationship with the church. I've had a consciously love-hate relationship with it for fifteen years, like a bad family relationship. It's been very hard for me to accept the need to permanently separate the religious from the spiritual. A political community is not a sufficient substitute for a faith community. And I've reestablished a sense of social and political community. It comes to be a spiritual community when I include shared values as part of spirituality. There would be a real fine line for me: between a powerful commitment to values and my experience of what's spiritual.

But I miss a faith community. In the last sixteen months I've been visiting the Quakers. I was intrigued by the connection of social values and activism and silence and a community of people that share values around all those things. And have a form of worship that's silent, that includes no printing, no need to correct anyone else's behavior, but rather a shared quiet listening to the wisdom that we hold within. That makes sense to me. People know what they need to do next if they get quiet enough to hear it. A whole group of people being together in that way, quietly, can fill a room with an incredible kind of power, like a collective meditation experience. That's probably the closest thing I'm experiencing now to what I would call a faith community.

Yet for some reason I'm on the outside. In every way I can identify, in every way I can point to, I believe the same things. But for some reason I'm not a Quaker. Even as I describe it to you, I'm visiting that experience, and I can participate, and I can enjoy it, and I can value it, and it isn't me. It's the thing I'm the most like of anything I know, but I'm not a member. You don't become a member of the Quakers. I mean, it's a very funny thing. When I look all around me at spiritual communities, there's just no doubt that that's where I fit the best, and I don't belong there. It's just very odd. The only other place I've had an experience that's that queer is around issues of class, when people would let you come, but it's real clear to you that you don't belong. I had that kind of feeling about the Friends; I can go, but I don't belong even though I share the values. I don't have it figured out yet, but that's probably about as clear as I can get it.

In some sense music epitomizes the tension Mary feels between her roots and her journey and between wanting community and needing to find her own answers.

The most spiritually opening collective experiences that I've had have been in music. I was in a vocal group for three years when I was in high school. I had experiences singing with this group that were deeply spiritual. I think the kind of experiences people describe as oneness with all life I had doing music. I felt connected with all. It was more than feeling connected with the people I was doing music with; it was feeling connected with everything living. The only place I've ever had that experience has been doing music. Now the thing that's missing in my life is music. I don't have this experience listening to music. It's connected to singing, for me, connected to voice. But I know that it's possible. I don't know who I would be if I hadn't ever had that kind of experience; it was one of those shaping experiences. I have had, easily since I was fourteen or fifteen, a feeling of being on a path that was taking me away from the world I knew. I've always been on that path.

The language has been important. I've reacted to all the he-God language. And there's a lot of he-God language in the music. It got to where I couldn't enjoy music anymore. Lyrics I know, lyrics I can sing in my sleep, are no longer enjoyable to sing. Brenda and I had a long conversation about this. She grew up in a very similar kind of family, and she went to Biola University, where she was a missions minor. She was on her way to being the Protestant version of vocationally religious, but she can't be that as a lesbian. So she really lost her sense of vocation, her place. We have a sense that all the music we knew and loved growing up has no place anymore. It no longer fits, and we're too conscious to enjoy it. There's not been a collection of music to replace it. Because we didn't grow up with peace and labor music, it doesn't move into the same place in our souls. I very much wish that my music experience as a child had been substantially broader, like I wish I had grown up loving classical music. I would still have that.

It's kind of odd. I think it's probably foremost the inclusive-language issue that I feel uncomfortable with, and the next one right up to it, for me, is the military images. Religious military metaphors in Protestant theology are immense. And then there's the big sacrificial thing: it's better to die. I would come away from church angry; there I was engaged mentally in a critical process—good exercise, but it's not a comfortable way to go to church. What I come away with is, "My God, why did I waste my time doing this?" Instead of feeling any kind of value of gathering, which would be a nice part of what I associate with the religious community, a sense of not being isolated in one's life experience.

But I have a whole collection of good friends now who are estranged from the church. A different kind of community. The people who are closest to me are a mix of Christians and spiritual people. Spirituality is more dominant than Christianity. I have four friends that have been in seminary. And the two that are out of an evangelical background, we talk a lot about issues of Christianity. The two that are Quaker by background, we don't ever talk about Christianity, but we talk about values and issues of spirituality a lot. Let me tell you about my friend Michael. I laughed when I told my dad a few years ago that I thought God sent Michael to my life just to blow on the embers. Michael is passionately committed to his spiritual journey and is a deacon in the Episcopal church and periodically comes down the hall with coffee and sits in my office and asks me spiritual and theological questions because he knows I'll engage them. There aren't very many people I'm having these conversations with. And he and I and Brenda and two other people here are getting ready to start a theological reflection group, so that we have a context for an ongoing conversation, instead of just conversations here and there. I'm really looking forward to it.

I attended a meeting about a month ago on feminist spirituality, where a group of women get together, and it was very interesting to me that a couple people in the group identified themselves as post-Christians. I keep trying on that phrase because I read Carol Christ and other people who identify themselves as post-Christians. I'm probably an estranged Christian and, as Cornell says, "grounded in a prophetic tradition," as opposed to an institutional tradition. I'm estranged enough that I don't identify myself as a Christian anymore because what the word evokes is no longer what it means. That's pretty seriously estranged. But when someone like George Bush says he's a Christian and stands for family values, I can't use the same words. It's almost made family values a despicable phrase.

We conclude with Mary's reflections on where she has come in this journey. This piece functions as a bookend in relation to her opening remarks, which described her experience of coming "headway up out of a hole."

I have had to reexamine everything I was taught. The average Christian assumes they were taught the truth because they were taught it by people they trusted and respected. And if you're a gay or lesbian Christian, you have to find another way to understand scripture, to engage it. Bishop Spong's piece *Living in Sin* has been as useful to me as anything I've found. He really does tackle the question, If we believe that the Bible can be meaningful to us as Christians, how? How do we reclaim it as presenting something about sexual ethics that is useful to us in this day and age?

How do we keep from throwing it away? And that's about both integrity and critical thinking. The average Christian doesn't do that. I suppose when you have a life experience that doesn't fit what you've been taught, you have the opportunity to either suppress and deny the life experience in order to sustain your worldview or use that life experience as a catalyst to reexamine your worldview. And if you're an awake gay or lesbian person, you have to keep examining your worldview, I think. Especially as a gay or lesbian Christian.

I don't identify myself as a Christian anymore—and I'm not different on the inside. But I'm unwilling to fight those battles. I don't want to deal with everything it evokes, all the emotion that comes up. I have no need to defend Christianity. I don't know; maybe I'm chicken. It just makes sense to pick my battles. I think I get farther authentically describing my life and values and issues of spirituality in the gay and lesbian communities without putting it under the whole rubric of "let's have a discussion about Christianity." The fundamentalists have just about ruined the word.

So Christianity is more of a theme for the people who are trying to deal with themselves in relationship to it. It just doesn't come up for most other people who are still dealing with value issues and issues of integrity and all the same kinds of issues, but without the junk. I hear people say that they are so thankful for their Christian background. I may live into that experience, but I think I would have a less garbage-filled understanding of the gospel and of grace if I wasn't trying to deal with all the junk that I've gotten with the church and with Christianity. The grace can hardly come through the oppression.

My understanding of God has changed a lot. And it's probably not finished changing. What I'm not resolved about is how seldom God acts. And I don't know how to resolve that. [Long pause] I no longer picture God as someone who's intervening all the time to make things work out. There are too many important things that don't work out. So God either has considerably less power than I thought or considerably more constraint about the way spiritual intervention should be done. I don't have that resolved. But I no longer count on miracles. I no longer assume that because it's important, God would make it work out. Because people aren't safe and they do starve, and they are hurt, and they are killed, and no one is making it work out. There's too much of that to be naively in the world assuming that God'll make it work out. The only way I understand justice is with almost a karmic kind of perspective. And justice is real important to me. The only way I can imagine justice occurring is over some really long period of time. It certainly isn't occurring in my lifetime or the lifetime of the situations I've seen without justice. So it takes a really long view to imagine justice really existing. It's so different from, "I'm good and God blesses me, and you're bad and God punishes you."

I used to be compulsively oriented to making everything fit. In fact, as an evangelical I was quite entranced with systematic theology. I loved all the pieces going together. Once they got all thrown up in the air, I had to rebuild with a much greater sense of not understanding, so I had to let go of the assumption that I should have it all figured out, which I'd had for a long time. And I had to identify some basic things I was going to hold onto: my sense of myself as a good person in the world, my sense that God doesn't make junk. I don't think I'm some kind of bitter cosmic accident. I'm actually part of someone else's cognitive dissonance. I'm proof that the pieces aren't all fitting together. I have to figure that a long view, in terms of time, matters more than I can imagine. I can only imagine what it would be like to see things in thousands of years, how it must really alter how the day to day appears. I really had to let go of the jigsaw puzzle; all the pieces are here. And one of the shifts in terms of understanding scripture was that I had to decide that everything that was true wasn't in there. Instead of figuring that this was the big clue book, the big riddle, it was all here, I just had to figure it out and interpret it. If I understood it, I would have all the pieces. I don't think that's true. There's clearly more going on than's in there. Because I exist. And I have life experiences that aren't expressed adequately by that book.

PART THREE

CHOOSING TO LEAVE THE MAINSTREAM

FOR some of the participants, distancing from the religious authorities of their youth and searching for a gay-positive community led them to explore nonmainstream belief systems. In some cases this exploration was a step on a road that eventually led back to the childhood, or similar, tradition. One man, John, still reflects on Buddhist insight into his Christian practice. Another man, Bill, grew up Lutheran and left that denomination to explore Nichiren Shoshu Buddhism, shamanism, and the occult before he eventually found his spiritual home within the Metropolitan Community Church about ten years ago. When discussing these issues in his life and those of others he knows, he expresses a value for spiritual exploration: "A person may be a Zen Buddhist, or maybe this need, this yen [to explore other spiritual paths] is there for some [valuable] reason. Maybe this is some way of God working within their lives. Just because the traditions don't match doesn't mean that person doesn't need [to explore in this way]." Sandra, as we have seen, joined a coven on her path, though she now has found a spiritual home within a Metropolitan Community Church.

Many others seem to be committed to a nontraditional path as well, and there is no indication that they will be turning any time soon to the traditions of their childhoods. Four individuals will illustrate this orientation for the reader: Harry is drawn to paganism, Mark is a follower of Siddha Yoga (a philosophy growing out of Hinduism), Rachel is finding that the balance and flow of Taoism fit her natural beliefs, and Sheila—who has long studied Edgar Cayce and other New Age authors—integrates these and other sources in a complex, Goddess-based belief system.

Harry, at thirty-three, bottomed out from compulsive drinking and eating and "asked God, whoever or whatever He, She, or It is, for help. For the first time I realized I still believed there was a God." This renewed commitment to his spiritual life took him to AA and a desire to develop a definition for God that is meaningful to him and fits with his spiritual and political values; in the last year he has discovered a strong resonance with Wicca and paganism and is looking for a profeminist coven of men and women.

Mark is twenty-nine and lives in Connecticut. He grew up in the rural Midwest, where he lived until he moved to New England for graduate school. His father, an alcoholic, was Protestant and his mother, Catholic. Mark and his siblings went to Catholic schools, where the nuns told him he should be a priest. As he came to see hypocrisy and contradiction within the church, he began to pull away. At twenty-three he was given the book *The Impersonal Life,* through which, he writes, he "felt the presence of God within as [he] confronted [his] own coming-out issues as a gay man." Coming out was a sort of spiritual emergence for Mark, a rebirth not only of himself but also of a sense of spirituality. Two years ago a friend invited him to a class that aroused his interest in Siddha Yoga, which has been the main strain of his spiritual journey ever since. The intensification of his path has spurred him to do doctoral work in gay spirituality.

Rachel, thirty-three, grew up in a highly dysfunctional Jewish family, from which she is now estranged. Her spiritual journey included a return to Orthodox Judaism for two years in a period of great pain and struggle: "If I can just follow these rules, everything will be okay." But she found out that didn't work for her, and she abandoned her tradition in the realization that she had no faith in God or a "spiritual sense." About five years ago she entered an Al-Anon group, which allowed her once again to develop her own spirituality. She has found Taoism to be a natural expression of her philosophical beliefs, and she integrates the rituals of Judaism into her current spirituality.

Sheila, forty-eight, is a preoperative transsexual. She grew up in Tennessee in a Southern Baptist family and attended Catholic schools "because they were better." Her mother and father divorced when she was a teenager. When she went to college in the mid-1960s, she found herself attracted to philosophy, and by 1970 she was beginning to read and study the work of Edgar Cayce and other New Age literature. Her study eventually freed her to explore more than her spiritual beliefs. She says, "I had had spurts of where the transsexualism thing would be trying to surface and I kept fighting it because it was terrifying me." As a way of moving away from those urges, she entered a marriage that did not succeed in keeping them at bay, and by 1978 she could no longer deny them. She went to see a Jungian analyst, through whom she came to accept the need for the transsexual transition, but she has not been able to find the money for the operation. Meanwhile, she has been pursuing Wicca and Goddess worship.

Harry: Recovering and Looking for a Coven

Harry grew up on an isolated farm in northwestern Illinois, the son of conservative, second-generation European immigrants; a "menopause baby." He has two older sisters. He describes his parents as regarding their Lutheran religion as an "insurance policy—just in case all this is true." Harry left home right after high school and began college at a state university, where he came out more fully, with his sister's help and support. Since then he has lived on the East Coast and in Chicago and is just about to move to Los Angeles to begin graduate school.

Having left the church as an adolescent, he reconnected to a spiritual sense in his life through bottoming out from alcoholism and compulsive eating. Now, at thirty-seven, he is exploring paganism, Wicca, and other nontraditional paths as a way to bring together his gayness and his spirituality.

Today, Harry's childhood seems far off, yet even in its distance, those years set the stage, a ground from which he both evolved and rebelled. Here we can read of a time of separation and isolation, of struggling with and coming to claim his uniqueness. As an introduction to this period, let's hear from Harry as he describes his feeling of "being from another planet." This piece also reveals his disdain for, and rejection of, the family ethic of appearances that runs through his life story.

I grew up in a very small and very conservative community. There homosexuality was clearly a bad thing, unspeakable. It just didn't exist for those who lived there. And I was one of those people who didn't think that any other homosexuals existed, until I went away to college, when I was quite shocked to find out that there were others of us. But in the community it just wasn't, and still isn't, something that people even talk about. Subsequently, I've found out there were other kids I went to high school with, in this little bitty high school, who were gay. But I had no clue at the time. One of them died of AIDS not too long ago. I happened to get a copy of the local paper—I really don't know any other newspapers that strictly avoid saying this person died of AIDS, but you could tell that they had gone to great pains to avoid saying it. And I knew it was a fact. So it's still not okay to be gay there. It's not accepted; it's not talked about. When I spend any amount of time there, I feel a great deal of ostracism. I really feel like I'm from another planet, which is how I always felt there. It still hurts, I guess, but it doesn't surprise me. It's not an unexpected feeling; I understand it.

Even before I knew I was gay, I felt like I was from another planet. At the time it didn't make much sense to me. I couldn't figure out exactly what it was that was going on here. But I always felt that I didn't belong with my family, that I didn't belong in my high school. I always had a real sense of being not in the right place—and of not being like other people there. I just knew that. I didn't particularly like it for a long time, but it was always more important for me, though, to somehow try to make it, so that I could be comfortable and do what I wanted to do. I was never stigmatized to the point of totally wanting to conform. I never wanted to conform. I just couldn't do it. I didn't have conformity in me. What I wanted was to get away with it. I knew people that were football heroes and everything else in my high school that turned out to be much gayer than I am, and they said that they played along, basically 'cause they felt like their parents would have killed them. And I replied that my father was a maniac, and I just didn't see it as any kind of choice. Clearly, to me, I was this way, and they expected me to be another way. And always, in my mind, it was not my problem; it was theirs. So consequently I felt pretty out of it.

From the beginning, he lived a life apart: his family home was isolated; he was the youngest by many years in his family; he was not what his father wanted in a son. This was a time when Harry learned the value of "appearances" in the family ethic.

My parents were both raised in European enclaves, and they are both still very "old country" in their attitudes, very conservative. I was the youngest of three. I was a menopause baby, so there was a big generation gap between my parents and myself. I felt really isolated. Never happy. [Chuckles] We were not a happy family in a lot of ways.

My parents were not risk-takers. They're both children of the Depression, and they value safety and security and the sure thing. They value fitting in, not being noticed, not drawing attention to yourself. I guess they valued hard work, and family loyalty was also big to them. On one hand, they talked about family loyalty, but practicing that was another matter. But that was something that was very important to them. Neither one of my parents liked their family of origin very much, and for good reason. And yet at the same time, they talked about loyalty and how family was most important. Now I always felt like they secretly felt very trapped by that; maybe that was the reason why they stressed it over and over again—if they heard themselves say it enough, they would actually believe it.

My immediate family was very close because my parents didn't have a lot of friends and neither one of them was real close to their extended family. And we lived way out in the country, way back from the road, so we pretty much only had each other. In a way we were very close, at least looking at it from the outside. In truth, there were a lot of family secrets. The system of our family was that you never confronted somebody or never told them the truth. You instead tried to manipulate them into doing something or otherwise control their behavior, but you never actually confronted it head on. There were never lots of arguments per se. My father yelled and screamed a lot, but there weren't really arguments. It was more just subtle control and a lot of martyrdom. So in a way we were close, but there were a lot of things that were left unsaid. And there was a lot of hostility beneath the surface.

We weren't a happy family. We tried our best to pretend that we were, but there was a lot of underlying tension. My father's mother virtually lived with us; she was at our house from midmorning to dinnertime at night every day. She owned the farm my father farmed. And so she pretty much looked over my parents' shoulder their entire married life, every day of it. She was a very, very, very manipulative woman, not in a land baroness way, but just very emotionally manipulative. And she thought in black and white terms, constantly: it was either her way, or it was not right. There was a lot of tension between her and my mother and between her and my father. And that was one of the things that we never talked about. It just was "never there."

Even his grandfather was not what he appeared: by accident, Harry discovered that his father was illegitimate and not the son of Harry's grandfather.

Part of the problem between her and my father was that he had been illegitimate at a time when illegitimate children were a very big deal. And she had basically defied her family and kept my father rather than giving him up for adoption. And as a result of defying her family, she was exiled. The rest of the family lived in central Illinois. She lived in northern Illinois. The exact circumstances of how she ended up marrying and how they got the farm and all that is so very much a mystery, nobody really knows what the story is. We suspect that the person that played the role of our grandfather was not really our grandfather and that basically it was an arranged marriage. And that part of the deal was he was given the money to buy this farm. But you know, we don't even know what the real story is. The only way the secret ever came out in the first place was that our family physician had a bad habit of talking about children as if they weren't right there in front of him. And I remember, I was going into junior high school, and I was there for a physical. And the doctor said to my mother, "Gee, isn't it amazing how much this kid looks like Otto"—meaning my grandfather—"but of course that can't be." And my mother gave him a dirty look at the time, like, "You have just dropped a bomb." Sure enough, when we got in the car, I said, "What does he mean by that?" And my mother told me. And so I was the first one in my family to know that secret. Outside of her, I mean. Later on I thought my sisters knew, and I let it slip, and they both said, "What are you talking about?" So we've come across my father's birth certificate, and it bears all this out. But there was a lot of underlying stuff. My father had a real complex about being illegitimate. And I think that was part of the reason why they didn't socialize a lot. There was some self-esteem stuff going on then. So there was this weird undercurrent beneath a perfectly normal-looking salt-of-the-earth farm family. We were one thing on the outside and quite another in the actual group, something quite different.

I have two sisters. My oldest sister is ten years older than me and left home when I was in third grade. And I didn't get along with my second sister when we were growing up—I couldn't stand her. But somehow, when I was about a junior or senior in high school, we got very close and have stayed pretty close since that time. When we were growing up, she was a very heavy-duty tomboy. In fact, I thought she was a lesbian for the longest time; I really did. And I still wonder sometimes. But she was a very heavy-duty tomboy and very good in school, and she was constantly thrown up in my face as an example of what I should be. So I really resented her for that, but we got over it.

His father's expectations of how Harry was to be were strong—as was his mismatch with those expectations.

It's interesting 'cause I've been writing a lot about the messages I got about homosexuality in my family lately. I read this essay recently; I think it's by Keith Thompson. It's in this book called *Gay Spirit.* And he talks about how his father looked at him and knew that he had "one of those." And it was the closest I'd ever come to having anybody describe what was the deal with my father and me. Because my father had this innate sense that I was gay right from as early as I can remember. He was really bothered by me, by everything about me. I was just not what he expected, and he knew what he had, and he didn't like it. And when I saw my image reflected back from my father, it was always, "This is just not acceptable." It was a "change or die" kind of message. My father really set about trying to find every possible way to make me something other than what I was. He really, really, really was upset about my being a homosexual. And so it was always an issue, and we were always at odds about it. It wasn't really direct. It wasn't really "You are a queer." It was, "You have to be good at sports; you have to, have to, have to be good at sports. Boys don't listen to records. Boys don't wear any jewelry. Boys don't! Boys all wear their hair this way, this exact way. Boys are interested in this. Boys aren't interested in this." It was like the world was divided up into what boys were or were not interested in, into what boys did or did not do. As an example, both my sisters took piano lessons, but I was forbidden to take them because girls took piano lessons. My father had a very, very rigid sense of gender. He was the kind of husband who made it so my mother never wrote a check, never knew where the bills were, never knew what was in the savings account. That was man's stuff. Women were supposed to do x, y, and z. When my oldest sister expressed an interest in going to college and getting a degree in business or law, he said, "No. Girls become nurses or secretaries." My second sister, who's now a Ph.D., had to go in this big wide circular path to get to where she was going because she couldn't tell them directly what she wanted. She became a dental hygienist. Then she got a degree in vocational education, and now she's a social researcher. But I think she had to go way around to get where she wanted to go in order not to get short-circuited by my parents. So, yeah, there was a big, big emphasis on what a sissy I was, and it was a big deal. They never called me gay or fag or homosexual. They never actually said those words, but that's what they were thinking. My mother, too. It wasn't quite as big a deal to my mother; I don't think she felt she had a lot at stake. See, my father felt like he had a lot at stake because this was his chance for some glory, for a quarterback or a basketball center or whatever. And he wasn't getting it, so he was not reaching his desired status in the community. The stakes weren't quite the same for my mother. I think my mother was mostly just irritated because my father used to bug the shit out of her about it. And it became just a complication in her life. I don't think that she saw things as being quite as much of a crisis as my father did.

My second sister used to make fun of me for being a sissy, and she's now one of the most gay-supportive people I know. I remind her often that she was very abusive to me when I was growing up, and she feels bad about it. But my oldest sister was totally out of the picture. She had her own issues with my parents, galore. She never really had any comment on the topic. And really still doesn't. I mean, she knows I'm gay, and she's not really upset about it; she just doesn't have much to say about it.

Harry describes both his feeling of safety in the church of his childhood and his disbelief in its faith.

I never got the impression that my family really believed in God. We went to church, and we went through Lutheran catechism, and we were confirmed members of the church. My parents had both been raised in the Lutheran church, my father more so than my mother. They felt obligated to go to church, and they felt like if they didn't go, they would be the subject of gossip in the community and that it would be detrimental to their social standing. So they went to church only the required number of times. And they didn't really approve of people who went to church a lot or of people who talked a lot about religion. It was just not considered a practical thing. Normal people didn't do that. So I got two different ideas about religion. One was that you'd better believe in God, and God was more or less vengeful. On the other hand, if you really believe in God and talk a lot about it, you're crazy, too. So there was a really conflicting message. And I always got the feeling like they didn't quite have a grasp of how they felt about it either. I felt like they never really resolved God and religion in their life, like they just never got around to it.

It was clear that appearances would not do for Harry.

I thought church was ludicrous from a very young age. I thought it was all smoke and mirrors and that people's actions right before and right after the church service spoke much more loudly than their actions while they were actually there. And I grew up in a church that believed in a literal interpretation of the Bible, and I didn't buy it. I said, "I'm sorry. I just don't believe that's true. I don't believe that, literally, that's what happened." And I learned pretty early on to just shut up at church, to keep my ideas to myself, to do what was expected of me, and to wait for the day when I could just not go anymore. At home I was welcome to be critical of the church. But I was also told that that was fine at home, but I should not say any of this in catechism, that I was supposed to mind my own business there and just do it. It was more or less like religion as insurance policy—just in case all this is true. . . . Even though I used to say, "Well, if God is omnipotent, he knows what I'm thinking, and he knows that I think this is a crock of shit, so what's the point of this?" You know? It's really even worse to be hypocritical and go and not believe in it. Isn't it really even worse to feel as I feel about it and go and pretend? And they didn't buy that, but when I got to high school, I just basically stopped going to church. And that was okay with them.

As Harry was beginning to come to terms with his homosexuality, he learned that "there was no place in God's house" for him.

When I was thirteen, we had sex education as part of Lutheran catechism. This was the first time I learned that homosexuality existed. Simultaneously, I learned that homosexuality was a sin. This began my disillusionment with the Lutheran church. That's really where I first diverged from the church, at that point. Up until then I had liked church; I liked the show of it. And church stuff was okay because there wasn't a lot of masculine pressure. There wasn't a lot of need to be real macho in church stuff. So in that sense I liked it. But, yeah, the sex education part—that threw me, threw me for a loop. We were the first group they ever did sex education with. They were uncomfortable down to their toes about it. It was very mechanical, everything had its proper anatomical name, and there was very little emotional content in this information.

One other message that I got from the Lutheran church was that being gay was not okay—it was practically unmentionable. And I didn't have a word for how I felt in high school, sexuality-wise. I didn't really have a sexuality. But I just had this feeling like there was just no place for me. I didn't ever feel like I belonged there. And even less so as time went on. And then once I came out, I didn't think that there was any place in religion for me. I couldn't get past the fact that I could argue 'til I was blue in the face, but they were still going to throw Bible verses at me and tell me this is wrong. So I just didn't feel like being a part of it.

It was senior year of high school when I really knew what was going on. You know how you know something is going on, but you're not even willing to say it to yourself? I knew that I liked other guys. But I just wasn't willing to name it. The other part of this was that I was smoking pot like a fiend and binge eating and all this other stuff, so I mean, I had lots of ways to keep myself in never-never land. I just never really named it. It was hard for me; reality didn't have much chance to get in much of the time, so it took a lot of push from the outside to get reality into me. In senior humanities in high school, we read Camus and Nietzsche and Sartre, you know. Reading the existentialists put me over the top, and that was it: I didn't believe in God. I declared that I didn't believe in God because God didn't believe in me. I knew inside I was gay but believed that there was no place in God's house for me.

Coming out really took shape when Harry went away to college. This was perhaps the beginning of reclaiming himself and, ultimately, God.

My second sister knew I was gay probably before I did. In fact, she was the first person I told, and she said, "Oh, thank God; you finally figured it out. I've been throwing clues at you. I've been introducing you to gay people, telling you where the gay bars were. I didn't know what else I was going to do to get you out of the closet." And so she knew, and it was okay with her. When she was in high school, she didn't understand. I think she really had opened to it when she went away to school. Her best friend in college ended up being a lesbian, and I think that changed her whole attitude toward everything. It was quite a revelation to her, I think, when she found out Linda was gay. I don't think she had any idea, and I think it really changed her whole attitude.

I was about nineteen when I first put the word *homosexual* and myself in the same sentence. It would have been my freshman year of college 'cause that's when I lived in a twenty-story dorm, all male, with close to two or three thousand men. And that made the pot boil right over because it was real clear to me how different I was from them. It was also real clear to me that I was very attracted to some of them and not in just a purely physical way. There were some of them that I really felt an affection for because I loved them the way they loved their girlfriends. And I understood what that meant; I could sort of figure out that's what was going on. It took awhile before I was able to confirm that to myself or before I knew exactly what to do about that.

How did it happen? Well, my sister lived in Carbondale at the same time, where she was on the faculty. And she peripherally knew some of the people in the gay community there and where the local gay bar was.

She knew where the resources were. And so she kept throwing information my way; she'd throw out the bait and see if I would take any of it. And I mean she even went so far as to have a Thanksgiving dinner and invite every gay person she knew in Carbondale over. And I just didn't get it. I just didn't get it. I didn't understand. I didn't want to understand, I guess. I wasn't quite ready then to match it all up.

Spirituality became a nonissue for a long time . . .

I really didn't consider the whole matter for a long time after that. During the next fifteen years of my life, I was really busy surviving. I had some heavy-duty neuroses. [Laughs] I was pretty crazy. And, no, I didn't. I just didn't really think of matters spiritual at all. It just was not something I felt; I was getting wrapped up in day-to-day life.

. . . until Harry hit bottom.

It was Sunday afternoon in August or late July. I was at the fishing pier off Morse Avenue. And I was at the end of the fishing pier, and I said: "Either I'm going to commit suicide, or my life is going to get better, one of those two things, but it cannot go on the way it is; it just can't. I can't stand it anymore." And then a couple weeks went by, I guess, and nothing really happened. I called a psychologist then and decided to go see him and give psychology one last chance. And this psychologist just said, "You have to come and see me twice a week, and you have to go to OA meetings, and you have to go to AA meetings, and you have to go to as many of them as you can get yourself to. And do you live alone? Do you live with anybody? What kind of medications do you have in your house? Do you have any prescriptions?" He really took me seriously. He really thought that I might very well commit suicide. And he told me a couple years later—I wasn't his client for very long; we ran into each other at a meeting—and he said: "I really thought that you were going to kill yourself. I really thought you were very, very close to suicide." And I didn't realize it at the time. I guess I knew it, but I didn't know it, you know? But I remember that day just saying, "Well, God, I'm not really at all sure that you're out there, but if you are, how 'bout throwing something my way 'cause I'm at the end as it is?" And I really think that things did start to happen from that Sunday forward. It was awhile before really significant stuff happened, but the wheels were turning in here, and the wheels were turning outside, too—things were happening. And then when I lost the desire to drink and when I stopped bingeing I knew 'cause I had not had any control over any of that. I was really clear on how powerless I was. And that's what was making me so desperate, too, that I just couldn't stop. And when I lost that desire, then I knew: "Okay, this is confirmation 'cause this is something I cannot do alone." Obviously some other power has stepped in, through nothing I've done. And so it was just very clear to me at that point that there was God, that there was something greater than myself. And that's where I left it for a long time.

When I first went to meetings, I was afraid that they were going to be a repeat of church, and I really didn't want to be in church. I was also concerned because people had all these definitions of God that they would talk about at meetings. They had their definitions of their higher power, and I really didn't have an idea; I really didn't have a definition for God. That's what I was concerned about, that I didn't have a definition of God, and was that okay? And people just basically said: "Honey, you can make a lampshade God if you want, if that's what works for you. That's all that's important right now." And that was very helpful; it helped me stay sober, but it also was a very good first step in getting a spiritual life 'cause it pared things down to the bare minimum. It was going to be okay to put everything else on hold. And nobody had ever done that for me before. As I was taught about God as a kid, it came part and parcel with Martin Luther, you know? And this was different in that here we were back at the essentials. There's a power greater than yourself, and you believe in it, period, end of sentence. And that really worked. It worked in ways that I didn't understand at that time 'cause it enabled me to build from there a very different way of approaching God. I say that as being of the ultimate importance. I could create my own definition, one that made sense to me. And at the same time, in this very beginning, here I was getting absolute proof that there was, at least in my mind, a power greater than myself. So it was very simple, and I had proof. And I could take it from there.

Right after the first meeting I can remember walking out onto Sheffield and thinking that it was very real and, at the same time, very strange to me 'cause I was a very pragmatic person. Painfully pragmatic. And so I could hardly talk about this 'cause I felt it was so much hocus-pocus. But yet it was very real. And I had a hard time. I had to assimilate those two things, and it took me awhile to accept the idea that some very transcendent things were happening to me. And I didn't quite know what to do about them. [Laughs]

His current explorations have taken him in a completely new direction.

My sense of God didn't go anyplace for a long time, and then a class got me started on all this—actually, the instructor herself. I thought she was a screwball, but she really fascinated me. She fed us so many bits and pieces of things. It was a theological, philosophical, metaphysical salad, you know? Eat some of this, and see if anything happens to you. That's what her class was like. And I really took off with it; I really just exploded with it. And I got very fascinated in a whole bunch of stuff that I had really pooh-poohed for a long time. I had really thought all this New Age stuff was a bunch of crap. And then I started reading. The first thing I read was *The Aquarian Conspiracy.* And I don't know, I started just hanging out at Transitions Bookstore and buying all kinds of stuff, and I got interested in the men's movement, in the mytho-poetic thing, at about the same time.

And then I got interested in the whole idea of witchcraft. I really don't even remember exactly what happened. I think I may have just been at Transitions looking at books, and I found one that I liked, and it took off in my head. I also started reading *RFD* about that same time. I thought, What is this Wicca stuff? What are they talking about here? That was in the spring, and then that whole summer I wasn't working; I was just taking two classes, and they were both pretty easy classes, so I did all this reading on my own—just a lot of exploration that summer, and I was very turned onto this. It was like a buzz that I had never gotten before. I was really absorbed in all of it, and there was a whole bunch of different levels of things happening. What appealed to me was that I would read what they said about the feelings of disenfranchisement in Christianity, and I was just relating all over the place to this stuff. I thought, "Finally somebody has said this in print. Thank God." I still have a hard time with the images of all this. I still have a hard time with ritual. I'm much more intellectually into it. I think I'm in the process of connecting intellect with action. But I was just very, very, very, very, very turned on to all this and in a way that I couldn't explain, really. It was another one of those things that I just couldn't really explain why this was so fascinating to me, but it just felt right, and I just kept wanting more and more and more. And that's where I've been at with it, is, I think that I see it now much more in terms of matriarchy versus patriarchy. And I tend to see it now as much more than just a spiritual idea; I see it much more as a social idea. I lay the ills of the world at the feet of patriarchal religion. I feel like in order for gays, lesbians, women, minorities, anybody, to ever get more of the pie—it's not even more of the pie; we need a different pie. I really see it as just a great deal more than spiritual. My own personal feeling is that there is no liberation unless we liberate this, too. That's a new idea for me. This is still something I'm sitting with.

I've just recently taken this another couple steps further. I guess what attracted me to it was that I felt like a lot of the sex role, gender stuff that's embodied in typical religions, in patriarchal religions, was dropped. That's a lot more equal. I also like the lack of conformity. The people who write about witchcraft all have very different sets of ideas, and they all disagree about all these different points, but they all are headed toward the same place, and they know it. So it's really okay to have different sets of ideas, and that doesn't necessarily make you bad. Most of all I just got a big spiritual buzz out of it. I felt very, very connected. And it feels very, very powerful to me.

I haven't checked out the radical fairies, and that's a lot out of shyness. I guess the main deal with that is I still have a fear of gay men. If you want to see me uncomfortable, put me in a room full of gay men. And the idea of not only being with a group of gay men, but really letting myself be vulnerable in this group of gay men scares the hell out of me, and I've not been ready for it. I'm also not sure to what degree the radical fairies and I mesh spirituality-wise. I'm not sure exactly where and if I fit in there. But I'm certainly challenging myself to move on that. It's not a dead issue. It's not beyond my consideration. I've really thought about it a lot.

I'm also working, in another direction, toward finding some people that are doing rituals here in Chicago. I have a friend who's a heterosexual woman, and we're running parallel in our little paths, so she and I are going to the local neopagan center to check that out. So I'm taking some steps to get it out of the purely intellectual and out of the realm of just reading and actually getting involved with some other people that are into it. And I do have some fears that I'm going to encounter lots of people that I don't approve of. I'm a misanthrope at heart, and I know that, and I know that I'm going to have to get past that some. That's an area where I really want to grow. I really want to get involved with some groups, but I also have to honor myself in that I take my time and I reel myself a little bit at a time and get into it a little bit at a time. And it's on the horizon; it's just not been here yet.

I would like to find—and this is real new—a feminist coven with men and women in it. I don't know if such a thing exists. But I'm really interested in exploring feminism some more, in exploring the whole idea of total changing in gender roles. And at the same time, I'm interested in doing some ritual and getting some real connection and learning the mechanics of what I know in my head. The idea of ritual is—and this is a seed that got planted in the course—the idea of ritual was really new to me. I didn't get it. I didn't understand what ritual was all about. I didn't understand why people made such a big deal out of it until I took her class. She really, in a very short time, shed a great deal of light on all that for me. I think much more so than she had any idea she was doing. And so I've been exploring that whole idea a little bit at a time. And I'm interested now in making some big steps with that. The problem, as we all have, is that we all need forty-eight hours in a day: this is one aspect of life, obviously, and there's nine million other things going on. I just wish I had more time to work on it, more time to address it, than I do.

Looking back, Harry reflects on the impact that being gay has had on his spiritual journey.

I think that being gay was at the heart of my disenfranchisement and my feelings of alienation back when I was eighteen. And also I think that I gave mainstream religion another chance in sobriety, and there was just nothing there for me. I didn't feel comfortable; it just didn't do anything for me. And I think it's because I felt like no matter how we try to reconcile this, there is still no place in this religious life for gay people. Even with the best, most liberal reconciling Methodist minister—a Jeff Smith clone; I don't care—there's still at some point the feeling I still don't belong here. I'm still not quite right with these people, no matter how good their intentions are. I'm still making excuses for myself and who I am, and I don't feel that I owe anybody those excuses. And I couldn't get past that. I wasn't really looking for something else, but when the idea came along, it caught fire because of that. It was worse than catching fire; it was an explosion.

Another class really helped me, picking up the whole idea of gay liberation again and of self-liberation and self-disclosure. I could pick up those ideas again and say: "All right, now, how do they look in the light of who you are now? If you hold them up to the light now, what do they look like?" And I feel, as a result of where I've gone spiritually, a new energy to think and act on these things. It's hard to describe, but it's like my spiritual ideas are making me feel like I also have to work toward this. The two go hand in hand. It's made me take a whole new look at gay liberation and self-disclosure and feminism and my own racism. And the other part to this is also an environmental awareness, which really goes hand in hand with a lot of witchcraft. A lot of people that are into witchcraft are also very heavily involved in the environmental movement because they see the earth as our mother, as a very real creature. And those ideas are still settling in with me. I'm not, I feel overwhelmed by the amount of personal change that it would take to put myself in line with that. And so I sit on the sidelines with it, and then I don't like that. But I also know that I can only change it so rapidly. There are only so many things I can do at one time.

I wonder if I would have explored other avenues if I hadn't been gay. I wonder if some other circumstance would have put me in the same spot if I had been heterosexual. If I were a heterosexual man, I don't know that I would have any reason to question all of this. Because, hey, I got it made. Why should I? Why should I question the status quo? I'm in charge here. So I don't know. On the other hand, I know that there are heterosexual men that come up against the wall at some point and look at the stuff for other reasons. Maybe they're on their third marriage and their fourth job and they're tired of it. Or their own alcohol and drug problems. I don't know if I had been a heterosexual man that I would have questioned all this. I really don't think I would have.

Prayer, a relic in some sense of a religion he has rejected, has reentered his life as he works to claim a spirituality that fits.

Meanwhile back at the ranch, while I've been busy defining and exploring all this stuff, it gets to the point of, okay, I really don't know what it is, absolutely, positive, that's out there. And for awhile that made it very difficult for me to pray. 'Cause what am I supposed to be doing when I pray? I had to go back to square one and say: "You're praying to a power greater than yourself to help you today because you are powerless. If you don't do this, you're going to drink, and you don't want to do that." So very pragmatically, I had to go back and just pray, the way I'd always prayed, and pray to something greater than myself, and it had to be okay. So, meanwhile, I've been journeying in a new way, and I've had to go back and just continue praying the old way, to the old God, and maybe to the old image of God, a little bit. I got stuck in that for awhile, and I had a lot of problems as a result of it. So I think that it was really important to be able to just say, "Well, we're looking at all this over here, but meanwhile have your safety net." And I've also had to be willing to be wrong at the end of all of this. My partner has been very good about this because he said, "You know I wouldn't become too vehemently anti-Christian if I were you, Harry, because you may read and read and read and read and read and five years from now you may say, 'No, I don't think any of this is true, I've changed my mind completely, and I've gone back to Christianity.'" His basic suggestion was a two-parter: (a) "don't burn your bridges behind you," but (b) "Excuse me, but I'm an Episcopalian, and I intend to remain one. And you're going to have to learn to live with that. And I won't bitch about your stupid rituals if you won't bitch about my going to church in mink." [Chuckles] So we've just had to let each other be, and let each other's spiritual ideas be, and I think that's been a lesson for me in letting other people do what works for them. I'm welcome to have my own ideas. And to want to change that, but there's only certain ways that I can go about changing that. Otherwise, I'm just as bad as the rest of them.

Prayer is important to me. If I don't pray every morning, I stay in the swamp. I can get very hung up, very much into fear and into wanting to control everything and hold on and build tremendous resentments. And if I don't sweep out the house every morning, if I don't get centered somehow before I really start dealing with people, I'll be a mess before the day is over. It's not that when I do that I don't get angry, or that things always go well—that's not really the case—but it's that things that aren't a big deal don't become a big deal. And that's really what's important, and it makes me able to just say, "You don't know what the answer to this is. You don't know if you're going to get into grad school. You don't know if the job is going to go smoothly the rest of the week. You don't know when you'll get your paper done. It's not important today. This is what you have to do today." And I really can live that way. I can't live this other way. And that's why prayer is so important—because if I don't do it, if I don't get myself centered, then . . .

I read a lot. Once or twice a week I try to go for a long meditative walk, preferably in some kind of natural environment, like along the lake or out at night if the sky is clear and I can look up at the stars in the winter. I just find that I can get a lot of energy out of that. When my head clears up, that's when I can really get some energy out of that. That's really about it, though. My spiritual life is pretty simple.

Mark: A Gay Spiritual Ancestry

Mark is a therapist in a partial hospitalization program in New England. Also working on his doctorate, he is exploring gay spirituality, and so this story reflects much of that very active and reflective thinking.

Mark grew up in the Midwest in a small town and went to a Catholic school. His first identity religiously was as a faithful (but sometimes questioning) Catholic boy who wanted to grow up and be a missionary. Yet some significant experiences when he was an adolescent disillusioned him, and he left the church. It wasn't until he left home to go to graduate school in New England that he fully addressed his gayness. Thinking at first that he would be forever celibate, a book given him by his twin brother triggered a total change in perspective. Now he practices Siddha Yoga; is in a significant and spiritually grounded relationship with his partner, Leo; and is on the verge of completing his dissertation.

Mark thinks primarily in spiritual terms about his life. Once seen as a boy who would become a priest, Mark now finds his spiritual meaning in Siddha Yoga, meditation, and a broader sense of the spiritual. In this first piece we hear him talk about a recent pilgrimage across the country that in many ways marked a significant point in his internal path.

You don't notice the significant changes in your life until you leave and come back, which is what my year has been about. Leo and I drove cross-country a year ago; we left in mid-December and got to San Francisco about Christmastime, right after Christmas.

I can recall as a child and growing up in my environment that there was a sense of fear about taking risks, both from my father and my mother; there was the doctrine that you make money to be secure. My father grew up in the Depression, and all of that stuff carried over. And so, for me, taking that risk was always something that was scary, but necessary for further growth. And although Leo and I had traveled before, there was a lot of pressure on this trip in that I was going to be leaving him for awhile and there were issues in that. So the whole thing was about risk, for me: here I had this secure relationship, a very good job, close friends. But I knew if I didn't do this, that stagnancy would grow for me.

There was the whole process of being in the car for that many hours and being together and dealing with the people that came to us. And there was a real beauty about going back to the Midwest. Prior to this trip I had had this sense of, "Oh, yuck, going back home, to that small-town way . . ." But in some way this time I could appreciate that this was so beautiful, and I really experienced people in a really friendly, caring way. Maybe they always were, and I wasn't available to that. But there was a sense of really appreciating where I'd come from. Part of my therapy and development around being an ACOA was really about acceptance of what I was handed, and I've worked on that for awhile—and I felt this trip really showed that I had done that work. And although my father was drunk and there was the typical family scene, it was not something that upset me anymore to the degree it used to. And we would meet people in the diners and the cafes, just on the road—I noticed I was more open to being friendly, which had been difficult for me out here. When I first moved out east, it was really hard to connect with people. But in that trip I felt it. Naturally, I didn't have the same pressures this time, but I can't explain it except to say that I was just being pleased with where I was going and trusting that whatever comes was part of my path—versus that constrictual, gotta-get-here-to-do-this-and-do-it-well mentality. That wasn't as much of an issue for me anymore.

I returned May 1st, so I wasn't out in San Francisco a whole long time. I had planned to stay six months, but some things changed. I also decided that it would be better to leave early and have time on the road to really do the things I wanted, to be free instead of rushing back. I needed that transition time on the way back. My trip back, west to east, by myself, was much more beautiful, and I didn't have to plan. On the way out we had more plans about where we were going to stay, what city, how many miles, a definite pressure that I didn't have on my way back. On the way back I was kind of flowing into adventures with people. It was clearly the best trip I've ever taken, although we've done more, I guess, exciting, trips.

To have a better sense of where Mark came from, to see where his pilgrimage began, let's start by exploring his roots.

I grew up in a small town in Michigan on a family farm. We lived in the country, in the same neighborhood as my aunts and uncles. My grandparents had their own house, too. We had a family plot, the whole bit. I never lived anywhere other than that until I was a senior in high school and spent a summer away.

The first chunk of my life is always the Catholic church, Catholic school phase. I went to a private Catholic school from second grade until twelfth—and almost to Catholic colleges. There was conflict there in that my father was Protestant and my mother Catholic, and we all went to the Catholic school my mother went to. And there was always this ridicule from my father's side, this sense from early on that came from something that happened when they got married. We never knew the full scope, but I guess that it was something like, "Omigod, you're marrying a Catholic woman." And so there was always that shadow in the family, and as a small child I would go to my father's church every once in awhile, but I always knew in a way that I was doing something bad. It was a strange scenario.

I grew up with five kids in the family. I'm the youngest, with an identical twin brother. My father worked as a mechanic, and we also owned a farm, which we rented to my uncle, who took the family farm. My father was the oldest and was entitled to the farm, but he didn't want it. So he ended up supporting my uncle, and we all kind of helped out on the farm at different times. My father worked as a mechanic for the city and worked on snow plows and all that stuff. And then he would work early hours for my uncle. That was another family conflict 'cause my mother basically always had issues with him devoting time to that for very little money and no interest. The religion and the family business, which is now bankrupt, were two of the splits. In the last year my uncle went bankrupt, so that's been a big trauma for my father.

My father always used to say, "You work, pay taxes, and die." And he said that a lot when he'd be drinking. If he wasn't depressed first, he had a depressive disorder from alcoholism. And I never got a sense from them that life was joyous in any way. I always have to sort out which was alcoholism and which was real; there was a sense of we don't buy anything we can't pay for. That was part of the family ethic. That kind of stuff about money was clearly there. Along with that, however, I had some respect for them in that they didn't have airs about themselves that were false from who they were. And they were good, honest people about this life. I can't really express that in a clear way. For instance, I noticed they didn't have many friends, and clearly, they had given all that up as the kids were growing up; then occasionally someone would stop in, and you'd see them laugh and be joyous, which was really nice.

There weren't any really strict rules. They never had harsh rules about anything—for instance, how late you stay out. There was none of that kind of structure, which I think would have helped us some—I knew full-well that my brother was downstairs smoking pot. And they kind of knew, too, but denial was so rampant there. It was very rare for them to ever scold us or say, "You did something wrong." And I think a lot of that came out in us as kids in that we didn't have anything to rebel against. So we did take care of ourselves, and we did do well, all of us. And I used to think, "God, they're lucky none of us really lost it or became dropouts" because in some way there wasn't that kind of guidance. But that is where I do have thanks for the structure of the Catholic school, that it brought to us. When my mother was back at work, it's interesting that we all had to take care of things, like cook dinner. I frequently started dinner, as an adolescent, at ten or eleven. And all of us had to pitch in. My oldest brother hardly did anything. His role was to work on the farm with my uncle, and he got some money to do that. He never really did any work around the house. But the four others of us did.

Were we close, my siblings and I? That question's interesting—how you think of it differently at different times in your life. And I guess, looking at that system, I thought we were close. And then as I moved away, I thought we were less close than I had believed before. We weren't close in the sense of being affectionate or of sharing intimate thoughts. I never told anybody anything about what I truly felt. I can clearly recall a sense of going through a charade and being fake about things in order to survive. Like when I moved here, out east, I remember how new friends or people I'd meet would greet me affectionately with a kiss or a hug. And that was very rare at home. I can remember the few times when we had to do things like when you go away on retreat, and you'd write letters to your parents, they'd write a letter back, and it's like, omigod, what are they going to write, you know? And it was very touching. I did slowly start giving them credit because they were able to start sharing that part of themselves and writing that. The one time when real affection was shared was at the holidays, in mass, giving the sign of peace. They would change a little bit, to say, "I'll give a hug or a kiss." And I'm going, "Weird." So I never knew how to deal with that, and I really had to work on it when I started getting close to other people outside the system of our family—the anxiety would really come. So I guess we were close in that we kept all the family secrets, that kind of closeness. And we functioned pretty well unless my father was really bingeing and made some horrible scene. Now, I think we're truly close. In my coming out to them—I always phrased it in that way—that you really don't know me, and if you want to know me, and you want to be close, this is the way. Otherwise, I just won't be a part of your life. And that hit them.

The messages I got about homosexuality when I was growing up were all negative. I can remember one particular scene, of Truman Capote being on TV and my mother saying, "That's a sick man." And I remember being very clear that she's sharing that to me, specifically. She must have picked up on something—she denied this, of course, when I came out. But there was this sense that this was a sick man, certainly. It was a very closeted kind of community, and we didn't have a real sense of gay people. Nobody usually does, but sex in general was not really expressed as healthy or positive in any way. It's a Catholic upbringing. I can recall as a kid, maybe in early adolescence or just before that, when I'd go to movies with my family, the drive-in or whatever, and there'd be a sex scene; Roland and I—that's my twin brother—knew we couldn't act as if we were conscious of it. We'd have to pretend like we're sleeping or maybe make some other kind of acknowledgment that we shouldn't see this. So that was always there. More so for the two of us as the youngest in the family. And I can recall reading *The Book of Lists* when that was a big hit. And in that book there's every sexual list you can have: it had various sexual positions, people who have so many partners, and so on. My mother found the book, and she made a did-you-read-every-single-page-in-here? kind of comment. In general, my parents were very permissive and not controlling at all. So this was very atypical for her to be saying clear things like that. That's why the message was stronger.

But it wasn't she who taught me anything per se. The Catholic school was that for us. And my mother was as devout as you can be in celebrating the sacraments and all of that. But she eventually did leave the church also. In the whole family no one practices Catholicism anymore. My sister got married in the Lutheran church, where my father went, and that was a big thing. But right before then the priest had run away with the organist, and there was all this stuff going on in the church, so my mother said, "What's the point anymore?" But in terms of being the one in the family who supported that the most, who acknowledged the teachings and practiced them, it was primarily me and my mother.

In my family the scenario was that I was to become a priest. That was the process, and it was really weird—all the nuns that I was close to in school would always confess to me—it was really bizarre. I was thinking about this, this morning, in fact; they would say things like, "Mark, you're going to be rewarded in heaven; you're such a good soul." I think my being seen as a priest goes along with the territory of being the perfect student. I always had straight A's, where my twin brother was also very bright but didn't achieve as much as I did. And people used to say things like, "You're the good one." That somehow just developed. And I also recall doing really stupid things as a kid with my friends. We were into music, and we would go in everybody's classroom and play Christian music and sing; it was really uckkk. When I look back at that, I can't believe I did this. And we also would talk about being missionaries. We were going to be missionaries—this is so gay, omigod—who were going to go into these communities and perform drama and music and spread the word. [Laughs] And we used to have this little ritual of going into the cornfields, kind of making our path. This would be similar to the prophecy of going into a community and spreading the word among the new people in this exotic place. And I can remember this transition happening from asking, "Do missionaries get married?" And when the nuns said, "No," my zeal kind of went away. I don't know why I got into being a priest, as if they could get married. But there was this focus I had as a small kid about getting married at eighteen. And I don't know where that comes from at all, except maybe sensing that I was gay and that was compensation of some sort.

Church was a "do the right thing" activity, I think. Typically, it would be my mother and most of us kids—not my older brother. I don't know if I'd call him the bad child. He never acted out officially, but he never really was a part of the family; he was older and had that privilege in some ways. I can recall, as a younger kid, my sister and I goofing off in church secretly; like we'd look so devout, but then we'd be manipulating it, having a little bit of fun. And it just happened to be one of those things you had to do. And I knew the rhythm very well, and I could play the part very well, I guess. In high school and the start of college, I had been the one who, with my mother, was identified as the most devout. That's when I was the only one that really went to mass with her anymore.

Mark's views about religion changed as the result of a series of childhood experiences.

I would say that as a child my view of God was pretty traditional Catholic, going by the book, so to speak. But when I was in religion class, I would challenge that. I used to get in arguments with some of the teachers. I was doing things in high school that were clearly against my religion. I was on the debate team, and I would be debating these topics; they'd find out about it, say, "Mark, what are you doing?" One of our debates was supporting using fetuses for experimental testing. And I remember being pulled aside by the nun of the day, who you did not want to have any difficulties with, and holding my ground with that. But yet I probably didn't have the sense or knowledge to know what it was, outside of that tradition. I knew something was changing, but not exactly how it should be. I probably couldn't have come up with a whole lot that I would be proud of now. And it's fascinating, now, when we get together with friends or whatever and I realize how much I either have forgotten or didn't know about my own Catholic church history. I'm sure a lot of that is, as I moved away from it, I didn't pay heed to it and pull it in anymore. So I guess it depends on which year, but for the most part I would have said what I was taught. And I would have talked about the tradition of my mother and the family being involved in that way. And it would have been a sense of, you do things because it's in your breathing; it's what you've taken in. And I clearly went along with that charade for quite awhile.

I can remember looking around at all of my classmates in high school or in early college years, at that scenario: you go to four-thirty mass on Saturday and then you all go out drinking. And to me it was a contradiction that I still had difficulty with. I couldn't rationalize the two. And I can recall in high school my twin brother got drunk once, and this was triggered by "father shit." I reacted: "How can you do that? Look at what we live with every day. How can you be a traitor?" And then, somewhere along the line, I just kind of let go of that and started partying, too; mostly in the summertime, partying and working, breaking free of all that religion. It was a sense of noticing, as a junior or senior in high school, what happened to me because I didn't go along with the peers. Throughout school my identity was more of class president or student council or something, leadership-wise. Lovely perks from the Knights of Columbus, Boy's Club, and all that junk, and I noticed I was being more identified as straight-laced, and I wasn't having fun with it. I had peer recognition in a positive way, but I wasn't part of it anymore. That disturbed me, I think. I conformed to the peer pressure. How to fit in was to drink, so . . .

At seventeen my friend committing suicide was probably one of the biggest things that opened up the charade, so to speak. That's when I was class president, so a lot of the responsibility of dealing with his death came back to me. When my mother went back to work, Roland and I would go to school very early in the morning, 'cause she worked very early and we got dropped off together. And this friend John and Roland and I were very close, throughout much of our middle years of school, 'cause we had that tradition of every morning hanging out since both our mothers worked and this is how we connected. And when we got to high school, he was known as a big drinker. He was also the famous jock in the class, and he clearly would have gone on and played professional basketball. As he was a drinker, the abuse that was going on among his closest friends became clear. At that point I wasn't in his crowd anymore; I was more of the academic high achiever, whereas he was bright but clearly wasn't achieving academically. He was in more of the jock/partyer role, which I was in some way crossing at that time. I felt like I had respect from that group, but I couldn't be one of the clique, so to speak. And that distance opened my eyes to how separate everything seemed there among my classmates, and that bothered me. I recall the class just totally losing it and crying and wow, all this aspect that was genuine; it wasn't attitude. And I remember the closeness that came of that. With all this affect was a real sharing, and it really pulled us together. And I recall, here we were in mass, just our class, after we learned of his death. And we're crying and people were having a really intense time. And the question, of course, for the priest was, "Will he go to hell since he killed himself?" And I remember the priest saying, "No, he won't." I said, "Wait a minute; this is another contradiction." So, he gave a lovely, caretaking message to all of us, and on one hand I really liked that because I didn't want him to go to hell. But on the other hand, it was like, this is all political bullshit.

So that was a big awakening for me. Mostly it helped to break the limitations of how you're supposed to relate to people in an unreal way 'cause that's what I saw happening to our class. I, as class president, had to be a certain person, too. You know, we visited his family and did all the dutiful things. And we saw how much pain people were in. And then I started wondering, What really happened for him? I really wanted to understand why he killed himself. And there was a lot of talk that he had a DWI—driving while intoxicated—and that jeopardized his whole career as a basketball player. There's that theory. And then I looked more; maybe he was gay. Sometimes I wonder about that now. And the charade he had to play was bigger than any of us in the class, by being the jock. It was incredible. And the charade at home, the pressure. We started to understand a little bit more of what his parents may have put on him. He had all these older brothers who were all excellent basketball players, but he was prophesied to be even better than them, so, the pressure was there. Up until that time I was still doing the right thing; now I was starting to look at other realities to life. And that was perfect timing in that regard.

The growing awareness that came from "learning about what's out there in the world" continued to chip away at his childhood beliefs.

The pulling away from church was more from really learning about what's out there in the world, I think, and particularly what I saw as the contradictions and hypocritical thinking. And I was realizing things, like this nun who kept coming to me all the time, Sister Carmella, who's a sweet little soul, would tell me about her love for this other priest; and I was really coming in touch with the fact that the priest was gay—I knew this—and I'd wonder, What is she doing, and what is he doing? And then, I think, all at once, everything crashed. The priest ran away. My sister got married outside of the church. Mother becoming disgusted with the church made some difference, I think.

And then as I started college, I would go to the university religious services, which I thought were more heartfelt in a way. But they also seemed kind of "touchy-feely love-and-peace," and I didn't buy it. It all came to, "What am I going through this ritual for anyway?" They didn't really make sense to me, and I really didn't feel anything in my body. I was realizing I was doing things because of the reinforcement, I guess, coming from the Catholic institution acknowledging my progress and my leadership. I never really got it at home, clearly. I don't know why I was such a high achiever. I don't totally understand that piece to my life. When I got awards or had to go a dinner or something, my mom would say, "Omigod, we have to go to another one of these things." I'm sure that was also my way of surviving the system, in some way, at home.

Church never felt really celebratory; I never really liked the music, never thought the messages were that important, except for those from a few priests. I never felt a part of the community in mass, except in the sense of how we all fit an image: "Oh, here we all are, and there's that person; there's that person." The way I can explain this to you is—I saw this in a movie where you see the beautiful woman marry the ugly guy. And I thought it was horrible, like, "Omigod, they didn't keep up; the prom queen should have dated the jock"—it was that mentality. Now I think what a joke that thinking is. Now, I don't ever think in that regard. But at that time that's how it all came to be. There was a sense of, Do I belong, or don't I belong? How do I fit in? I think part of it was the shame of the alcoholism and making the family picture look fine. None of my friends knew the horror that I put up with, with my father. They always thought I had the best parents, I pulled it off so well. So the picture had to look good, and clearly, living that way you can't totally feel the essence of things and celebrate. There's always this rigidity you have to watch out for. So I'm sure that had something to do with it and that maybe I was robbed of what ecstasy could have been there for me. I think the moments that were most powerful in the church were at Christmas—for example, when a lot of people were there and you could feel some of that energy. But mixed with that energy was the thought, Where are all these people the rest of the year? The message I had was, I'm good when I'm here, and you are never here, so you are not good. It was really judgmental. So that was kind of sad about the church.

What's fascinating is that the value of looking good was never verbalized. Clearly, it was my own shame that created that. Or maybe it was carried down without a verbal message. If that was a family ethic, my father broke it all the time with his drinking. He couldn't control himself, and I think that was more of my way to deal with the shame. So it was self-created.

Mark left the Midwest to go to graduate school and, as it turns out, to come out.

I came to New England for grad school. I knew, on many levels, that I had to get out of the Midwest. There was a sense of not finding my true identity there. And at that time I think I was certainly becoming more clear that I was gay. I always knew on a certain level, but never acted on it or admitted it.

But there were also other issues, chiefly that my father was an alcoholic who had never been in treatment. There was always that bingeing and family conflict with that. So when I moved out to Connecticut, I knew on many levels that was not just for school. It was really to be myself—and you know the typical scenario—I went away to come out. And I can consciously recall driving in my car, when I first moved here. I moved here to the East Coast the summer before school started, and I worked at a camp for emotionally disturbed kids. And I started having these sexual dreams about my roommate, who I had already met in Fairfield. It's not like I was never aware of that part of myself. But I remember them coming up and being aroused and then when I moved here, being conscious of that and saying to myself, "Okay, you are gay; you know it for sure now, but you're never going to do anything about it." And when I think about that, God, it's so different from who I am now. It's totally naïveté.

That was a powerful time. Slowly my roommate came out to me, so I was picking up the energy of that. And that was my first relationship, in fact. We hooked up, and I never had any difficulties coming out, really, in terms of depressive disorder or anything in that regard. The only difficulty for me was that I was in a relationship with a woman and him at the same time. The tri-relationship theme had to be played out a little while there.

I came out to my family at various stages. I had to come out to my twin brother and my sister about five years ago. I used to rationalize, in a way, that I had no reason to come out until I had someone in my life to come out with. And then Leo and I were together—although I had had other relationships, but not of that depth or security—and it hit me to express that in a letter. Now there were other times, like when my oldest brother, who's in the moving business, came out here kind of on the spur of the moment. He was in East Hartford, right over the river, twenty minutes away, and he wanted to come over. And that was so horrible; Leo and I were living here, like we do now, and he was going to spend the night. It was like "Wake up. Be roommates in an apartment; he had to sleep on the floor of the office." We needed to break up the household. I can't believe I had to do that. I would never do that again today. But this was the brother who I was least close to. And I think maybe it was shortly after that, that I mailed the letter. And it was a whole scene, my sister was getting married at the time, and they scapegoated me for coming out and ruining the wedding. The wedding was nothing formal, just the whole family coming together. I wasn't even really truly invited, I think. So they had a lot of issues with that. My mother was crying and wouldn't talk to me. I felt like, "This is amazing: you, of all people, know more than anyone else."

But my father talked to me then, and it was fascinating. He was drunk, of course, when he called me, but he at least talked to me. And I learned a lot of secrets; my coming out clarified some of the things about sex that were there in the family. I remember feeling that, wow, this is really breaking the facade. And in particular I had had that sense of, or lack of sense of, Do my parents have sex? My mother had twins at the age of almost forty. That was a difficult thing for her, and I'm sure it caused a lot of trauma. And shortly after or right before my birth I thought an affair took place. There was this man, in particular, who was very close to my mother at mass. My father never went to mass with us, of course; he still practiced a Lutheran following. And as a little kid I was thinking, this is the man; I don't like him 'cause whenever my father got intoxicated, there would be this talk of infidelity and rageful kind of shit. So anyway when I came out, my father seemed to be expressing to me that he was impotent for a long time. And the way he expressed it, I think, was that he had kidney stones or some medical problem that was very severe. And then it all kind of hit: the impotence and the paranoia about my mother being with other people 'cause he couldn't have sex with her, perhaps. And there was a weight taken off my shoulders about that. She probably really didn't have an affair.

And I remember really feeling like, "Of course, as you become more real, the people around you become more real." I think it went in stages; I talked about moving to California and my parents got a little scared and made a visit out here. My parents and I took this drive up to Maine, and this was after I had written the letter. You know the experience, you clearly write this letter, and you know shit's happening back home, but no one's bringing it up with you here. And we took this trip, and they didn't say anything until we got ten minutes from Hartford, when my mom asked a few questions about Leo and about children and his family.

And we virtually said very little, even though I've sent them literature about being gay or asked them to inquire.

Last winter when Leo and I drove cross-country, we had Christmas with my family. And that was the first time Leo had been with the whole family. It went very well. And this year before the holidays I made the request that if they were going to put my name in the sibling draw, they had to put Leo's name in, or I didn't want to be in. So I started making these expectations, and they delivered very well. My mother got us these matching necklaces, and we decided to hang them on the tree. They're not something we really care for, but it's a very sweet gesture. And matching socks, really acknowledging the relationship, and they got him a sweater. Early on I said, "You need to ask about Leo and find out about his life," and so much more freedom and expression have been resolved.

Before this I reached a point, I think, when I said to myself, "This is all a joke." Catholicism seemed like a joke. Family seemed like a joke. And I would go home on the holidays, and there'd be this kind of quivering, I used to call it. We'd sit around; maybe we'd go out to lunch, my mom and my sisters and me and my brother. And there'd be this talk back and forth about Dad. Or about someone who never was there.

Leo and I had similar roles in our families, the one that was the caretaker—"Talk to me anytime." And then that just got really sick 'cause no one was talking to anyone else. So I'd come home for whatever, and it'd be the same scene over and over again, people bitching about this one who wasn't there and couldn't defend him or herself. And then my father was getting drunk every single time. And I reached the point where I decided, I'm not doing this anymore. The statement of saying, "I don't want to hear it" was the big step. So I became healthier. And then I just kept going.

The book The Impersonal Life *was a powerful catalyst in Mark's coming out.*

This story is totally fitting of synchronicity. It's probably one of the peak moments of my life. I had come back home—this is when I was just starting my master's program—for Thanksgiving or some other holiday. My brother had read this book, and he gave it to me. A woman that I, you could say, had dated and then had left—before we had sex or anything, of course—became his partner, or girlfriend, and they ended up getting married. So somehow there was an energy around us being together that was starting to grow into a spiritual sense with the three of us. And I was certainly beyond the words to speak of spirituality in a real way, like I feel I can now. I recall I had this book, but I didn't read it right away. At that time I was starting to confront that statement I made about "you know you're gay, and you'll never do anything about it." The energy was changing with Paul, my roommate: the sexual energy was building for both of us, I think. And there was a sense of wow, this was all new territory; what do I do with it? And I remember sitting in my room one day and seeing the book, and I just picked it up. And the book opened and made statements about "how I am God"; every line is God speaking directly to you in a religious or spiritual way that I had never read anywhere. It was so powerful. And quickly—I may have been conscious about gays being bad and the culture we live in—it hit me right away: if God has talked to me, it was talking from the context of God living inside of me. And at that time it just hit about being gay—that it's very powerful and good and honest and real. And I literally can remember energy going up my back and tingling all over my body, similar to how kundalini energy is, which I was just on the brink of discovering. It was incredible. I couldn't put this book down. And I remember just sitting in my room like nothing else mattered in the world. Even career, job, anything. This was it; this was the true essence of what it was about. The sense that it doesn't matter what any of us are—talk about the charade totally being broken—how things look didn't matter. And the risk of being questioned about being gay or not. That's why I think my coming out was not difficult, interpersonally or intrapersonally, because this message was so heartfelt. I can never describe it, but I remember just those words. I still have it, and I ended up ordering that book for friends, and that became "my" book, my message. Few experiences in my life will match that moment. It was this sense that everything I viewed was totally changed. Here I was working as a substitute teacher with very difficult kids. There was a lot of stress in doing that. Children, of course, will push you; they know your stuff in a powerful way. And I can remember, I was starting to look into counseling and psychology, and I had a sense of, How can I ever relate to my clients? There was a time when I thought I had to work with kids because maybe I'd never fit in sexually, or I never had that straight identity that I thought most people had. And so this book totally said, "Whoever you are, it doesn't matter." The energy was there. It was very freeing. And if I look into that relationship with Paul, I'm sure it helped me tremendously in working through the first gay relationship with a man who couldn't be a nurturer, a giver, to the extent that I might have needed in my first relationship. And it really empowered me to take care of myself, after a history of taking care of my family and other people, never looking, really, at my needs. That was not part of the agenda. Taking care of myself is always something I'm working on, but then it got to be where I would almost overcompensate, I think. And so I had to find a balance there.

A little while later I broke up with Paul, the guy I just talked about. I recall I knew either he wasn't able to meet the intimacy needs I wanted, or he was distant at the time. And now I believe, in some ways, I was more than I think he bargained for. Paul is not a person who—I don't know how to put this—knows what he wants for a life. He has no desires or things he's working on or a sense of direction, or he probably very much does, but he's not clear about that. It got in this back and forth game where we'd go to his family's and have these really powerful times—they lived in Rhode Island—and then he'd push me to take the next step: we were finishing our graduate programs and might live together. I was shocked. "What are you talking about?" And then as I started to think about it, I realized that maybe that is something that I wanted to do. Then he pulled back. It was the typical pursuer-distancer all the time. And it drove me crazy for awhile. But then I noticed, I would get really romantic about things. I worked a midnight shift in the crisis program at the time. And so I would go and see these full moons and have these experiences. And I would love to call him up and share. But I knew I couldn't do that with him. I knew he really wasn't there to share with me the intimacy I wanted. Although we had many powerful times, we had reached our peak. And I knew he would not be the person that would really end the relationship. It would be one of those things where he would grow distant and distant and ignoring me enough, so I said, no, I don't want it to get horrible. It was a really beautiful time, my coming out. It really flowed beautifully. And I never had really terrible hardships with the coming out. And part of it, I think, was having that intimacy at that time.

There was such a beautiful artistry in the movement, from reading the book and understanding the concepts of God living within in a real bodily, felt way, to the transition time of finishing my master's program and moving out into the world. We literally lived on campus, and both of us worked for the school. And then I started my first position. It was at a time when I was planning to move to Boston, but I never made it because I interviewed for this job and got it. It was incredible how I entered this real, live, living, sharing group of people, a quality which had not been conscious for me in my life. But this was. And a woman on the team and I became close quick friends; a very sexual component developed there in terms of her wanting to be a sexual partner of mine. And I was dating this other guy, and it became a new triangle.

She and I were introduced to Siddha Yoga by a woman who was teaching a course in psychological theory. We had been approaching spiritual themes after reading the book and starting to look into meditation. The woman who taught the course broke up all the theoretical approaches and was about to present the transpersonal approach. And Amanda—who's the woman, the friend of mine who I work with—said, "She's gonna present transpersonal theory, and I think you should come." And so I went, and the instructor started talking about meditation, about different layers of consciousness, and we totally got aroused and interested. We ended up talking to this woman, and she connected with me 'cause I was a therapist and so was she. And then she invited us to her home, where she had meditation sessions, 'cause she was one of the district leaders of Siddha Yoga. It was really bizarre. There was a lot of judgmental stuff that came up from me about it, that some of these people there were really weird. And clearly, I still had the facade. You never totally get rid of that. That's how it felt 'cause it was totally different from anything I'd practiced before. You'd be in a room meditating, and people would just start screaming—I mean bloodcurdling screams 'cause that was part of their process. And it was alarming.

Eventually, a few months later, we did go to South Fallsburg, which is the national headquarters, and that's when we met Gurumayi. Then it led into weekend intensives. And that's really where, I would say, the kundalini awakening occurred, being initiated, bodily touched, by the guru. And the essence of love, whoa, I'd never known that. I can't really describe it. It's like I'd be listening to those sappy songs on the radio and having this whole new relationship to the music. It totally blew my mind. There must have been fifteen hundred people in this hall, and the guru went personally from person to person. That whole gesture, to me, was so moving and loving. And after that I had all of the bodily felt stuff, sickness and throwing up and the purification, and it was very scary. But I also had a sense of, wow, this is real; this is not going through any rituals that make no sense to me. There are a lot of rituals in Sanskrit and all that, that I didn't really understand, which I think was helpful because otherwise my cognitive part would've gotten in the way. And that led to daily practices in my home and setting up my own kind of altar. Yeah, that was very powerful. Those are experiences beyond words, really.

I'm not, I want to say, as devout as I was. I think I've incorporated it more into my awareness of everything versus having to sit down and meditate. Sometimes I'm concerned that my practices are not as regular as they used to be. For example, one of the reasons I went to San Francisco was to be close to the ashram out there—I thought it would help me get back on track—but what essentially happened was, I was open, and I think when you're open, people come into your life, and you meet people who take you further in your journey. And that happened a lot, powerful moments with people, which was the thing I really didn't have; here I have all these people around me, but we were never really celebrating together, and I think that's more of what the trip was about. All my friends were scared of my getting into a cult: "I don't understand why you're doing this; it makes no sense to me." It was totally the opposite of everything I'd been trained in, in the world. And part of me wanted to say to myself, "Are you really losing it?" But for the most part I knew that I wanted it. I look at it in terms of total balance in my life. When I got involved in Siddha Yoga, I had the perfect job, if you can ever have it; I was surrounded by people I really loved; and I was doing the work I really loved. I was feeling, How can life get any better?

And Leo came into my life at that time. I don't think there's any mistake there. He was a little scared in the beginning, when I'd talk about my practice, and he'd see the pictures; if you look in the bedroom, there's this huge picture of the guru. He was scared, but I think he also knew not to push that 'cause it was so important to me. But now if you look at Leo, things have totally changed; we were sitting here with a group of friends, and this friend said, "Mark, you've done a marvelous job with him." Leo was talking more spiritually than anybody in the room. It was just beautiful to see how we had come together around that theme. So in that regard my practice is more whole; it's more a part of everyday life.

We talk about the exchange in our relationship. And he does acknowledge that there was a time when he couldn't even bring that up. He would tell me, "Don't say anymore" 'cause I would challenge his beliefs about death and life. It was a total paradigm change for him, and he would kind of get freaked out. But now it's beautiful.

Another significant experience in Mark's journey happened recently, a "Body Electric Workshop."

I had been given a flyer or an article about the "Body Electric Workshop" two summers ago, and then I just did it this last summer. So I had this information for a whole year. And just reading about it was like, wow, people really do this. You know, all the training's done in the nude. A friend had given the flyer to me, saying, "Look at this, Mark," and we kind of joked about doing it, some friends and I. And when I went out to San Francisco, I had planned to do it in Oakland, which is where the headquarters were, but I had to do something else for graduate school, and it just never worked out. So I ended up doing it in New York City last summer.

And a lot of things developed before I actually did the training—I was focused on it and talking about it, and people would inquire about it. Leo and I have an open relationship. And it's been that way for a couple of years now. And during the time of talking about it and thinking about incorporating this work in the Ph.D., people came my way to talk about it with. And that even turned into opportunity for sexual experiences, which for the most part never happened. There were some very positive, but also some really negative, things that happened. I met this person at graduate school, and I clearly thought this guy was gay or bisexual. And he's telling his story about being a minister and his family and his wife, but yet he kept trying to engage with me: "Tell me about that," and "What is it that they do? Can you show me that?" It was very provocative, yet it was just so indirect. . . . I almost said dishonest, but that's not really fair; it was a sense that he had incorporated his sexuality, in a comfortable way, with my sense of it. Maybe he just wanted to have sex with me. I think, clearly, he did, but there was this hypocritical quality that came up again. I started challenging him about his life, and very clearly he didn't like that. And the same thing happened again at another graduate school thing, where this time I was talking to someone about it, and I think this guy picked up on it, and he was married, same kind of thing. I wasn't even attracted to him, but we really hit it off as friends. And it was very beautiful in that we really connected. He wanted to know, Is it much freer? And here I am telling him this story about this previous experience, which this time turned into a powerful one. And I don't know if you could say we had sex, but we engaged in some kind of sexual play. And he had, clearly, limits and issues about that, but I was more able to accept where he was at that time. So just talking about this thing brought this energy. All these synchronistic things happen again.

I went to New York City, which is where the Body Electric training was, with my friend Amanda—it's going to sound like a soap opera, but Amanda's the friend that had sexual interest in me and still does, and this is going on six years now. And here I am going to this training with gay men in the nude, and she's going with me to New York, and we're staying at a friend of hers, who we think is a lesbian; all of these boundaries about sexuality were not as clear-cut. And she buys me flowers, which were the favorite flowers of this friend who I was losing at the time, and then I go to the training, and all of this stuff is incorporated into the process for me. There are various parts of it. It's a two-day intensive. But one thing that Kramer talks about is that some people will have near-death experiences. Some people have kundalini experiences—there's the whole gamut of what comes for people. And clearly, that is what happened for me, the near-death experience. I really believe that ritual of the combination of sexuality and spirituality helped me deal with all these forces around me because it was a very intense time. Amanda and I, in our relationship, have had to try everything in the book; it's very complex, but I'm technically her supervisor now, even though we were colleagues at one time. She's twenty years older than I, so it's all those issues, combined with the intensity of who we are as people and at work and our myths. And so I would try to set more limits, and she would see that as more rejection. Then there's how Leo viewed it, and this was so thick, you cannot imagine. A certain trust really happened. And her understanding and acceptance of what I needed and who I was sexually was powerful. If you look behind you to see the print of two men embracing, she gave me that for Christmas. It's incredible. She's come a long way. So on many levels in my life that energy before, during, and, now, after continues to be operating. And it's also just looking at heartfelt experience. Certainly the importance of ritual to get you there. The group of these men and what happens and how easily it was for me to let go of that judgmental view of how things should be. I think that was the experience; there was an affirmation that you are able to move on from that.

And I would sit there, and I would giggle at some of these people 'cause in that experience, people come to you; your spirits kind of come to you. And I don't know how to put this except to acknowledge how different my view, my perceptions were. Prior to that my twin brother visited me in San Francisco. And he and I have always been close; it's really that kind of telepathic kind of closeness. But we never have verbalized things in terms of loss, in me coming out, in his loss—he's now divorced from the woman who I had dated—and we started talking about that, and then we talked about my coming out, about the sexual aspects of that, which I think my family in general is pretty uptight about. And I didn't feel maneuvered like I had. When you verbalize that to someone in the system you grow up in, they're like, wait a minute. And he started questioning my love for Leo because we had this open relationship. And so that pushed me to understand it and verbalize, "Wait a minute; they're your views, you know." And so that's where all of a sudden you say: "My God, I know I'm not the same. I do see things quite differently."

Mark wrapped up our discussion by describing how his journey has been affected by his being gay.

Is there a relationship between my being gay and my spiritual journey? Definitely. I come from the premise that I think our ancestry is one of being a minister, so to speak, in a spiritual sense. And that goes in many realms: of healing and spirituality and teaching and guiding. And I think part of that is based on the presence of difference, of not really fitting in. I think that, clearly, is a lot of what my life has been about. So I don't think there's a mistake that as a child I was guided to being a priest or that I was very much into the rituals, although I didn't feel it. I'm a firm believer in past lives and journeys in that regard, and a lot of my readings and understandings indicate I did have those existences as a priest, and some of that I think I'm working through. A lot of the message for me was, yes, I would jump into it, and I would spread this word, and then something would happen to challenge me further. And I'd get rejected or abandoned or ostracized and then pushed into that pilgrimage. It's the same journey again. And I really feel that is there for me.

I used to think, "What if I was straight, how would my life be?" And I think, you really can't do that, but as much as I do it, I would have continued with letting things look a certain way: work towards that BMW, maybe, and be a high achiever to get those things in life. To fit in, in a yuppie sort of way. And I really believe that being gay pushed me to challenge things more; I went a long time accepting stuff, and then I said, "I couldn't take it." I don't mean that straight people don't go through a place where they challenge, but for me I think it made a lot of sense that I needed that to break through and push further about what is reality, what matters. It's a weird position I'm in 'cause I can compare myself to my twin brother, who is straight—and who is spiritual. For myself, I think maybe I would've fallen into a different frame of going along with things more so; it's just part of who I was.

The interplay of gay and spirit, I think, is so frequent if I look at everything. Somehow I'm drawn into that mystery of the church and that intrigue of the shadow side. I don't know if there's a connection in terms of our ancestry: falling into that experience and breaking through it, for rebirth, to push further. I also think in my work as a therapist, if I look over time—where I was in coming out and where I am now—it really has pushed me. It's fascinating when I think I used to believe I couldn't become a therapist because I was gay and because I couldn't relate to people. Now looking at it, I think I'm so much more there for people because I challenged more things and didn't have this image, so to speak, that I thought a therapist should have.

I have this friend, Victor, who's always challenging me, "Mark, there's not meaning in everything." And we'll play back and forth with that. What is meaning, you know? I know one thing: I am much more of a believer in the power of the mystery of life. For me, mystery is sacred. Victor clearly taught me this.

I think, from my connection with other gay people and my own work, that there's a frustration when people come out. When you come out, you have this expectation that you will connect with gay people and they will welcome you into their arms and [claps] you will feel your community. I have asked people if they felt that, and for the most part, they don't feel it. And I believe, in my thinking about us as spiritual beings, in a gay essence, and the challenge it provides for spiritually, I think, why not have that experience? Why can't we just feel that essence when we come out? And join it.

I think that's the missing piece, for me, in my journey. Like when I go to the ashram and I feel a total gay presence, and I know it's there, but it's not verbalized. And then that bothers me, and I say, "But Mark, you know, at some point we get beyond that in terms of our spirituality." I'm clearly not at that place; to me the gayness and the spirituality are right there together. Eventually transcending that is something that I hope will happen for me at some point. But that's clearly where I'm at in my development, and I think being there is for a purpose: for people to combine being gay and spiritual. So even though I look at these positive experiences that have put me in touch with my gayness and spirituality, it wasn't in the context of other gay people, really. And I guess maybe that's not usually where it comes from. But I also have this sense that maybe there is this gay spirit around us that guides us to where we need to go. And it doesn't have to be on a conscious level between gay people, too. I

"The interplay of gay and spirit, I think, is so frequent if I look at everything."

wonder about that. 'Cause I do believe that there is that ancestry for many of us. Those are some of the questions I'm asking.

I keep hearing this from people I work with who are coming out that there's something missing. So I wonder if we're developing that missing piece. Is that what might be happening for us now, to have more gay spirit? If you look at what's happening in the world now, what with Clinton and being a gay-positive president, and with the many years of AIDS, where is that going to lead us? I really do believe that it's pushing us, maybe, to a more real celebration, gay and straight, in a spiritual sense. But it's about putting that out there in a more direct or a more conscious way.

If today someone asked me, "What do I really want to do with my life?" how would I answer? There are different times in my life where I've thought about this retreat place for gay people, not where you go in on one weekend, but one which you know is always there; slowly, many people come in, and that's part of the energy that's acknowledged. There are few places, I think, where that exists. It's in the consciousness now. And I'm sure it's been there for awhile, but maybe the times haven't been there to create it yet. I want to be part of that vision, that place.

Rachel: Culturally Jewish, Naturally Taoist

Having lived in both the Chicago area and Ohio in a Jewish family, Rachel relates that she has few memories of her early years. She left both the home and the religion she grew up with after high school and has had little contact with her family since. Now a social worker who has spent a great deal of time trying to make sense of all of this, she talks about her life in a powerful, honest, and reflective way.

Rachel's spiritual story includes significant contributions from three different traditions: Judaism, Taoism, and twelve-step philosophy. In a very strong sense, she has rewritten the "story" she was given by her family in her childhood, reclaiming that portion of her roots that remain meaningful and combining this with new elements. We will explore both the old and the new here, beginning with the ties she keeps with her Jewish background, but first let's orient ourselves to her current perspective by noting why she chose to participate in this study. Here she tells us about her reconnection to the Jewish roots she had denied for some time.

One of the reasons that I was very interested in being part of this study, and to focus and think about my spiritual journey, is that in the last year and a half to two years I've had this spiritual awakening. In the sense that if I could let go of things that would happen, then I wasn't feeling so crazy. I am finding this really huge connection in the various pieces of my life, but I don't know how they're going to come together; I've had so little experience of it. I don't know. All of this is very new for me. And my interest in doing this is I don't talk about it that much. It's been very private. It was very embarrassing to say I wanted to go to temple to the same people that I had said, "You guys are kind of crazy." So that was a really big thing for me to say, "Okay, this is what I need to do." And I have some friends who have been very cooperative in re-Jewifying me. My best friend brought me over this little Jewish star sticker in my window. And I lit my Hanukkah candles in the window. So it's been an interesting kind of turnaround. I know that people go back to God or whatever in times of distress. One of my own pieces of my psychology is I hate to be part of the mainstream. It just kills me when what they write in the books applies to me. I just want to be the exception. I am the exception.

In many ways Rachel has moved a long way from her family, yet there are ties.

I was very close to my dad's father, who brought me to temple. If I got any kind of religious anything, it was from my grandfather. Last night in therapy I was talking about the connection that I got from him, which was so strong—and probably the only source of positive anything from anyone in my family. He and my grandmother are Russian immigrants. They met on the boat. My grandfather sought out my grandmother for two months. All he knew was that she worked in a shoe shop on Montrose Avenue. I never saw them argue. He got sick with Parkinson's disease when I was about seven or eight, which is at the same time we moved to Ohio. And so we came back from Ohio in '70. He was already very ill and not functioning very well; he couldn't work anymore. And he died in '77. I look back now, and I really grieved his death. I was away at college, and I came back, and he died ten minutes after I got there. And I think that connection has been important for me in terms of trying to keep a spiritual sense; later when I was a little bit older, I think I tried to reconnect to him by living in orthodoxy for a couple of years. I tried to understand how all this fits together. I always thought of my dad's parents as very religious, although I think that they weren't.

As for my mom's parents, I think my grandmother was an immigrant from Russia or Poland. Her father was born in Austria, and he came over here as a child, after his father was killed. I really don't know much about his mother; what my uncle told me is that she was in a mental institution for women's problems. My grandfather's family is quite wealthy, and he was like this disdained child who was passed around. They're a publishing family, and they would never quite let him up to the top, so he is very, very angry. I don't have any emotional memory of him, just distance. I remember my mother's mother died when I was six, and my mom was traumatized. And then my grandfather remarried a year and a half later and moved to California. I really don't think about it too often.

The contrasts between my mother's and my father's families were stark. My mother grew up with a Christmas tree because my grandfather was a businessman. And I remember, when I was about four, we had a Christmas tree, and my dad's parents came over, and I thought my grandmother was going to kill my mother. My father's family never liked her. And so I grew up with this weird combination of orthodox rituals on my dad's side and no religion, anything, on my mother's side—except for my grandfather. He used to belong to Temple Shalom. To connect with my grandfather, like a yentl girl, I wanted to be a rabbi. I was the only girl in the orthodox Hebrew school, and the intellectual pursuit of it was really important to me. I'm pretty sure that there was no faith involved anywhere. That was pretty amazing to me: how much ritual I could do without a belief in God.

I think that part of my eventual dispersion of Judaism is somewhat connected to what happened when I wanted to be a rabbi when I was younger. I was going to be bat mitzvahed, and my mom called the rabbi and canceled it. And so I had a clandestine bat mitzvah in Hebrew school. And I really struggled; I went to a religious school four afternoons a week and Sunday 'til I was fifteen. I wanted to go to the academy, but my mom wouldn't let me go because they found pot in someone's locker. So I went to New Trier, where people were doing cocaine in '75; her rationalization was so bizarre. And when I told my rabbi, who was very young and very cool in every other way—I read him the Torah; I did everything that the boys did—that I wanted to apply to the yeshiva, he told me that I should rethink my plans. And that as a woman I would never get a congregation. If I wanted to be a theologian and scholar, that would be fine; maybe I could teach one day. But if I had thought of getting ordained, then the only way I could get ordained would be as a reformed rabbi. That would be very, very heinous.

The easy way to explain why I would not be reformed would be to say it's 'cause my mother's father was reformed. That's the easy answer. I think it's truly because my sense is that if you're going to do it, you should do it. Don't fuck around. If you're going to take a stand, take it; don't be a mush. You know? I think that when I'm uncomfortable it's because I'm being a mush and I can't make a decision, and I think that is like reformed Judaism. I understand the sociopolitical thing behind it. But there are five hundred and ninety-six, five hundred and ninety-two—it's one of those big numbers—commandments; how can you throw half of them out? [Laughs] That's how it feels to me. I could compare it to my sexual identity; it's the same discomfort I feel if I have to change pronouns. This is who I am, and I'm not going to make a concession to the general population because that's denying myself as a human being. And I think that's much more articulate than I felt it originally. It was kind of like, we're Jews and we do things differently. Our Sabbath is not on Sunday. We don't have choirs; that's not what we do. That's not how it was set up. Temple Shalom is not quite that reformed. It was just like Cliff Notes. [Laughs] It was enough. The rejection of it really has more to do with my family and how they expressed religion.

Anyway, the *Tribune* wanted a cover article on the rabbi for their magazine because he was the youngest ordained rabbi to have a congregation in the Midwest. He was something like twenty-two when he was ordained. And so he was probably twenty-six or so when he made this remark to me. And [sighs] although I don't think I felt it at the time, I was devastated. I think that a big part of what fueled my rejection was that this man had not a clue as to what this meant for me. He didn't get the meaning of what it would have been like for a girl to be in this Hebrew school, to go against her parents, and have someone say she couldn't. I think that was an important incident for me in terms of rejecting all that stuff.

Here was someone who I really believed in and trusted. I don't think it has anything to do with my sexuality. I don't even perceive—as most of my women friends, especially lesbians, do—Judaism to be a very anti-woman religion. The way that he explained it was very liberating. What I was taught was that men had all these tasks they had to perform because they couldn't remember. But because women lived the lifestyle—which is what Judaism is, rules for living—they didn't need to have so many reminders, and so they didn't have to do so many things. Keeping a Jewish home was enough; that kept them spiritually in tune. Men had to perform all these rituals because they were too dense to get it and too distracted by other things. Now, to me, that doesn't sound sexist. To me, that sounds very prowoman. But I don't know that anyone else got that interpretation. I don't even know if anyone else in the class even got that interpretation. That's what I got. And then to have this man say, "You know, it's not a good idea for you to pursue this any further" was such a contradiction.

The first hints of her lesbian identity came during high school.

My sister's friends in high school used to call me a lezzy. I had no clue. I was engaged to a man whom I'd known since I was seven; we met when I was living in Ohio. Total mistake. He got some girl pregnant. I think that I was in survival mode for so long, but people that I talk to who knew me in high school, knew that if one of my girlfriends started dating some guy, even though I dated guys, that I would break up their relationship. I don't know how, and I don't remember doing it. But I do remember someone telling me that when I was around twenty.

I think my coming out came very intellectually. I always defended gay people. I grew up knowing gay men, though I didn't know any lesbians. Alice, who was the best friend of my Aunt Beth—who I lived with—is the queen of the fag hags. Her gay friends became my aunt's friends. At my cousin's bar mitzvah there was a table of gay men. It was like, so cool. My two cousins in Miami—they're my cousin's cousins—one's a lesbian and one's gay. I have another cousin who's gay.

I think my first real self-knowledge came on New Year's Eve '78 or '79. I was at a New Year's Eve party with a friend. And it was midnight, and all these couples were kissing, and I just felt repulsed, men and women. And I just remember thinking to myself, "I don't belong here." And my cousin Sara—we grew up together, and then our families moved away—she was in town for my cousin Jeff's bar mitzvah, and we hit the town. We were both nineteen, and I had never been to a gay bar before; we went to Coconuts, and it was great. I didn't get a clue. It was so exciting.

By May or April it was there, and it's not been a struggle for me. It was just okay. Cool. I was dating a woman. Bad relationship. This is like the most bizarre coming-out story. We were watching *Soap,* and it was the episode when Jody meets the lesbian. And I just said to her, "Wouldn't that be just so much easier?" And she said, "Yeah, it would; we get along so well." And that was it.

Rachel left home after graduating from high school and only returned for two very brief periods after that and only for financial reasons. She began college at Northern Illinois University, but as she said, "I got high and failed all my classes." She returned home to junior college and discovered an interest in social psychology.

I really hooked into Erving Goffman and couldn't get into U. of C. And so I went into social work, which I'm glad for; I love it, but it wasn't my intention. I think—this is my therapist head talking—that studying Goffman was a real fringe way of connecting to some of the theories I had about being in my family. My family kept telling me what a waste of time I'd had since I'd been going to school for a couple years. And I worked, and I lived on my own in an apartment. My first lover and I broke up, and I wasn't making any money, and I went back to my parents' house and went back to school to get the bachelor's degree.

I was in undergraduate school for social work when my father had a heart attack, his third. And while he was in the hospital, my mom just flipped out. I know I had a basic understanding of what was going on with her at that point, and this is before she was diagnosed, but I just reacted to it. I went to go stay with my dad's sister—I stayed with them on and off during high school when my mom would really get violent with me. And my aunt made me go into therapy because I was getting migraines whenever I heard my mother's voice. So I went to therapy, and as I started to get better—with very, very minimal improvement in asserting myself and figuring out what my needs were—they began to reject me.

As I really got into social work, my politics started to shift—I'd always been somewhat left-leaning, but then my politics began to shift fairly hard. The two years I was in undergraduate school at UIC were very radical—the twenty-eight people in my undergraduate school were very tight, and we had a boycott (there was a lot of political action on campus) against things that were going on in the social work college. And that's where I met my ex-lover, Mary, in Social Work 100. I fell in love with her on sight. She's a Mexican-American, ex-Catholic Marxist. She helped my politics shift, but it all made sense to me.

The first conflict I had with my family, having to do with my lifestyle, my choices, and my politics and theirs, happened around Rosh Hoshanah and Yom Kippur in '83. I went to temple, and I just remember reading the prayers and thinking, "This is stupid." And I was in a lot of pain about that. I don't remember much; I just remember the pain feeling. I didn't want to be there. I was staying with my uncle at the time, and I had to be there—my uncle was active in the congregation, so we all had to be there. I couldn't stand it.

The conflict between us just kept growing as I was getting ready to get my bachelor's degree and go to graduate school. I was getting more and more involved with Mary and her family, who were accepting of me without knowing I was her lover. They felt more accepting to me than my own entire family, and I gravitated toward them. And as I began to say that I have needs and to be an adult—I was twenty-two or twenty-three at the time—they began to tell me that I was ungrateful and that they could see why my mother beat me. Anyway, the huge conflicts were around the Jewish holidays with my family, my aunt and uncle, and my grandmother. I was spending most of my time in the city and not with them. I stayed over at Mary's house a lot. And I stayed at other friend's houses. It was just closer for school. I didn't really want to be at my parents' because, like I said, as I was getting healthier, they were becoming more rejecting of me or more scapegoating of me. It was just something my family always needs, the target. It shifted to me. And I'm still in the midst of it.

The end of any decent relationship with my family happened during Passover in '84. I came in from work, to my cousin's and my grandmother's house, to stay with her, and they were halfway through with the Seder. I walked in and my cousin called me a beaner, and he asked why they didn't get the tortillas out for me—just horrible kinds of racist things against me because the person I was spending my time with and her family were Mexicans. And while they were eating dinner, they were talking about lazy Mexicans and lazy blacks and welfare cheaters and people who just don't want to work. They also talked about a friend of my cousin's who had gotten thirty thousand dollars of public aid fraudulently; that was okay, but not these lazy people on welfare. Later on that night the conversation I had with my grandmother was, "You really should be with a Jewish person." It was no issue that it was a woman. That she wasn't Jewish was first, and that she was Mexican was this whole other layer of weird stuff. It was that I was doing this horrible bad thing by connecting with this non-Jewish person and her family. There was nobody on my side in all this. This whole thing was such a huge mind-blowing thing.

The strangest thing about that memory, for me, was my cousin, who was like my big brother—he's fifteen years older than me. He lost his business because he gave away too much medicine. And he was buying into this racist thing around this holiday of liberation and oppression. The political and emotional for me were just extreme, and so my connection to my family just went off a cliff.

So it was over. I moved in June, with a friend from school, and I've never had any contact with them since in general. My mom called me a couple times when my sister disappeared for six months. Other than that the only contact I would have would be from my youngest sister, who would call me when my mom would beat her up. And then she'd get mad at me 'cause I was angry that she was saying she deserved it.

I had a friend who called me to tell me that my sister had beaten up a teacher and they had gotten this huge staff meeting together and finally got my mom to come into the school. They had been trying to get her to come into the school since my sister was in third grade because she was learning disabled. And now she was a sophomore in high school and violent. And they had psychiatrists and clinical psychologists diagnose her at this meeting. I don't know what happened, but I got a phone call after that from my sister threatening me and my boss with physical harm if I ever got into her business again. And then I called my dad and told him what happened and that he needed to get her in check or do something 'cause she said she knew where I lived and described my apartment building and that she was going to hurt me. My father said, "You should just stay away from us. You just cause trouble." And my dad is kind of a wimp; he's so distant from me he wouldn't come to my graduations because my mom would be angry at me.

When I think about [sighs] trying to get a handle on what I was raised with, I think I lived in survival mode. We had a really definite "we versus they" kind of thing, my whole family. I can't distinguish, myself, how much of my experience growing up in this working-class, trying-to-be-middle-class Jewish family had to do with its craziness and dysfunction versus that my mom was mentally ill and my father, God knows what he is. You don't go to temple even if you believe in going to temple; you don't go out on the holidays 'cause we have to give that appearance of solidarity or observance, things like that. And then part of this really crazy system of my grandfather's father was killed in a pogrom, and then he came here and had a Christmas tree. It's such a jumble; I can't pull it apart.

Going to Al-Anon was a major turning point for Rachel.

I think in terms of my developing sense of spirituality it's very tied to going to Al-Anon. When I went into Al-Anon, at the suggestion of a friend, I had no clue as to my mother's use or my sister's use. I mean, I knew my sister was using drugs, but I never thought of her as an addict. My mom and my sister used to drink together. My sister, who's younger than I am, is her favorite child, and she and my mom were drinking buddies. A friend who knew Mary and me and watched our relationship in tumult said, "Is someone in her family an alcoholic?" I said, "Well, her father died; I think he probably was." And so I started going to Al-Anon because I couldn't deal with her weird stuff. It was embroiling me, so I went to Al-Anon, and then I realized about my mother and sister, and I quickly felt, thank goodness it's not just me who has had to live with this. That was the positive part of being in the mainstream.

In the very beginning I used to use Al-Anon and powerlessness over concrete things. I would always be frantic, waiting for the mechanic to call. And I would call other mechanics while I was having my car repaired at my one mechanic to make sure he wasn't cheating me. This was crazy.

The twelve-step programs have been very helpful. They helped me figure out I don't have to do everything, I don't have to believe in God, God our father, or God Jesus, whoever people want to call God. But that there are answers outside of myself. That is an internal conflict for me because that's what I teach people—that they can find the answers inside them—when I do therapy; I couldn't integrate it in any way in a spiritual sense. And I had a problem with praying, and it was very difficult for me to work with religious people because I couldn't grasp what they were talking about, going to church and praying about things. And I started to get there little by little.

I don't think that I could have looked at anything outside of myself without Al-Anon. The first thing I hooked into was the serenity prayer. To do those kinds of things I could do was difficult, but I wasn't going to keel over. I look at the way that I caused myself a lot of financial harm. When I got out of graduate school, I made no money, I had huge bills, and I tried to outsmart all the government agencies I could and screwed up my student loans and my taxes. I was so afraid of dealing with these things that I ignored them, and I tried to manipulate them. I was very good. I did a really good one with the IRS—I even called a tax consultant on it—but it wound up costing me a few thousand dollars because I was so afraid of dealing with the mistake I had made. Had I been able to say, "I'm going to be okay" and deal with it, it would have been a $400 error. And I think that all this stuff came at me at once. I just said, "My way is not working. Something about me trying to run everything is not working. It's just bringing me more and more chaos." Hearing other people talk about these same kinds of things was very powerful. Even though I don't like to be part of the mainstream or the textbook answer, the negative self-image that I had was so well integrated for me that I needed that kind of salvation. I needed to know that I wasn't born this way and that when I think back, that the events around me—my family, my mother's mental illness and her drug use, my sister's drug use, my misuse of foods, all that kind of stuff—they weren't all things that were wrong with me. To say that I couldn't figure it out or that I was a victim of the same forces is very difficult. And it was Al-Anon that allowed me to look at those things, that helped me to look outside of myself. To say: "This is really screwed up. It's not just me."

See the lava lamp on the table? At the beginning of my own sense of defining "higher power" for myself, an image happened to come to me in a guided visualization about sliding around in my brain, and all I could see was warm orange stuff. The message was that we were supposed to find within ourselves the answer to what we needed. So I probably knew what to look for. And I saw this real gloppy stuff. The only way I could describe it was the insides of a lava lamp. So I have one. I would never buy it—I'll spend money in weird ways, but I could not get myself to spend $60 on a lava lamp—so my best friend, Sara, who I know from Al-Anon and never would spend the bucks, and my other friend, Dianne, who is someone I work with, bought it. Dianne's been very helpful for me in terms of breaking out of traditional spirituality. The very interesting visual connection is that my first therapy was reconnecting around my emotions; the first thing that I saw was anger, and it was the same thing when I got the lava lamp visualization. The sense that I think I was beginning to develop at that point was warm and fluid and soothing.

In the last phone call I had from my younger sister, she told me she was going to AA and was in therapy. But she wasn't going to have a relationship with me, and I haven't heard from her. I'm listed in the phone book, so that if she ever wanted to contact me, she could. My other sister—this is weird to me because I don't think about them in daily life—she must be, about to be, thirty-one. She disappeared and turned up married to a guy that used to work in the Mafia. It's like an *All My Children* family.

A few years ago Rachel discovered Taoism to be a natural fit with her developing spirituality.

When I was thirty, I began exploring Taoism. I know something is true for me when I read it and I feel it intensely to be painful; it's weird, I don't understand it, but it's like this intense emotional kind of clenching, and that's how I got Taoism. It came from my therapist because I really didn't have a clue to it at all. She's a Buddhist, and she used to tell me about this extremely excruciatingly Buddhist meditation group she used to go to. You'd sit in a white room for forty-eight hours. I thought, I don't know if I need to do that kind of physical thing at this point. But I was explaining to her about my spiritual sense being very physical, that there was a universal energy and that everything was connected. And she suggested that my natural belief system sounded Taoist to her. I resisted that for six months, and then I bought a book on Taoism. And it was describing how things are connected and that somehow there was balance—and here I was trying to figure out how to get there. Those Taoist principles have been really helpful to me.

In the last year or so Rachel has been on a journey of reconciling the past and weaving the pieces together, given impetus by a time of deep pain.

What happened to me is that my relationship had ended, we got back together, and it ended again in a really disastrous kind of way. And we had to live in the same house together for nine months, and she was seeing someone else. I felt like I couldn't be with her and I couldn't be with her family. I have felt almost propelled in the last year toward what happens religiously on the high holidays by just feeling this accumulated grief and not being able to talk about it.

I had thought about going to services last in '91, and I couldn't make myself go because everyone I knew, knew how vehemently opposed I was to these kinds of things. I felt like I needed to connect and to figure out more of who I was. I have some Jewish friends, and I tried to connect with them. And then this last year I just needed to go to temple. Or Chadash is a reformed synagogue. Whatever hold and connection I have to orthodoxy and traditional Judaism has made it very difficult for me to go to Or Chadash, when Yom Kippur services are two hours long. I don't understand that connection unless I look way back; however, I don't think I could have stood more than two hours this year. But I went—on Rosh Hoshanah and again on Yom Kippur—and I could not stop crying.

The recall that I had from these services—from the time I was six, and going to Sunday school and having the children's service, until I was twenty-two—was incredible. What happened on Rosh Hoshanah was that I hadn't been in a temple for eleven years, and it was very overpowering for me to hear some of the older members of the congregation chanting. And then on Yom Kippur, the counting of our transgressions against each other. And this was the first time that I *needed* it. And again I felt this pain of really wanting to let go of those things. These are really big feelings for me, about what has gone on with me.

Religiously, I'm not involved in Judaism now, and I don't know if I have to straighten it out. It's been a big struggle for me to reconcile the fact that I live religiously without a belief in God. I'm sure I'm not the only one who's experienced that. And I know I'm not the only one who's come back to some kind of spiritual belief. But I think that now [sighs] I was raised in Judaism and I don't believe in Judaism. I think, culturally, I like to experience Jewish things. I feel more comfortable returning to my own cultural things as I reconcile my past. They're the rituals that I know and that I'm comfortable with. What is most important is that as I continue to work my twelve-step program, that the spiritual part of it, on an individual level, is still really very based on the Taoist kind of thinking. So those are the kinds of things I need to live my life. But when I need a ritual, I think that if I can reinterpret Judaism and the rituals of Judaism for my own needs, but have that congregational sense, that's going to be really important.

I like the folkloric explanations they still have in Judaism, like the people who die at the end of the year who are blessed because they got through more of the year; I don't think that's really written anywhere. I really like these kinds of folkloric beliefs; I've always liked those. I had so little experience pulling these things together. I can't see myself all revved up, except at women's holidays and Passover. I haven't been to a synagogue in a long time where I've felt any kind of spiritual sense. I've gone for the social kind of things; I really do have this thing about oppressed people fighting for their own liberation

As she concludes, Rachel speaks of finding her way.

I do some spiritual reading, but I'm not very good at it; I'd much rather read fiction. I think the deliberate part of this movement is that when I challenge myself, I have to stop myself and do things differently, to not react, but to find that balance, to find what the natural way is—it feels kind of cliché to say "find my way"—or find what makes it my own way. But I have to be deliberate in that, because my anxious buttons can get pushed, or my caretaking or my social work professional "let's make the plan" buttons. Instead of just letting things happen and feeling them. I want to jump in and fix it, and change the course of things. That's my job; that's what I've been trained very well to do at all levels. It's been a very slow integration process in terms of action and the way I do things.

But there's another kind of thing that goes on for me. These kinds of changes make sense to me intellectually and emotionally first, and then I start to work hard at integrating them into how I do things because my action is usually guided by instinct, which is so much older. I never studied in graduate school. I wrote papers, and I did some intense research, but I didn't ever have to study the principles or the theories I was learning because it—the old social work principle—immediately made sense. It was the same thing with Left politics, the way that I experienced them, and that's kind of how some of these things make sense to me now; they just become integrated in how I do things. I think what that intense feeling was when I started to read about Taoism.

I think my spiritual journey has also changed how I work. It's helped me be more patient. I used to say that I couldn't do long-term therapy 'cause I couldn't manage the middle phase. And now I'm much more tolerant, and as I become more tolerant, I get more clients doing long-term work. I work with teenagers. And now I have clients who I can see for a year. I never thought I would see clients for a year because I wouldn't have the patience. And I used to be very task oriented, and now I'm very much into letting the process evolve and not trying to control it. Eight years ago I was the controlling bitch from hell. I ran my supervision meetings. Now I don't. I convene them, and I give them the news. What's funny for me is that I have done some work as a mediator, which is something I never thought I could do 'cause I could always see my own stuff coming up in people. I used to be the person who needed to get her own things out. Now I can sit back and listen. And kind of figure out where the gaps are and redirect the stuff going on in the group. And to me, professionally, that's wonderful, being able to sit back and not be so

"I do love being a lesbian, though. I really do love it. I'll be driving . . . by Women and Children First, and I'll just think, 'Ohhh.' You have to be cool to be queer."

directive. It's pretty amazing when I think about how I can sit there and I don't get wound up, even by their energy, that I can just see it. You know the movie *A Tale of Two Cities?* You know the woman who's knitting? She's like [laughs] how I used to be. I can just be up there, and now I'm much more comfortable sitting back. The secondary gain for me is when I sit back and watch everybody else putting their own shit on the table and then I make one statement that seems so absolutely brilliant. Really all it is, is that I don't have that same kind of emotional investment. You can see the obvious. And I like that.

I do love being a lesbian, though. I really do love it. I'll be driving down Belmont Street, and on Clark Street, by Women and Children First, and I'll just think, "Ohhh." You have to be cool to be queer. There has to be a certain level of self-acceptance to really just be okay. And this is pretty cool. It's been one of my stronger points of self-esteem, is being a lesbian.

Sheila: ALL THAT IS

Sheila, a preoperative transsexual, was born in Tennessee and raised in a family with Baptist roots, though she left the church when she was thirteen "and never went back." Virtually her whole life she has been on a journey of discovery of herself both transsexually and spiritually. My experience as I listened to her, and read, and reread, her words, was that these two strands were profoundly and intricately interwoven.

Discovering philosophy and the New Age after she went away to college, she has pursued a journey that has embraced Edgar Cayce, the channeled (by Jane Roberts) messages of Seth, Wicca, and other approaches as she has worked out her own set of beliefs and values. Now she works for a local MCC, takes phone sex calls, and acts a channel for Goddess energy. In this interview she speaks eloquently about her evolving spirituality and sexuality.

To understand Sheila's journey, it's important to know her roots, who and what have influenced her. In her first few pages Sheila describes her Southern Baptist family and childhood and the beginnings of her commitment to question and challenge the received authorities of that time.

I am an only child. My parents were Southern Baptist. My mother's side of the family came from five generations of landed gentry that lost everything in the Civil War. My father's side of the family came from the other side of the tracks. The two met at public school. In the South there's this whole thing about, "Well, we may not have the money, but we do have the breeding, and everybody else is just Johnny-come-lately. They would really like to move in our circles." So you have a bunch of broke people living a hundred years in the past. My mother's living right now in Columbia, South Carolina, with some of the family that's down there. The reason she picked that place to move to is because it reminds her of the way Nashville looked just after the Second World War ended, before civil rights, before everything started going downhill and the social structure started fragmenting. So she's tried to live in the past while still in the present.

My father was a salesman at that time, and my mother was a fashion buyer for department stores. They got divorced in 1958. After that she continued doing the buying, up until about '65, and then switched into real estate, where she has been ever since. I am an only child. My father was IV-F during the war due to a head injury in sports, which he got in high school. That frustrated him because he really identified a lot with Tom Mix and Buck Jones when he went to the movies, and it looked like he had a promising career as a professional baseball player. But after he got cleated in the head playing football—in those days they didn't have the steel plate thing down very well—he had to hang up his spikes and forget it, or he would die on the field. His next option was that he wanted to go to Hollywood and become a cowboy movie star. But the lights were too strong, with heat from 25,000 watts, and he would die on the set. So then he wound up selling dog food and a line of glass and home cleaners, bleaches, things like that, for the next twenty-five or thirty years. For someone who had put so much emphasis on their physical prowess, this was a tremendous ego slap.

I think he possibly realized unconsciously what was going on as far as my transsexualism was concerned. We never discussed it. I'm not even sure if he knew there was such a thing, but the chemistry between us was such that my presence seemed to make him nervous, to threaten his masculinity, and to get this compulsion for him to make me conform to some macho ideal. There also was a slight bit of sadism involved in it. Since my mother had read the Dr. Benjamin Spock book, they had decided there would be no corporal punishment. Well, he was raised with lots of corporal punishment, and now he couldn't do it legitimately under the family constellation. So what he would do is take me out to the backyard for sports practice. By teaching me how to block at football, he could knock me all over the yard, and he could work out his aggressions. I would much rather have been inside reading a book than out chasing a stupid ball around the field, but he couldn't have cared less: "You must do this." "Why?" "Because I will beat your ass if you don't." Strong argument, okay. I generally only saw him on weekends; he was a road salesman, so he was gone five to six days a week.

My primary influences were my mother and my grandparents, who were living with us. Both my grandmother and my mother were very strong career women. My grandmother had gone into the workforce while her husband was overseas in World War I. My grandfather was a very quiet man, and he put in some thirty-five years at General Motors. He started out on the assembly line and worked his way into an office. He was in an inventory-type position by the time he finally retired; that wasn't bad for someone who had to leave school in the sixth grade. He never was strong about a lot of things—he didn't like fights, so he did not squabble. The only time I ever saw him really get hard-lined was when my parents split up and my father came by to pick up some of his things. My grandfather went out to the car to talk to him for a few minutes. My mother went into a rage about how he could be so disloyal to her by going out and being friendly with the adulterer, and he just turned and said, "Daughter, he's never been anything but nice to me, and the least I can do is wish him well and shake his hand, and I do not want any lip out of you." He was very quiet when he said it, but extremely firm. My grandmother liked the struggle. Whenever she would start that, he would just back off from it because he didn't want to squabble, but when it was really important, he would take a stance. The thing that impressed me most about him was that he was an opposite to my father. My father, I think, had to compensate for not being able to go to war by doing all these macho things, even when his health was bad. My grandfather had been in World War I with Pershing's regiment in France, at Verdun and Chateau Thierry. It wasn't until I was in college and started reading about the battles that I found out exactly what he'd been through with some of those battles. But he never told war stories of the combat kind. He would talk about jokes they had played around the barracks. I remember my grandmother saying that when he went over there, his hair was coal black. He came back three years later, and it was snow white, and it stayed that way until the day he died. And when somebody asked him what being in the war was like, he just said: "Well, I got through it, and I don't think I killed anybody. I tried not to." That was his only real statement about what World War I was all about. He was a very modest man.

Messages in her family about sexuality were largely unspoken.

I did not get any messages in my family about transsexualism or lesbianism. They didn't joke about it. My mother was so naive; she didn't know until after she had been married for two years that there was such a thing as a gay man or a lesbian. She heard somebody make a crack, in passing somewhere, and asked my father what that meant. He told her, and at that point she looked and said: "You're joking! You're making that up. People don't do that." And, he replied, "Yes, they do." "You're just putting me on because you know I don't know anything." She had no exposure at all. Very stilted. If we can believe my father's sister, he was not sheltered. At the time of the divorce she made a reference to pubescent incestuous things that had happened between them. It was never verified. It wasn't anything he would ever want to discuss. And his sister, when she had a mad-on about something, she would say anything, so I'm not sure how valid it is. I get the feeling it probably was valid, but I have no proof of it. There was a lot of repression there. My grandmother was very frustrated sexually because she found my grandfather's bedside manner boring. He had never learned what to do; to him, it was just jump on top three times and boooop, go to sleep. And she was sitting there going, "Is this all?" She did that for forty-five years of marriage. It made her a very bitter woman. Very bitter. She had tried to teach him, and he was like: "You can't teach me anything. I already know everything I need to know. I learned about it behind the barn." And so he was very stubborn about that. After the divorce my mother did some dating, did not have sex with anyone, and according to her accounts, never even masturbated. She felt that even though there was a legal divorce, she did not have the right to remarry so long as my father was alive. He finally died in '71. She still hasn't gotten married, had a serious date, had sex or anything else. She has not had a sexual relationship since 1958, when they split up. So she has spent the better part of her life denying herself out of a misguided sense of morality. 'Cause she's been always more concerned with what is fitting and proper, how it looks to the neighbors, rather than what she feels.

Speaking of her growing self-awareness, Sheila describes being the target of teasing and abuse by other boys.

I knew at about four or five that there was something going on with me. I did not have a name for it until I was about ten and I first heard about Christine Jorgensen. And all of a sudden a whole bunch of things clicked, such as why, from the first day I started public school, I was the immediate target. The whole group of guys wanted to beat the shit out of me, and I didn't even know them; it was my first day and I hadn't said, "Boo" to anybody, but it was just TARGET. I think they were picking up on the transsexual vibe unconsciously, and I was scared 'cause they always came in packs of six or eight or ten, never one on one. I experienced that throughout public school, at every school I went to. When I would change schools, if we would move from one area of town to the other, I wouldn't be in a school more than two days before a pack would be after me. At the same time, I was able to get in and make friends quite well with all the girls in the school—until I started, in my teen years, to feel peer pressure enough to want to cover my act by trying to ask one of them out. And all of a sudden, I would get this blank look like: "We can't go out. I'm not a lesbian." And the boys were all threatened by it. At about age eleven I started very deliberately and consciously repressing it because I realized that was the source of where most of the beatings and everything else were coming from. And of course my father's attitude to the whole thing, when I came home and said that I had been beaten up at school, was, "Well, the next time they do that, if you don't beat the shit out of them, when you get home, I will beat the shit out of you." So, hmm, Father knows best.

The roots of Sheila's draw to philosophy were in what she calls "Romper Room Philosophy 101"—that is, ethics classes for non-Catholics in the Catholic high school she attended.

I was brought up in the Southern Baptist thing. I went to a Catholic high school because it was academically better, or at least that was the feeling at the time. And, in '58 and '59 they probably did have a better standard than some of the public schools in the South: a lot more rigorous academics, a college-prep curriculum, smaller classes, more individualized instruction. And instead of making us non-Catholics take religious classes, they had us take ethics, basically Romper Room Philosophy 101. We were barely getting our feet wet, but it was starting me to want to look around and carry on. And when I would go back to the Sunday school, I would have some of these other things I had been working with all week long with the ethics class, and I wanted to get some different viewpoints rather than just what I had heard from the Catholic school. I tried to find out if we could in some way approach issues like this in a Sunday school class because they seem to be very applicable to daily life to me. But I was told, "No, because the Sunday school book said we had to cover Paul's second letter to the Romans; that's what we had to do." And at that point I said, "Well, if you're not willing to even try and address the questions I need to have answered, I don't need you," and I walked out of the church when I was thirteen. And I never went back.

My mother has essentially stayed traditional Baptist all of her life. She's read a little of the New Age stuff, but it has not rubbed off. She just went: "Oh, yeah, that's a nice book; that's interesting. I'm reading another interesting book now, okay." She'll read, for instance, *There Is a River,* the story of Edgar Cayce. She read that probably three or four years before I did. She never said anything other than it was a nice story. Then she went on and read whatever one of her other bestsellers was—James Michener or something. She treated the Edgar Cayce book on the same par as the James Michener book; it didn't make her want to go find out more about it or study it or incorporate it into her worldview in any way. It was just a nice book to read.

Philosophy became an abiding interest, which she further developed in college and afterward.

I stayed fairly quasi-agnostic, or at least unchurched, for most of high school and up into early college, '65 or so. I started taking a lot of philosophy courses in college again because I found out that for a bachelor of arts degree you needed college algebra, trig, and calculus. For a science degree, which would seem to be more technically demanding, you did not need all that math, and you could even—if you picked the right catalog to come in under—substitute some philosophy classes for the math. I had been out of high school about three years, and I had not done that well in higher math in college and high school; it was mainly because they always had football coaches teaching it who were more interested in a double switchback on the end field than they were on the material for class, and they were reading the book the night before they tried to teach it to us. So I did not learn geometry and algebra very well, and there was no way I could cut it in college, so I took philosophy classes again. I loved it; I had a blast. I took philosophy of comparative religions, all sorts of things like that, and at that time ran into the Ayn Rand books. They pushed me very heavily into agnosticism. At the same time, I was going to major in theater, which on an unconscious level was coming out of the mystical ritual thing, and they rubbed against each other a lot.

It must have been '70 when I first ran into the New Age stuff, with Edgar Cayce. What happened was my local grass supplier came by one night and said I did not get a lid because the town is dry, but here's this book; it's a real hoot, and you might like it. And he gave me a copy of *There Is a River.* He was involved in one of the Cayce study groups. I read the thing, and I said, "I'd like to find out more about this stuff" and asked, "Are there any more books?" He said, "Oh yeah, come on down here." I wound up doing a study group program with that. Just about the time I was getting into that, in late '70, early '71, was when my master's degree was blowing up due to some departmental politics. I had stepped on a few toes in the department over seven years there, and it was time to get even, so my theater degree, which is where I had thought I was going in my career, blew out from under me, just as the New Age stuff was being dropped in my lap. Something said: "Wait a minute. This New Age stuff is basically what you've been looking for in theater. It's more direct, it's not covered up in a plot or anything, but it's the same ritual basis, and it's coming at it cleaner and with more depth. And so it's time to move from kindergarten into the real stuff."

So I started working with the Cayce material in a study group for a few years where we'd go through the material, kick it around, try applying it, and then come back the next week to explore how we were doing, what successes or failures we had had in trying to understand or apply certain concepts. There was a lot of sharing that way. It was a fairly close-knit group of about eight people—there were about three hundred involved in the entire program in Nashville at that time, all of them in really small groups. I was getting an urge to do something ministerial with it, but I wasn't sure what. I had heard about Unity, which was fairly close to the New Age I was familiar with. But I talked to a Unity minister in Nashville, and she said: "Now you don't want to fool with Unity. They've turned it into a standard mainline diploma mill now. Go out to Denver and talk to the Divine Science people; they're closer to what Unity was back in the old days when it was really solid, where you had to learn how to apply everything before you get your degree." She said: "Now they just cranked them out in three years, like any other seminary. They have gone just for the bucks, and the feeling is gone."

In this next part of the interview Sheila tells us about the resurgence of her transsexualism.

Intermittently throughout this I had had spurts of where the transsexualism thing would be trying to surface and I kept fighting it because it was terrifying me. I had never met anybody else who had gone through it, especially in Nashville. What gay and lesbian community there was in Nashville was extremely closeted. You knew there were a few gay people in the theater department; one motivation for me going into theater was protective coloration because I felt the transsexual vibe wouldn't stick out as strongly among the other people in the department. And theater folk tend to be a lot more loose and accepting about a lot of things; what with jumping in and out of different worlds, you wind up wearing lots of pairs of shoes, and you develop a certain amount of tolerance the longer you're in theater. So it had been attractive from that point. But I kept feeling the urges, and I didn't know anybody that was doing the change; the only place I knew they ever did so was over in Europe, and I didn't know anybody there. At that point I was still working part-time for something like $2 an hour and going to school. It was like, "Yeah, how am I ever going to get money for an operation and a trip to Europe working for $2 an hour?" I couldn't deal with this.

Marriage became a possible way out, but in the end it didn't work.

I had tried at one point to put my transsexual feelings into the box of "Well, fate has done this to me, or God has done this to me." This time I did the New Age rationalization trip, which was, "Well, maybe I spent several lifetimes as a female, and there's some carryover, but it's my karma to have to put up with this shit." In '71 I jumped into a marriage as a last-ditch way of trying to hold onto my male identity. The first six weeks or so that Susan and I were together, we did discuss the transsexualism thing because it jumped out of the closet about two weeks after we were married. It just hit me with an emotional brick. I'd spent about six weeks reading everything I could get my hands on concerning it: Benjamin's book (*The Transsexual Phenomenon*), Jan Morrison's book (*Conundrum*), everything I could find. It caught me by surprise because I thought I had successfully rationalized it away, put it under where it wouldn't bother me.

Now the thing that was so interesting, as far as synchronicities go, was when I first came out with it to her. She sat there on the floor and said: "Uh-huh. Well, I guess Edgar was right. You run away from a problem, and it gets worse the second time around." I said, "What do you mean?" She said: "The person I had a relationship with before you, in a different year, was born on the same day that you were born, and he was a bisexual who didn't know how to deal with it, and I couldn't handle that. I ran from it and came down here, and now I get you. And it's the same problem, but more extreme." And she was very supportive, saying: "If this is what you need to do, we'll go and get an annulment or something. I don't want this if it's not going to be right for you." I didn't have enough self-confidence to be able to say, "It's gotta be this, or I'm going." If I had to be gone, then I'd be left dealing with my transsexual stuff, and I didn't want to deal with it, so I had to keep plugged in with her. So I put it back under the rug and thought it was over and done with. I really rammed it down solidly under the rug and sealed it up with super glue.

It didn't come out again until '78. And then the lid blew off the rug.

Everything came out all within a three-month period: the need for the transsexualism, the marriage falling apart, everything. I had known the marriage was getting rocky. I didn't want to face what the problem was. Susan kept saying she needed a stronger male energy in the house, and I was already acting as much as I could, and that obviously wasn't cutting it. So we moved into an open relationship, and I went out and did some screening and found her some guys. I screened them for her to make sure they were okay people and not psychorapists or something. And then finally she said: "Look, I feel like I'm living with a lesbian, and I've had bisexual fantasies, but I don't want them in reality. I need male energy, and you don't have it. You've been trying to do it, and you've been making yourself miserable trying to be something you're not. So we need to split up, and you need to go do whatever it is you need to do." She was very supportive. She could not join me in it because it bothered her too much to see me start changing my role. She didn't want to have to change the way she thought about me. But she realized the necessity for me to change and was totally supportive of me doing it.

Leaving the relationship, she entered therapy to help her in the "transition."

Anyway, after we split, I went through eighteen months of analysis with a Jungian therapist, and he's the one who initially helped me into the transition. He said he would not accept that as a foregone conclusion; we'd just have to see which way the therapy went. He would frequently say, "Well, what makes you think you're female?" To which I would say something, and he'd say, "Bullshit; go deeper." So, he was pushing me down to the point where I was dredging up all sorts of stuff, memories that I had repressed. Dreams I had had when I was twelve, thirteen, about being transformed. Even prepubescent dreams about going through a sexual transformation. Sometimes we did it through technology, sometimes through magic ritual, but it was always the same thing. And then when I would wake back up in the body, it was like, "Wait a minute; I thought that was real because it was such a strong feeling." He pushed me into bringing all those back up. At the end of eighteen months he said: "Well, you just need to get your money together. I don't think you have any more problems. Now that you've made your transition, I'm hindering you getting your money together by coming here and paying me. If you need to come by, make an appointment, and I'll be glad to see you, but don't just come out of habit. I think we've done everything we can do at this point." And so by mutual consent we terminated the therapy at that point. He did do informal spot checks because he was a customer at the natural food store where I was working as an office manager at the time, and I would see him infrequently on a social basis, three or four times a year. He wrote the letters for me to Dr. Biber—perhaps the most famous surgeon in the U.S. for the TS procedure—to start the program out there once I can finally get the money. And that's what's been holding me up for twelve years. The economy has not been doing great things for acquiring $20,000, which is roughly what it costs: ten g for the operation and ten g for if a kickback sets in. You never know when you come out of the anesthetic if you're one of the fortunate people who heals up in six weeks or if you're one of the other group that takes six to seven months, where you hurt too much and you're actually physically incapable of going out and going to work. So you have to have a living cushion just in case. And that's why it takes twenty. But I've got my little lotto ticket, and I'm working three part-time jobs right now, so I do what I can.

Coming out transsexually and developing a more sophisticated New Age paradigm were interwoven.

In the process of coming out transsexually, I was around some of the New Age community because of the natural food store. And as I got deeper into my feminine center, I found myself working a lot more, or being attracted to reading books a lot more, that dealt with the feminist approach and with Goddess worship, Wicca, things of that nature. I'd also gotten into the Seth material books by Jane Roberts, which approach it on a very personal level.

And then I was also reading the Don Juan books by Carlos Castaneda. And the last five or six years I've picked up on the Lynn Andrews books, which were Native-American mysticism from the female point of view. I like looking at both the similarities and the discrepancies between the Don Juan path and the Agnes Whistling Elk path because there are some common grounds. There are some role-playing gestalts that are part of both traditions, although emotionally there is a world of difference. The male tradition is all about being stalwart and forcing yourself to open, whereas the feminist approach is just lay back and relax and see what happens. Even Don Juan mentions this in his books; he says men have to work to access the level of consciousness that women carry with them all the time, and he relates it to a difference in biochemistry. The only time that a male shaman does not want to have women in the group is when they're in their period. They say it messes the energies because of the biochemical changes. Any other time they want them in there as a facilitator for the other males in the group. So they do acknowledge that there is some kind of a difference, and the two structures reflect that. They're going more for emotional depth and the texture of an experience in the feminist Native-American tradition, whereas in the male tradition it's more the whole warrior path thing. They're both equally valid approaches—and they even use some of the same words to describe what they're doing—but you come out of it with a different emotional context. Blending the two together works really nicely.

So I've been working with that, with the Wicca thing. I don't work with an organized group as such, but occasionally there are some specific individuals whose energies, I know, work well with mine, and we may on occasion get together and do a working. I haven't found anybody up here yet that I am willing to do that with. I had a couple of close friends in the Savannah area before I moved, and we would get together on the quarters to do observances; we also had a site in a local park that was essentially virgin territory, and at one time had been an Indian medicine ground. And once every quarter I would go spend a whole day walking around in there, and I would be very aware as I was walking through the woods of changing the labels on the file drawers in my mind and recategorizing experience and processing. I could just wander through there for a whole eight hours and come out feeling great. I wouldn't have any idea sometimes what the subjects were; I would just realize there are some things happening. I can feel the movements, and then I would wait a day or two to find out what the movement was—something would come up, and I would think, "Whoa, change that one around." I haven't found a place like that here.

The closest thing I had to that kind of experience here was this June when I had my piercing. I had been thinking about it for the last nine months, and I tend to run a nine-month cycle before I actuate something. Nine to ten months is a normal pattern for me. I wasn't sure when I went in there if I was going to be able to go through with it or not. So in a way what I was trying to do was push my limits, find out what they were and see if I could push them. It's a very strange thing because you're lying on this table waiting for somebody to stick needles in you, so you're obviously a little bit submissive, but you walked in there and handed somebody money and said, "Do this," and that's a dominant thing. So you're doing both at the same time. And it stirred some energies up, and for about three weeks afterwards I would wake up in the middle of the night feeling like I had been working. I didn't know what about, but I knew I was moving file drawers again. I had no idea what it was. After about the third week it finally came through to consciousness; it was an emotional-level thing on the incest trauma that an uncle had done on me when I was about fourteen. And I could only approach that, when I was in therapy, abstractly and intellectually. I could not get a gut level thing on it because it was too loaded with fear, anger, all sorts of things. Primarily, this was not because of what he did, but because of what he didn't do. He had been in the gay community in LA before coming back to Nashville in '58 to help his father, who had gotten ill. He was probably the only person in Nashville at that time who had enough experience to pick up on the transsexual vibe and identify it and to offer some kind of assistance on how to deal with it; instead of doing that, he chose to try to manipulate me through the divorce trauma my parents were going through. Here he was being Mom's support and keeping her from having a breakdown, so he could have a nice little closet fuck in closeted Nashville. That I blame him for more than anything because he could have helped, and he made things worse. But I finally got an emotional thing on it the third week after the piercing, and what really surprised me was that when the material finally came up, the anger and fear had been dissipated already by the unconscious, and it came up already healed. And so that is probably the strongest spiritual transforming experience that I've had since I've been in Chicago.

There's something about us living in a society that doesn't have all that many actual rituals anymore; if the culture doesn't supply them, people make them up from the grass roots. So there is a psychological need for them that our societal structure doesn't fill, is incapable of filling, at this point. The people are starting to do it on their own. And they're going through transformative processes, either to make the decision to go in for a piercing, or as a result of having it done; they're making their own rites of passage. I didn't realize how widespread it was until I heard a speaker mention this last year at a leather meeting, and then when I went through it myself in June, I realized, "Yeah, he does know what he's talking about." I was expecting some physiological changes, but I did not realize that when I had it done, it was going to do the whole bit with the incest trauma. If I had known that consciously, I would have probably shied away from it for another three or four months because I didn't think I could deal with it. But then what amazed me was that the trauma was dispersed by the time it came to consciousness. And I'm sitting there; well, the work's been done.

S&M has had a major role in Sheila's evolving spirituality.

I had been doing most of the lighter stuff in S&M, either in my head or just a little bit of experimentation with Susan prior to our divorce, a little bit with another friend in Savannah—the scene there is extremely closeted. Even in the gay papers I couldn't find any ads for any group like this. I moved to Chicago, and I picked up one of the Chicago contact papers. I see all the ads from the people in Georgia. They don't advertise in Georgia; they advertise in the Midwest. They don't want anybody else in Georgia to know what they're doing 'cause they're in Pat Robertson's and Jerry Falwell's backyard. All those kinky people there and I lived there for fifteen years and never knew it. I could have had fun. But, no, I had come here, and last year, in September, I got in to a group, and it's been my first chance on a fairly large scale to be involved in the scene. There's a wide diversity of people, and they've got to be the best group I've ever hung out with. Some very, very sensitive jobs. At the meetings we just go by first name and last initial, like the gay community was in the sixties. Or sometimes total pseudonyms. You wind up totally redefining friendship because you're not even sure if you know the person's right name, and yet you feel perfectly comfortable talking about some of the things that are in your most private urges, or secrets, and know that they will respect them. Whereas normally you start working friendship from the periphery in, with the hello-how-are-you, and finally get down to the more personal level. Here you cut straight to the chase and say, "Well, I'm into hanging upside down." "Yes, so am I." Whoa . . . and then you say: "Yes, this person is a very good friend, but I only see them at meetings. I don't know their phone number, their last name, or how to look them up in the book. I don't even know if their first name is real, but yet I know they are a friend." And so it's very strange to have a very close friendship when you're not even sure you know the person's name, but you relate to them much closer than people you've known twenty years. It's a totally different way of looking at personal relationships and friendships. And especially in the scene, there's a very high premium placed on trust and respect because they have to respect the safe word [a word by which the bottom signals that he wants the top to stop]; if a top doesn't respect a safe word, the word gets put out, and then no one will play with the person. So it's one of those things where in many ways they're being more honest than people in just about any other kind of group because the honesty is required for the play to be done safely. To me, that's the fascinating dynamics of having a whole different way of looking at friends and just seeing where it leads.

In August I did a lecture for the group on the spiritual aspects of S&M play—that's the main thing with being in the scene, that I find is quite interesting to me now. Sometimes it doesn't even have to be really extreme play, if you hit a psychological trigger, either with the equipment or instrument, or maybe it's even on the soundtrack, a tone of voice, anything. But it can suddenly kick the bottom into an altered state, and they can have a transcendental experience right in the middle of a scene. Now some tops will encourage that, while others are frightened by it and will try to pull the bottom back out of it because they want to keep them in the here and now, but most people do recognize that it does occur. I knew it did under fairly extreme settings; what surprised me was that I had a partial out-of-body experience from an extremely mild scene, and it was something more of a personal chemistry between the two of us. She was just using a very lightweight flogger, hardly doing anything at all with it, but there was something about being on the St. Andrew's Cross (an X frame) and the chemistry between the two of us that night. I kept alternating between being on the cross and on the ceiling looking down at myself, just in and out, in and out, as the rhythm went. I couldn't maintain it because there was so much other action that was all new to me going on at the party room and new people in a strange space. So I kept getting distracted, and I didn't feel totally secure, and I couldn't fully leave the body. But I did have that in-and-out experience from a purely, almost vanilla scene, so these kinds of things do happen, and that's part of what's very attractive about the S&M scene to me; it's another doorway to open yourself to the transcendental experience, if you choose to use it that way. Or you can just play. It's most essentially the same thing Timothy Leary said about acid. You can either just get stoned and sit around and listen to tunes, or you can use it to see God; it's whatever you want to make it to be. Regular sex is like 90 percent in your mind anyway, and 10 percent in the body. S&M sex is 99 percent in the mind because you're playing very heavily with fantasies and expectations and wish fulfillments, much more than you are with the actual physical manipulation. You don't actually have to hit anybody that hard if you've got their mind in there in the right place.

The times I will bottom—I do switch on occasion—is with other females. I'm still not enough over that incest trauma that I will bottom with a male. I can see maybe in another year or two I might. And I've picked out one or two people that I consider trustworthy that when I'm ready to experiment, I know that if I had to call out the safe word and say I can't handle this emotionally, they would stop. I have gotten to the point to where I can top a male; for awhile I was scared to death 'cause I was afraid that all the anger at my uncle would come out on an innocent person. After this thing kicked off this summer, and I knew the anger was discharged, I felt it freed me up to be able to do some cross-gender play without fear of hurting the bottom inadvertently or losing control of myself. So it's widened my area, and I'm essentially functioning a lot more in a bi-capacity right now as far as scene play goes.

Emotionally, I still relate primarily as a lesbian. I guess that's because I've never really been savaged emotionally by another woman, but I've had several male figures in my life—my father, several of my bosses—who every time there was a point of vulnerability it was like poof. And it's made me very leery, but I have met a couple of very responsible fellas that I think I could do something with in maybe another year. I want to simply because it's another one of those hurdles to get over; if I can do it and deal with whatever the backlash is, it will make me a freer person in the long run. Whether or not I decide to go with a particular partner, I want it to be because of whether or not I like them and not avoiding someone out of fear of what they might do because they remind me of something in the past.

Surprisingly enough, one of my part-time jobs right now is phone sex. And I have wound up doing more counseling calls on the phone sex line than I do in this church. People call up and say that they want to talk to a TS and they don't want to do a fantasy; they think they're TS and not sure, and they don't know what to do, and they just need to talk to somebody about it, to try and get their head straight. And they live somewhere out in the middle of nowhere and don't know anywhere else to get the info they need.

Once a customer asked for a submissive. I started to do the call, and he did not want a fantasy. He's got a girlfriend who's submissive, and she wants him to whack her. He's afraid that he would do it too much and actually damage her, yet he wanted to please her. He wanted to talk to another submissive to understand his girlfriend's head space and get some advice on how he could give her what she wants without really doing any damage: "What do I look for? How do we communicate?" So I gave him a quick S&M 101 about establishing safe words and things of that nature. It was a strictly informational call, and he did not want to do a fantasy one. And I get on the average one or two of these a week when the phones are ringing on a regular basis, and they're counseling calls, pure and simple. They're people talking about things that are so extremely private to them that they can't tell even their best friends, but they can call up a total stranger. That makes me feel that it's taking a lot of guts for them to be that vulnerable with me. You have to be supportive of them, even if it's something that you personally think is totally outrageous and off-the-wall; it's a very private thing for them, and it has to be respected 'cause they can't talk to anybody else about it. And you just have to handle them with kid gloves because you can do a lot of psychological damage if you reject them or ridicule them. So you can't go by whether you like the activity they want to talk about or not, especially if it gets into something that's unsafe. Then you try and educate them by saying something like "Oh, well, that's a nice thing to think about for a fantasy, but you wouldn't want to do that for real because such and such and such and such." And they go, "Oh, I didn't realize that," and so you start teaching them a little bit. You can even incorporate that, sometimes, into your fantasy; you can incorporate some teaching, safe sex, things like that. You educate them any way you can.

Sheila shares, in the balance of this interview, her present day spiritual journey.

Working with the Goddess is still very much a part of my spirituality. In '81 I went through an initiation as a priestess. I function in that capacity wherever I am. I don't need to be registered with the state to do what I need to do. I work as a channel for the Goddess energy, and so long as I'm in a position to be accessible, the people who need me find me. I haven't told too many of the people in MCC about a lot of what I do, as far as the New Age stuff is concerned, because they're not ready for it. So most of them don't know that. While I was in a Cayce group, I did a really heavy thing on working with dream interpretation, had a fairly good knack for it in our group, and I would have all these people in Nashville calling up: "Hey, I just had this dream the other night. What does it mean?" And I've had people come up to me, even in this church, saying: "I had a strange dream the other night. I wonder what it means." They don't know I'm into it, but they come to me with that concern. So if you're there, they will find you.

I haven't really planned on what I will wind up doing spiritually in the long run. I tend to just try to go into my center and see where it wants to lead me, and then I'll find out about it when I get there. It's like when I moved to Denver. I thought I was going to study at the Divine Science church, and they were boring. But that's where I ran into the Seth material, and I've been studying that for twenty years now. So, invariably, when I move to an area, the reason I think I'm moving there generally isn't it. Six months to a year later the real reason shows up. There had to be something to make me pack up the truck and move, so the ego was given a carrot to get me there.

I'm not quite sure whether I'll ever find a group here, in terms of Wicca, that I want to affiliate with or not; I don't gravitate too well toward institutions—I tend to work more with individual people. When the need arises, and when I do work, it's not like having a church service. I do work for a specific purpose. And that's the only time I do it. I don't really worship. To me, there's simply an affirmation when you do work of, "I'm doing this because I'm trying to accelerate or alter a pattern that's going on or to make myself open to the meaning of it." Regardless of the terminology you use, what you're really doing is altering your own consciousness, not anything else. If you want to change the world, you start by changing yourself and changing your perception. And that's all ritual work is. A way of getting you out of your normal everyday frame of mind and into an altered state where you can accept information from other levels of your mind.

When I talk philosophically about cosmology or theology, I tend to use a Seth term, *ALL THAT IS,* all caps, because I don't like the g word; it's too personified and too anthropomorphic. Also, it always has a sense that you're talking about me over here and god over there. When you use ALL THAT IS, nothing can exist that isn't a part of ALL THAT IS. There's nothing you can do to get it; there's nothing you can do that will make you lose it; you're always a part of ALL THAT IS. The only thing that you can do is, by your mental state, either be aware of being part of the process or unaware. But that doesn't affect the fact that you are, and so I work on that kind of abstract level, thinking about it. But when I do ritual work, I relate strictly to a feminine archetype because it opens doors for me; I'm aware at the time that this is strictly a mental construct that I use, and I don't know whether it ultimately has anything to do with the shape of the cosmos or not. It is a tool that works and provides me access. I was in a work situation several years ago where tension was getting rather high with some petty office politics. It had been going on for some time. And a friend of mine and I had talked about it, and I said, "Well, I know philosophically I don't get into anything that I am not capable of handling 'cause we don't do this to ourselves." The point is, I wasn't willing to handle it anymore, so we essentially did a meditation and a banishing ritual: I'm tired of this situation, and I want it resolved immediately for the ultimate best benefit of all parties concerned. And that was the end of the ritual. Within twenty-four hours the situation was resolved.

So if you access the energy, you can inject it into a situation. You earn your best results when you don't try to prejudge the outcome. Just open yourself as an input of energy, and let the energy sort things out. Most people get into trouble when they try to work at this level because they're not satisfied with just having a car that will get them from point A to B: it's gotta be a Cadillac, and it's gotta be green, and it's gotta have air-conditioning. They only need to go back and forth to the store once a week; they can make do with an old rusty Ford. By putting all the qualifiers on it, they probably wind up passing up a few rusty Fords that people would like to give 'em while they're waiting for the Cadillac to drop out of the sky. It's very similar to the advice we tend to give novices in scene, which is the worst thing you can do is take your expectations into the scene. Some bottoms are really pushy about it, and they'll come to a dominant and go, "Well, first I want you to do this, and then I want you to do this and this and this." They have a whole script worked out for you, and if you don't do everything exactly right, they'll say the scene isn't working, or you're too tall or you're too short. But if they just come up with a general idea, and don't get into tight specific expectations, they have a much better chance of having a good scene because the more tightly we limit ourselves, the more we limit our options.

This is especially true when you're doing ritual work. If you know what the end result that you want is, just state it, and keep the energy to it, but never tell us how to get there; all we need to do is to hear what your desires are at that point and your cooperation as a channel to facilitate them. You also have to be prepared to pay whatever the price is because sometimes we don't think situations all the way through. If you want a million bucks and you do a ritual that says you want a million bucks, and if you started looking at your life situation, and the only way you're going to get that million bucks is if Uncle Joe dies and leaves it to you in the will, do you really want the million bucks so much that you'd want to lose Uncle Joe? That's why you have to be careful what you ask for because you might get it, and then you'd be stuck with your guilt. So you have to think yourself through it before you do any kind of spiritual work; you have to realize you may have overlooked a couple of things. Otherwise, you carry that weight when it happens. You have to take responsibility for your own actions. You cannot shuffle it off on the will of God or the work of the devil.

That's, to me, the main attraction about New Age work: that you are the person in charge of dealing with your stuff and you cannot pass the buck to anybody. Nobody else can take the credit, either. And you're in a continual process of recreating yourself on a daily basis. Each day you are the best person you can be at that moment in time. The fact that a year from now you may be better in certain areas doesn't mean you're bad now. And you can't justifiably feel guilty because you're not out here yet. If you're functioning at 100 percent capacity, that's all you can expect of yourself. You just keep trying to stretch your limits in whichever ways they'll go; you never know when a situation is going to arise where you're going to be needed, once you make the commitment to be a channel. It's really serious when you say you want to be used as a channel because it takes you up on it, invariably at the weirdest times. You just want to go out and have a nice quiet drink, and the next thing you know, you walk into the bar and sit down and somebody's standing there talking about exactly the kind of stuff you know something about, and they're asking the questions because they want an answer, and you're right there. Well, if you're a channel, you deal with it. You don't go, "Oh, not now; I just wanted to be alone." You bought into it when you became a channel. So I just try to be as open as I can, and I look forward to surprises. I don't want to ultimately know what I'm going to be doing two, five, ten years from now. I still want there to be some rabbits to jump out of a hat.

Otherwise it would be boring, and why bother? If you already know what the end result is, then cut to the last reel and forget it. You should be able to surprise yourself on occasion. I didn't know I could do that, and in fact, that's one of the most fun concepts of the Seth readings, that ALL THAT IS has created everything. Given the free will to do whatever you want yourself, sometimes the way you combine the elements of your life will produce combinations that the rest of the universe hasn't thought of doing; the situation has never arisen, and you are actually able to teach ALL THAT IS something new about itself, something that it didn't know it could do. And this reverberates through all of creation.

That's an interesting thing to work with when looking at the value of one's own life. You may not get your name written on a monument, but the way you handle things and the attitude with which you approach them may be a totally unique way of approaching that situation. And if you at all share the idea of the collective unconscious, that experience is in some way put into a receivership account that other individuals can draw on as they have need and are receptive to it. So it can be transmitted, and even though you may not know it, you can affect people all around the world just by doing the best that you can do with whatever you're given. Your combinations may benefit people that you never meet in this lifetime, let alone any others. So you can have a much wider range than we normally think we can. There's a lot more interconnectedness going on than most people realize; it's like those nature shows that always stress the conflict of the predator and the prey. The battle. They never talk about the cooperation of the ecological balance and how each is necessary to the other, about the harmony of that cycle. They're always into the conflict. And I tend to look more at the cosmic dance than the conflict. Conflict is nice to look at once in awhile, but you have to remember: it's only a game. The dance goes on forever. And people, since they are part of that dance, can communicate their own exponential things on a non-verbal level. To me, sharing our experience is what makes the whole trip worth going for, and I just look forward to having more strange and wonderful experiences to grow into, and I'm not at all closing the door on anything that might come down. Whatever happens, happens.

Wrapping up, Sheila speaks to my question about the relationship between her sexuality and her spirituality.

My sexuality really hasn't affected my spiritual journey in many ways. It's been more of the reverse. When I was still in the Southern Baptist thing, I thought there was something wrong with what I was feeling. When I got into the agnostic period, I thought I was probably socially maladjusted or something like that. Finally, when I got into the New Age thing, I started reading material that emphasized variety and diversity. And I think that's what finally opened it up to where everything could finally come out and I could deal with it. It took me a long while to prepare the conscious mind to deal with what wanted to come out from inside. And it took me until I was thirty-five to get enough of the kind of supportive material, from a whole bunch of different cultures; all sorts of different things that I realized were saying really the same thing. So the sexuality didn't influence the spirituality in that sense. Spirituality either repressed or allowed room for growth. The main way the sexuality thing has impacted on it is in the choice of imagery, from having to go so deeply inside to a feminine archetype to find the feminine core that I had buried so long. But the philosophical was already there, to bring the sexuality out in the first place. The philosophical view did not change, just the imagery. I had been doing an almost purely abstract imagery thing prior to the transition. I did not have any imagery to go with it because I did not care at all for the patriarchal, and I didn't have anything else to put in its place. So the sexuality gave me something that I was missing by giving me an imagery thing that I could work with and utilize in ritual. But the spirituality itself was already there and more shaped the sexuality than the other way around.

How does MCC fit into all of this? Well, the way I look at it at this point is MCC provides what certain people need at a certain level of consciousness. It's all they're prepared to deal with. They're in the aerobic walking stage—they're not Olympic sprinters. They'd hurt themselves if they tried to do an Olympic sprint right now. They need to do an aerobic walk for awhile. Just because my needs are different doesn't mean that theirs are wrong. I do what I can to help them with what they're here to do. I don't need it for myself; I find myself elsewhere. But it's not just a job; it's a way of helping people, and it's also a way, very definitely, of making myself available, so I can do channel stuff when the people need me. I'm in a place where they can get to me if they need me, and they'll wander in. I like to be in a job where I am accessible, so that I can send out the vibe and folks that want to drop by can. So I prefer a public contact job like that: it lets me do my little thing for those who need me, and at the same time, it is helping the church. I don't think any one denomination has a lock on anything. Invariably, the rules of an institution are made up by the people who come after, not by the founders. And regardless of the stated purpose of any institution, its number one objective is its own self-perpetuation. I've run into this with New Age groups, too; when they're institutionalized, they're more than happy to show you how what they've got to offer is more than what you might be leaving behind. They're not at all willing to admit the fact that you might someday be ready to outgrow them and move on to something else. So they want to keep your dollars. That is the thing I respected most about Jane Roberts with the Seth materials. My first exposure to it was at a Church of Religious Science trial class. They wanted to pick up one of her books and use it as a textbook on pastoral counseling and psychology for their ministers. They wrote her a letter saying that they were going to use it in their denomination worldwide, and they would buy thousands of copies. They asked if she could either come out and give them a lecture or maybe write something and tell them how they should approach the material. She said, "No. I don't do lectures. I would not presume to tell anyone how to interpret this material. I don't know what it means; I just channel it. I have as much trouble understanding it sometimes as you do." And she specifically will accept—the source and she were both very adamant about the fact—that no organizational group will be formed for the material and that the books should just be printed and disseminated, and let people work with them on their own. She was turning down, or risking turning down, several thousand dollars' worth of book sales. I thought that was really somebody sticking to their principles. Some of the New Age groups have bought into it as heavily as the organized churches. Oh, well, you can spend lifetimes here and never learn. So they will play the same game. And you just have to trust your own inner instincts. When it's time to move on, you move. And you shouldn't feel guilty about it. It's not just institutionalized religion per se; any institutionalized movement wants to save itself first. They'll help you only so long as it doesn't interfere with their higher income returns. But I think they can all do a certain amount of good for the level at which they're reaching people. They serve a useful function and should be helped.

PART FOUR

DEVELOPING A MINISTRY

AN early reader of the interview transcripts was struck by what may seem to many a perplexing question: why, in the face of such religiously based antagonism as is found in our society today, did many participants opt to *stay* within the same traditions in which they had been raised and which were now rejecting them? Faith and community could potentially be found in friendlier places—why did they remain?

This is a compelling question. That gay men and lesbian women should move away from organizations that reject them—as have many of those participants we have already met—is not surprising. Yet there are others who stayed within—or at least close to—familiar traditions. Consider the words of Matthew, a former seminarian who is still a Catholic, as he discusses why he remains: "Even Mother Theresa's first attempt at an order was banished. . . . This ain't bad company. [He goes on to discuss the church's endorsement of slavery in earlier times.] It's not only comforting history; it's also appalling history, and you can find comfort in that history as well as what makes you angry. I mean, if I walked away, that's like not voting—I can't complain about the church if I just turn it over."

Those individuals represented by this part have felt the rejection of the institutional church as acutely as any. They were prayed for, damned to hell by, and alienated from the institutions that they had been a part of for years. One man was forced to give up his position as a minister; another ended up creating his own church to have a place where he and others could worship; a third, a seminarian, was not ordained because she is a lesbian. Although it is not the intention of this study to completely answer the "why stay?" question, the lives shared here give a sense of the rich and personal ways in which gay and lesbian individuals may move along in their journeys—even within apparently antagonistic contexts.

For these people, commitments to their roots were deeply felt. Virtually every gay or lesbian person in this study did experience some dissonance and worked hard to integrate sexuality and spirituality in a coherent way. Those who stayed within a particular tradition worked to find a way to continue participating with integrity. This typically involved profound and often painful questioning, reformulating old belief systems in a way that was congruent with what they were learning about themselves, translating language and symbols within a larger and more inclusive framework, and locating communities that were affirming of them as gay or lesbian. The time-out for distancing, questioning, and searching could range from a few intense weeks to many decades of movement in and out of a variety of traditions. Often, there was a period in which they explored other paths, such as Sandra's entry into Wicca, before coming "home" to a religious affiliation closer to their roots.

Claiming an identification does not automatically end the struggles, of course—a person's focus may shift, however, to a more open and outward conflict both within and outside of the lesbigay community. One man wrote, "It is harder for me to come out as Christian to my gay friends than to come out as gay to my family and straight people." His fear, of course, is that his gay and lesbian friends would judge him as internally homophobic, thereby denying the great deal of difficult and intense work he invested in defining his religious beliefs. And visible gay or lesbian Christians may find themselves at odds with their denomination's policy and values.

As they come to reclaim their spirituality within old institutions, some, including these three individuals—Gerald, Ann, and Vincent—have even taken leadership roles within religious communities, finding that they can define a ministry that supports their sense of who they are as gay men and lesbians. Their stories are shared here, for they represent the struggle within a heritage perhaps most poignantly.

Gerald, thirty-seven, after going through a very painful coming-out process in which he confronted his fundamentalist values, has founded an independent, charismatic gay church, which is where he finds himself today. He considers himself conservative religiously, but he believes that being gay is what God wants for him.

Ann, thirty-three, has left the traditional and conservative Bible church of her childhood but has pursued ministry within a more liberal Christian context. She has recently completed graduate studies in an American Baptist seminary but cannot find a church that will welcome her as an open lesbian pastor. In the meantime, she works in a Metropolitan Community Church.

Vincent, forty-one, is a Roman Catholic priest working outside his community. As he has grown, he has come to look on his institution's stance somewhat cynically, though his personal faith is strong: "Church, for me, is not the Vatican; it's more of a commitment to a Christian lifestyle than documents and things like that." He is questioning the appropriateness for him of being in community and is content to let rest the question of whether to leave. In the meantime, he is considering more direct ministry to the HIV affected.

Gerald: Fundamental, but Gay Affirming

Gerald is a social worker and the minister of a charismatic gay and lesbian Christian church. Raised in a Methodist family in a small town in Indiana, he took a turn toward a more fundamental understanding when he was a college student. He wrestled strenuously with his beliefs when he came out, reaching a point where he could bring together his sexuality and his spirituality. He describes that journey in this interview. His story presents a powerful challenge to those who say you can't be Christian (and especially conservative Christian) and gay or lesbian, for in these pages he honestly presents his life and beliefs as a "witness."

Perhaps what is most compelling about Gerald's journey are his trust and faith in the obvious struggles he has had: beginning as a Methodist, he consciously chose to take a much more conservative tack out of a sense that only in this way could he be faithful to the Bible. Then, coming out, he needed to confront, in a painful and intense way, the more literal theology he had adopted; eventually, he came to an understanding that his being gay was part of God's gift to him, and not a curse, yet doing the hard-fought work of integrating this into his otherwise fundamental understanding was not easy. To gain a better sense of his roots, let's start with a few paragraphs on what he learned in his family, beginning with the value that "everybody had to fit in."

I grew up in a small town not too far from Indianapolis where there was some industry, and it was all surrounded by farms. I'm not sure how many people live there now, but when I lived there, it was about twelve or fourteen thousand.

SmallTown was very segregated. In fact, the first black couple was—and I mean this exactly the way it comes off—*allowed* to move in, after I graduated high school in 1973. Everybody was expecting a lot of trouble. When I started high school, that was the first four-year class in the new joint high school, between what was the SmallTown high school and one of the county schools, where there were three or four black people. It turned out to be no big deal. Apparently—and I don't know this for sure—my hometown used to be one of the headquarters for the KKK. Very conservative, weirdly so, I mean it was largely, politically, a Democratic town, but it was very conservative. Everybody had to fit in.

His family reinforced this valuing of appearance.

I come from your basic dysfunctional family. I had three sisters, all younger than me. Both my parents are still living—my mom had a stroke in 1980, but that's been the only really major illness in the family. All three of my sisters are back in my hometown, so I'm the only one who has moved away and stayed away.

As far as morals were concerned, the odd thing about my family was they didn't really care what we did so long as we were in the "in" group. It was okay with them if I did drugs because all the people who were in the accepted group—this was back in the early seventies—did drugs. If I did drugs, that meant I'd be accepted. It was okay if I did anything so long as I was accepted. My father, especially, was very big on appearances—so we were told not to steal, not to cuss, to be honest. Those are actually the only rules I remember. As far as sexual discussions, we didn't have any; we just didn't talk about that.

I felt ostracized from my dad. Looking back, I see the pressure that was on me to perform, to be a man. I was to be everything my dad wasn't, I guess, and of course, I wasn't any of that. I didn't want to play football or softball. I wanted to be in the band. The pressure was really, really on to be a man. And I remember the one year I wanted to join the band, which meant you had to start in the summer. Well, my dad wanted me to play softball. To this day I will not play softball. I just hate it because it brings back too much. And I hated softball then, and I think because I hated it, I did awful at it. I remember the one time I got a hit, I tripped on the way to first base. It was not pretty by any stretch. I tried out for football, and I tried out for wrestling, and I just couldn't succeed. And the problem was I could never be what he wanted me to be. Finally, I got, oddly enough, into doing dramatics in high school, and some of the "in" group were doing that, so that was okay—there wasn't any problem with "appearances" here.

Still, my dad thought I was a sissy. Lots of that—sissy, lily, things like that. Right after I came out, when I was going through my anger stage, I just wanted to scream at him and say, "You said that's what I was, and look what you got." We talked about it a little bit, and I told him one of the things I knew I had to do was forgive him for all that, and of course, he just went and totally dumped on me; he had no idea what to do with that.

I would say my family was a Christian-in-appearance-only family. You were expected to go to church because that was the thing to do. We went to the Methodist church that my family had always gone to, and then the district closed it down because they'd built a new one. But then my family moved, and we went to an Evangelical United Brethren church; a few years later the Evangelical United Brethren and the Methodists combined to form the United Methodists, so I didn't go very far; I stayed in the Methodist church.

Church was an obligation. It was something that my dad wanted us to do; it was the social thing to do. I look back, and church just wasn't making it for me at that point in my life. I went through a time of doubting whether there was a God when I was in high school, but it was real brief. I would look around and I'd say: "I don't care what anybody says. This was planned by somebody; this just didn't happen," and I think that's what held me to believe in that there at least was a God somewhere. At that point I had no idea how to talk to Him, how to reach Him, or any of that kind of stuff; it was just like the great unknown. I honestly think intellectually I knew what they were talking about; I mean, I could spell off this creed and that creed, and so intellectually I knew what it was about. But I didn't really know what the spirit was about.

Actually, before I received Jesus as my savior I thought I was Christian. When you grow up in a Methodist church, and I'm sure it's this way for a lot of churches, you have summer church camps. Every year I'd go to church camp, and every Thursday night of the week when we were there, they'd have the Bible service. And, you know, this guy would tell you to get saved, and so every year I got saved. But when you get back to church, there never was any follow-up, so it was like I never really did anything with it. I don't think I ever really understood what it meant to be a Christian. I knew the doctrines of the church; I even preached. But still there was something—and I didn't even know it at the time—that wasn't quite there. I think, for me, church was partly about doing my service to God. And, of course, the youth group that I was in was just fun time; we did lots of social stuff, went to movies and outings and so on.

Still, I knew I wanted something more, and I wasn't quite sure what that "more" was at that point. About that time was when the Broadway play *Godspell* came out. I'd gone to see it and later saw the movie when it came out, and I'd sit there and think: "Okay, this is not what I thought Christianity was all about. This is weird stuff. These people are having fun; maybe that's what I'm missing, the fun." I'd go to church and sit there for an hour and listen to the sermon and sing the songs and do everything, yet something still was missing. And for awhile I looked around; I even considered becoming Roman Catholic because when I was a senior in high school all my friends and the girl I was dating at the time were Roman Catholic. So we'd go to mass and then go over to the Methodist church, and I saw something mystical in the mass. But even that didn't satisfy; I knew there had to be something more. And before I finally went up to college, I met with the pastor of my church, and he said, "Well, now, when you get up there, why don't you look up Campus Crusade for Christ?" I just said: "Right, right. I'm going to go away to college, and that's the last thing I want to do is get involved with some church group."

I need to add another weird thing. I look at it, and I see it as God moving, nudging me in His general direction. When I was in high school, the book *The Late Great Planet Earth,* by Hal Lindsay, about end-time's prophecy, was very popular. A friend—I was best friends with this guy from the Assembly of God church, which is a really wild Pentecostal church—gave me a copy of it to read, and I thought, "Well, this is really great; this is really neat." But that's about as far as it got. But I still held on, and I did believe. I started believing that Jesus was going to come back, but I never once thought that I had to do anything to get ready for it, which is really weird thinking on my part.

Moving away to college—and toward a more conservative understanding—followed.

Before I went to college—even though I didn't want to get involved in any church groups or anything, and certainly not a "fanatic" group like Campus Crusade for Christ—I knew I had to have a Bible. I didn't own one on my own, so just before I went to college, I bought one. I figured everybody in college should have a Bible. So I left with my bags packed, with no intention of ever reading the thing. But it ended up that in the residence hall I was in, one of the leaders from Campus Crusade for Christ was on my floor. It was really weird because Roger had put up an invitation to come to a Bible study. And I thought: "Okay, I'll go. I'll see what it's like. Why not?" And I started going and we talked—we were using some of the Campus Crusade for Christ literature—and we went through a book called *The Uniqueness of Jesus.* There came a point, when we were talking about the parable of the sower and the seeds, when it was as if God smacked me in the face and said, "Okay!" One of the questions was, "Which one of these—the rock by the roadside, the rocky grounds, or the good soil—describes your life?" And I think for the first time I just sat there, and I thought, "Well, I know it's not the good soil." So I talked to Roger about it—'cause meanwhile we'd go door to door and witness to people, and I didn't even know who I was talking about at that point—and I said: "My life isn't where it should be. There's something really wrong here." And he asked me, "Well, did you ever ask Jesus into your life?" And I said, "Well, yeah, I did, about twenty times already." And so we talked about what it really meant, and I think for the first time I understood that it's not just a one-time experience. I mean, there is that beginning point, but I never had anybody talk to me about what happens afterwards, the follow-up: prayer and Bible study, fellowship, things like that. And so it was that afternoon that he and I prayed together. That's when I asked Jesus into my heart, and it was really weird because from that point on, even like the next day, I was thinking, "God's called me to be a pastor." And for awhile I looked into going into seminary and stuff, but I never could afford it.

I had been witnessing door to door even before I accepted Christ in my heart because I honestly thought I knew. It probably goes back to coming up from a people where appearances are so important, so I could put up a real good appearance. Roger was really shocked when I told him that my life wasn't at all where God wanted it to be. "What? You know what to say." I said: "Yeah, I know that, but it's not real. It's just a front." And I think when we did that parable, that's what God said, "You're just putting up a front; you don't really know me." I also think part of it was self-delusion because I thought I did know, but it was all up here. Like I said, I could quote scripture, and I could quote the creeds, I could sing the hymns, but it was all up here, and it hadn't sunk down yet and become a vital part of my life.

I was dating a girl from my hometown, and the scariest thing for me was to write her a letter and say, "Well, I don't know that we can do what we've been doing anymore." So that was one of the first, immediate changes. And I think, looking back, I became really legalistic, having moved from almost no moral stance to ironclad, brick-wall, right-and-wrong sort of stuff. And in a way that was good for me at that time; I needed that security. And I still believed, yes, there are some things that you can do and some things that God obviously says no to. I think at that point I was so immature, and there was so much else going on—it was the first time I'd been away from home, a massive loss of security—so I immediately became very rigid. For a long time. I needed very, very firm boundaries; by being rigid, that provided them for me.

I think part of my experience was just to find out who I was. I knew who I wasn't, but I had no idea who I was, and I thought maybe this would help. It wasn't that my life was so empty; I just felt there had to be something more, something more out there for me, than I had. It really has helped me to find out who I am in Christ.

I had absolutely no idea I was gay at this point. Talk about denial, whoa, I look back over my life, and I remember times when I was really fascinated with adolescent sex play and wanting to be more than friends. During my senior year in high school—I was dating a girl at this time—my best friend started dating another good friend of mine that I'd known since seventh grade, and I was insanely jealous. I mean, I was insanely jealous. I had no idea why I was feeling that way at that point. I just knew I was incredibly jealous and angry. And his school was doing a play the same night that our school was doing one, and he'd gone over to his cast party, and then he came over to join the rest of us at ours, and he was really drunk, and for the first time the thought of having sex with him went through my head. Of course, I immediately stifled it, but at that point I didn't even think it was wrong; I ignored it like it didn't exist. And I remember looking at men and thinking, "Wow, he is really, really hot," and yet it didn't register to me that that was a homosexual thought. Maybe it was because I had no comprehension of what a homosexual was. At that point homosexuals were dirty old men who hung out in bookstores, or something along that line. I had received a message, I guess, that homosexuals were very effeminate and flighty, which is funny 'cause I never was effeminate. I never had any mannerisms or anything 'til after I really came out. I had never heard of Stonewall at that point: if somebody had mentioned it, I would've said: "Huh? What's that?" I think I had no comprehension.

Being baptized again was an important step for Gerald in his new understanding.

Maybe it was the baptism in the Methodist church that turned me gay. You'll understand when I tell you this. I had been christened as a baby, but then the minister we had—I think he might have been a closet gay—took a little crystal bowl, which, of course, had water in it, and he took a rose and would dip the rose in the water and sprinkle us on the forehead. After I got saved, I start going to an independent Christian church, and they talked about baptism. I'd never really studied the scriptures about baptism before, and once I did, I realized this sprinkling with the rose thing didn't cut it as far as the Bible was concerned. So I decided after reading the scriptures that I needed to be baptized; the church that I was going to at that time baptized by total immersion, which, as I see it from studying the scriptures, is the most general way the early church did it. So I prayed about it, and I felt that's what I needed to do in order to be obedient. So on March 17th, 1974, I was baptized. After I was baptized, I felt closer to God. I felt better because I knew I'd been obedient; I knew that this was scripturally what God wanted me to do, so I felt better about it. A really strange coincidence is that the woman that I later married was the one that handed me the towel when I got up out of the water. This has been one strange life.

I remember Ann handing me the towel. She was a biggie in the church I was going to and was dating somebody else at that point anyway. And we didn't even hardly talk to each other at all until my senior year in college, when we ended up going up to the wedding of two friends of ours. She was singing, and I was an usher, so we rode up with another friend; she and I got a chance to talk, and we started dating then shortly thereafter. It was at that same time that I started having homosexual experiences, so, I mean, this was a real, real crazy time for me.

"Receiving the fullness of the Holy Spirit" was another important step.

When I was nineteen, I received the fullness of the Holy Spirit and spoke in tongues. Again, this was another step in obedience, but it was also a step into His presence and power at a level that I had never known before. It was something I was scared to death of. I have to back up a little bit, to the Bible study I was in, in my freshman year. The makeup of this group was very, very strange. There was me, who was "the Methodist who finally got saved"; there was Roger, who went to a very conservative Presbyterian church; Larry, who was the resident assistant on our floor, who went to the Campus House, the independent church I ended up going to; and Joe, who was an Assembly of God fanatic. Joe and Roger were roommates, and they would yell and argue about speaking in tongues and such.

So the summer after my freshman year in college, I went to Joe's church, and I really enjoyed it. It was the first time I'd been in any sort of Pentecostal or charismatic church. I enjoyed it so much 'cause it's a really lively service, with people singing like they meant it and lots of clapping and tambourines and stuff. And while I enjoyed that, I said, "I like this, but this speaking in tongues stuff, I don't think I want that." But then the next year when I went back up to school, a friend of mine and I started talking. He told me he had this experience, that he had been baptized in the Holy Spirit and spoke in tongues, and I said, "Okay, that's fine for you, but I don't think it's for me."

But he gave me a book to read on it, which I read. It was really weird because that Saturday I was working at a residence hall desk; I had to open and I had to close, and nobody bothers you from eight o'clock to ten o'clock on a Saturday morning. So there was nobody around, so I took the book, and I took my Bible, and I was looking up all the scriptures, and I realized: "Yeah, I believe this is not just for other people. I believe that this is something God wants me to have." And I treasure the way that I received it because we all have this view of evangelists and Pentecostal meetings where people jump and shout and force you to speak in tongues, and I've seen that done in large meetings. On that Sunday morning—I praise God for this—I got up, was getting ready for church, and I stopped, and I just started praying, "Lord, I believe this is for me, and I want to receive it, and that was it; I started speaking in tongues. And it wasn't like this big emotional thing; it just happened. And I think the Lord knew that was the way I needed to receive it because I've never really doubted it since then. I can't blame it on emotionalism. I was by myself; there was no emotional buildup. I just prayed and asked and got it, and that was it.

I knew from what I had studied in the Bible in the Book of Acts that every time that Luke writes that people receive the fullness of the spirit, of the Holy Spirit, the common factor there was speaking in tongues. Every time they spoke in tongues. So I knew that would be the sign, and I prayed and I prayed and I said, "Lord, I believe this is for me, and I ask you now, in faith, in Jesus' name that baptized me in the Holy Spirit; Lord, I thank you for doing it," and I opened my mouth. It wasn't like a very fluent stream at that point, but a couple words were there. And it was neat because the words came first, and that's when I knew I had it, and the emotions came later. It was funny; I went down to find Gary 'cause we were going to walk over to church together, and he looked at me and he said, "You got it, didn't you?" I said: "Oh, yes, yes. How'd you know?"

I got really happy. I think that's probably what showed on my face when Gary saw me. It was just the joy because I knew I had taken another step of obedience, and there was something welling up inside of me. Jesus said, "Out of their bellies shall flow whole rivers of living water." And that's, I think, what I was experiencing; it was bubbling up from my spirit into my emotions, and I just got real happy. But what happened after that was I became more aware of the reality of the spirit world. It was almost like Jesus, when he was baptized and the Holy Spirit came down in bodily form as a dove, he was led out into the wilderness to be tempted and he faced the reality of Satan. For me—and I think it's fairly common to a lot of charismatics and Pentecostals—that part of it became very real, too. And I remember my first Easter after I got saved; I sat and cried all morning because I was so happy. I said: "Now I know what this means. Now I really know what it means to worship a risen Lord. I worship Jesus, who's risen from the dead." And I was so happy, I cried all morning long. Here was another step that I'd taken. Suddenly everything became much more real, and progressively, with each of these steps, the Bible became more real and more understandable, too. It just kept getting better and better.

As one might imagine given this background, coming out was not an easy experience.

My coming out ebbed and flowed. When I was a senior in college, before I did my social work practicum, I took two quarters of New Testament Greek. The class met on the second floor of the arts building, next to the men's restroom, which was the place on campus to go. I started going there before class, and I remember one time I was in there; they didn't have large glory holes, peepholes, but I was sitting there watching the guy next to me masturbate. And I got so excited, I mean, I got so turned on. And I thought, "Omigod," and then it hit me: I'm getting excited about watching this guy masturbate. Well, then, I looked down, he's looking through the hole at me, and he puts his hand underneath the partition, and I'm going, I wonder what he wants me to do; I don't understand this. That really scared me because I thought, "Omigod, I might be queer." And that was the terminology I was using at the time. You know at that point I wouldn't even have considered using the word *gay.* To me, it was "queer."

The next major thing that happened was I went in there one night after class, and this guy stood outside the toilet door, the stall door, and he approached me when I came out, and I left. This was too awful to even imagine. These are things that are burned into my memory.

Joe, who I mentioned earlier, later went on to an even more fundamentalist Pentecostal church as an evangelist. I told him I was doing my social work practicum on the north side of Indianapolis, and he said, "Well, stay away from Broad Ripple Park; just queers hang out there." Well at this point I'd begun to think that I might be a queer. I began to recognize that I was attracted to men. God has such a sense of humor. I remember going to a mall, which was in the same part of Indianapolis as Broad Ripple, where all the gays lived. One of the bookstores there, oddly enough, had all those magazines, which I thought was real odd 'cause it's a conservative town. But I remember I picked up my first copy of *Blue Boy* and looked at the men, and I thought, "Omigod, omigod, these men are gorgeous." And I thought, "I want to have sex with these men." That was the first time it crossed my mind that I wanted to have sex with men. And, of course, that was totally alien to my thinking. Well, I finally had that first experience; I went out to Broad Ripple Park and met a black man, of all people, and he wanted to be on the receiving end, and so did I, so that didn't work. But then the adult movie theater in Indianapolis was showing gay films that whole summer, and so I went there, and that's where it happened. This man patted the seat, and I said to myself, "I think he wants me to sit down," and he gave me oral sex. And after it was done, I expected that theater to be swallowed up and me to be cast into hell forever. But that was it; I realized, somewhere down inside me, "This is what I am; this is what I want."

And that began the struggle. All my Christian upbringing told me that because of what I'd just done, I was going to burn in hell forever. If I stayed this way, it was nothing but death for me. So I got married, and my ex-wife knew—I told her that I was struggling with this, and we went into the marriage. It got to be so bad at one point that we decided we would try to live celibate. It ended up that I couldn't. We have a daughter who's twelve now. And I thought, all these things—getting married, having a child, I did everything my church told me to do: I prayed and fasted; I went through deliverance services for this, read the Bible, went to counseling—and I was still gay. It didn't change, obviously. And some friends of ours from up here who eventually got me my first job up here came down and counseled with us and said everything would be okay; we'll just pray more. It didn't work. So we moved up here, and I met the man who would end up being my first lover. And you know, Ann had found out that I was sneaking out in the mornings to go see him, and so she left and got a divorce. And at that point I hated God; oh, I was so angry. I remember in the weeks after my ex-wife had left I'd go around the townhouse yelling at God, saying: "You were supposed to heal me of this. You were supposed to deliver me of this. I'm not supposed to be gay. You were supposed to do this, so either you don't care, or you don't exist."

I turned my back on God at this time, for a good while. Actively turning my back on God lasted probably about a month. For a long time after that I ignored Him; I didn't want anything to do with God: "You couldn't cure me of this, so I don't need you." But God wasn't finished yet. After I came out to myself, after I found out I was much more drawn to men than I was to women, there was nowhere and nothing I could turn to. All I knew was the Christianity I had been brought up on. And as far as I knew—of course, at that point I was living in a small town outside of Indianapolis—was that what I was, was wrong. I thought my being gay was terribly wrong.

But I couldn't ignore Him for long. I still wanted the relationship with God. My relationship with Jesus made my life complete, and it couldn't be complete without Him. And I thought, "Well, if I'm gay and I can't change, then I have got to figure out what's going on here." So I started going to libraries and getting books out—I found some books about being gay and Christian and on different people's views on what the Bible said about homosexuality—and the more I studied, the more I began to see: it's not the fact that I'm homosexual that offends God; it's how I use my sexuality, just the way that a straight person uses theirs, that's offensive to God. And then I realized, "I'm still a Christian." So then I tried a couple of straight churches. I tried a straight Methodist church because I knew I couldn't go into a charismatic or Pentecostal church because the minute they got wind that I was gay, I'd be out of there instantly. Either that, or they'd drag me to the front and try to cast a homosexual demon out of me. So, I went to a Methodist church, and I sat there and cried through the service—they sang my favorite hymns—and I thought it was wonderful. I found home. So I set up a meeting to talk to the minister. I wasn't ready to tell him I was gay, but I did tell him I was divorced. And he said, "Oh, we have this wonderful singles program." Well, I thought: "Here we go again. You know, this is not the church for me."

In looking for a more accepting place to worship, Gerald ended up at a Metropolitan Community Church.

It was funny because before—when I was still struggling with homosexuality and stuff—I had heard about the Metropolitan Community Church. "I'll never go to that church. It's the church of Sodom. I'll never go there." Well, God used MCC to get me back closer to Himself. My experiences there, overall, were really good. I met some really wonderful people, but even that wasn't it; MCC is very liberal, doctrinally, and I'm really fundamentalist. So there came a time when God told me to move on, and I did. It's really weird; when I left, nobody could comprehend that I was leaving to start a church because most people consider MCC to be it as far as gay-Christian ministries are concerned. But MCC was there when I needed it, and God used it to ease me back into being, to integrate. God helped me to integrate both parts of me because I had splintered it so.

Let me tell you about my time at MCC. I began there around Christmas of '86, at Christ the Redeemer in Evanston. Of course, MCC had really begun using inclusive language, which I was real uncomfortable with: I was used to saying, "Father, Son, and Holy Spirit," and they were saying, "Creator, Redeemer, and Holy Spirit." And I'm going, "I don't understand," so they told me about this liturgical church down in Hinsdale. I said, "Okay," remembering the time I wanted to be Catholic, "I'll go try this place out." And I really did like Holy Covenant. That was my main church I went to. I was in the choir, led a Bible study, and so on, but the time came when we had a rough time because one minister left and for awhile there was no minister and the church was falling apart. Then we got another minister who said he was real conservative. One Sunday when he was gone, I was able to take my ex-lover with me, and I thought, "Great, he's going to go to church with me; this is wonderful," but the guest preacher got up there and spouted out this stuff about Buddha being as good as Jesus. The way I interpret the Bible, that was just like heresy, and I couldn't believe this was happening. So when our minister got back, I confronted him. I said, "Daniel, you've got to understand, what was preached was not according to the statement of faith in our bylaws." I wasn't even going to tackle the Bible 'cause I wasn't quite sure where anybody stood on that, but I thought, "At least they'll respect the bylaws." And Daniel said, "You're right; nobody who's not a Trinitarian will ever preach in this pulpit." I said, "Okay," and we rented space in a Unitarian church, and sure enough, a few months later the Unitarian student minister got up and preached from the pulpit, and I looked over at my best friend and said, "That's it; this is the sign from God."

Not finding a congregation that shared his beliefs, Gerald knew it was time for him to start a church.

We had hooked up with another guy, who was in this organization called the Evangelical Network, which was a bunch of evangelical gay churches, and he had heard of a revival service being held in Dayton, Ohio. It was being held by a Community Gospel church, which is a Pentecostal gay church. So some of us packed up and went down there, and that Saturday night, the minister looked at me and said: "Gerald, you know what God's called you to do. Now is the time to start." So that's when we talked and decided God was calling us to start the church. So that was what we all considered the birthday of the church. I had been praying, "Lord, when should I leave MCC?" I didn't want to leave; I didn't want to just disappear. I didn't think that would be proper or appropriate. So after this Unitarian minister got up there, I gave letters of resignation to everybody, told the people in choir why I was leaving: that God had called me to another ministry. And that was a big step, to leave there.

What I found is there are independent, mostly charismatic or Pentecostal gay churches all over the country. That has been a big help to me because at first I thought, there had to be more of us, but I sure don't know of anybody. But there are churches all over the country—right now they're mostly out in the west—and a couple of different organizations, and we have big meetings. There are more springing up in the east. In Chicago there's two of us as far as independent churches in this area, but that's about it.

We started meeting in my apartment, which was very, very small; it was a one-bedroom that my ex-lover and I shared, and it was really, really crowded. After we came back from the revival at Dayton, Martha, who's one of my elders now, said we could use her apartment, and she had this really nice big front room, so at that point we started meeting in her living room, and it could only hold about six comfortably. But that was okay for a long time 'cause we were still pretty small. We got up to about eight, finally, and then we moved to Rodde Center. In fact, today was our last Sunday there. We're moving to a Methodist church; we're going to use their chapel.

We average now anywhere from nine to fifteen people at a service. One Sunday we had nineteen. That was strange; we'd never had that many before except for the Sunday after I was ordained. We did have quite a crowd then—we had something like twenty-one—but that was a special Sunday because we had a lot of out-of-town guests come in then. But the Lord keeps bringing people to us, one here, and one there. I think what I feel the Lord's been doing in the church is building us up, building the core group up, 'cause we've gone through a lot of infighting and personality clashes. Martha and I never got along; we'd fight like cats and dogs. We'd just gone out to Wichita, a bunch of us, 'cause there was an independent church out there and I was invited to go out and preach. So I went out to preach, and some of my people came along, and that Saturday night, Martha said to me, "Come on; we've got to go up and pray at the altar." So we went up and prayed, and she asked forgiveness for not seeing me as the pastor and running all sorts of power plays and such, which was really neat. And then I had a lot of repenting to do for her. I think that's what God's been doing. I think part of the thing that's been going on is we haven't been moving together like we should have. But God finally got in charge and said, "You will do this, and you will like it, so . . . "

Two of the guys who ordained me were themselves ordained under the auspices of Lambda Christian Fellowship. Sylvia Pennington ordained two of them, and one of them ordained me, so I'm sort of like Sylvia's spiritual grandchild. Which is great because I got to meet her, and she was a wonderful woman. The other one was Mark, from Christ Church in [the west], which used to be MCC; Mark was ordained a Baptist minister eons ago and then became an MCC minister, but their church just decided as a whole to leave MCC. So they were the three that ordained me into the ministry.

In the independent church there's really not a formal seminary or preparation process. One of the reasons I wanted Mark there is that I really respect his ministry. I had known Fred for a couple years, and he had kept a watch on my ministry anyway. And I think since I haven't been to seminary, people that ordained me were ones that had contact with me and had been able to watch how I minister. Frank was one of the ones that Sylvia had ordained, and he's my other elder, so he had obviously seen me and been able to observe me. And I don't suppose I really would have needed to be ordained, considering that the ordination, in the eyes of the state, gives me the right to marry people; the majority of people I'm going to marry are not going to be recognized by the state anyhow. But I wanted it to validate not only my ministry, but the ministry of the church. We needed somebody who had been officially ordained. And like it or not, a lot of people in our community like the official stuff, and as much as I hate it, I'm probably going to have to go out and get one of those funny-collared shirts. I know from my experience in MCC, you almost never see an MCC minister up in front of a church who has on anything but the collared shirt, and usually it's in robes, too. I usually have on good pants and shoes; I didn't even wear a tie this morning. But if I'm called upon to do something official, for whatever reason, we want those appearances, so I have a friend of mine who's going to make me a robe, a natural slacks sort of thing. So that was how I got ordained, and I haven't attended seminary. I'd love to. However, again, it's the same quandary: if I go to a seminary where it's okay to be gay, that seminary, chances are, is going to be way too liberal for all my other viewpoints.

I'm sure I could go to Garrett without a problem, but I'd have a real difficult time because I'd probably get hassled on a lot of my papers since my viewpoint would be totally different from the professors. However, if I go to where I want to go, which would be some place like Trinity Evangelical Seminary up in Deerfield, again, the minute they got wind I was gay, I'd be out of there on my butt. So it's a no-win situation.

Asked about being fundamentalist, Gerald speaks of conflicts and misunderstandings he frequently faces.

Normally, we avoid use of the word *fundamentalist. Windy City Times* interviewed me for an article, and I talked to the guy who did the interview and made sure he understood what I meant by fundamental. When I say fundamentalist, what I mean is we believe in the fundamentals in the faith. And I always try and clarify that because when people hear the word *fundamentalist,* they think of Jerry Falwell, they think of Pat Robertson, and it has such a negative connotation. We use the word as it was originally used back in the early part of the century: those that believe in the fundamentals of the faith. All this other stuff has been added on since then, all this political right-wing garbagey stuff. So usually when I talk to people, I clarify exactly what I mean by it when I call myself a fundamentalist because a lot of my social views are not anywhere near right wing. And a lot of them are; mostly I'm very, very conservative, even politically, but some of my views are not. I've written letters to Pat Robertson; I've written letters to *Christianity Today;* I've written letters to Jerry Rose, the president of channel 38, because they've had programs on that I didn't like, or articles, in the case of *Christianity Today.* Of course, from Pat Robertson I got back this computer letter, and I know he probably never even saw the letter; it probably would have scared him to death if he had because I said there's a growing army of gay and lesbian Christians. And I had put in there that I was a minister and that I was gay, and I got back this computer letter that said, "Well, perhaps you need to read Romans, chapter one, verses 18 to 32." So I thought to myself, "I put in the letter that I studied all these scriptures—did they think I missed this?" I guess, based on what I put in the letter, he pressed "homosexual" on the computer, and it spit out this letter.

You know, I never did get a reply back from *Christianity Today,* and they never did print the letter, although they did just print one on the controversy on whether or not you're born gay. And they did print a letter from a guy who signed it anonymously, "I am what I am by God's grace, I am what I am." They actually printed that; I was kind of surprised.

I never got a reply back from Jerry Rose. I call the station sometimes because they have talk shows and stuff. And I'm seriously having thoughts of writing Oprah because I know she does so much for the community, but she always has these wazoo people on to defend being Christian and gay. What I notice is they always bring on the liberals. Even this one guy who I did like, John Ankerberg, who has a show on channel 38, had Bishop Spong on. Well, any fundamentalist can discount Bishop Spong because he's so liberal; they're not going to believe anything he says. They should get a conservative person on there who believes exactly the same way most of these people do, who just happens to be gay. Of course, that makes us an oddity, because not only do we have enmity from the Christians because we're gay; we have gotten yelled at from gays because we're Christian, because we say we're fundamental, because we're evangelical; we're conservative.

The last three years we've had a booth at the rally after the Pride parade, and one year this man came up and screamed and yelled at us, saying we were worse than Jimmy Swaggart and worse than Jerry Falwell and all this because we were conservative. So we get it from both sides. And I talked to [local gay columnist] Rex Wockner when some of us from the church went on the antiviolence march last April; I said, "I need you to know I'm one of those fundamentalists you write about." He said, "Honey, if you're here, you're not one of the fundamentalists I'm writing about." Well, you're right. It's that sort of thing; it's very hard. I think part of it, too, is that we make a stand for things like sexual morality. As far as I know, we're the only gay church in this area that does. I'm not sure about Grace because I haven't sat down and talked to them about it, but I know what MCC teaches because I was there. We believe in monogamy; we don't all have it perfected yet, but we're trying; at least we're saying two people in a monogamous relationship is God's perfect plan. That's what God wants. And that's really unpopular. Even now, that's unpopular, which just blows my mind. You'd think we as a community would've wised up a long time ago.

I even get challenged within our church. There's one lady at my church who I still periodically go around about it with. She says, "Well, if you take the Bible to be literally true, then what do you do with these 'clobber passages'?" And part of me wants to shake her and say, "You've been through my seminar twice—and heard nothing?" In fact, that's what I'm doing on our Wednesday night studies now: going back through all those clobber passages. We just started last week; we talked about Sodom, and to me, Sodom's the easiest one of all. But even there I guess we look at it a little differently because I think it's strictly a sexual context: yes, they were being inhospitable, they wanted to rape the angels (that's about as inhospitable as you can get), but the context was clearly sexual. The sin was rape, and besides God had already judged Sodom. I think the important thing is for people to look at the scriptures, look at the context, look at the original languages. That's why I really praise God that, even before all this, I took Greek in college because at least I can look at the words and say, "Okay, this is what it means here."

If people ask what kind of church ours is, I'll say it's an evangelical charismatic church with a ministry for gays and lesbians. And unless I clarify that, people immediately assume that it must be some sort of straight church that's trying to change them. And when I say, "No, we're an evangelical church for gays and lesbians," that's where sometimes people just shake their heads in disbelief because it's difficult for a lot of people to accept that. If all we listen to are the Jerry Falwells and the Pat Robertsons, then we're going to assume that you can't be gay and Bible-believing at the same time. And we are. I think we've run into some negative stuff, but actually far less than I anticipated. I was concerned at the beginning that we might run into more than we have. Actually, it's been interesting. As of yet we've not had any run-ins with fundamental or evangelical straight churches. We've been at a Methodist church, and this fall they're going to go through the process of becoming a reconciling congregation. So that's wonderful. They love us, and I think that's neat. It was so funny because they were so afraid—not of us being gay, that was no big deal, but of our charismatic worship style. That's been it from churches like the Methodist church. It was just fine that we were gay. The fact that we were hinging on being Pentecostal was quite a worry to them.

Summing up, Gerald speaks of what it has meant to him to be gay and Christian.

Being gay made me take a big detour for awhile. But I think because I'm gay, maybe I feel more integrated. I've had to reintegrate my spirituality and my sexuality, and that's been a major struggle. But I think because of that, I'm more whole now. Maybe I just don't know because I'm not heterosexual, but I don't think there's so much to integrate there. At least with those of us who are gay, we have to integrate everything that we tend to tear apart, and I think being able to integrate that, for me, makes me feel like a whole person. I feel complete. I have a much deeper understanding of God's love and grace because I know just how far from Him I got when I turned away or ignored Him. And I know how much He called me back. I know how He kept calling me, like he was leading me out on my leash, and then He started reeling me back in over a length of time. I know He did that for love, and I have a much more, I think, profound understanding of that. I never really understood grace until I was able to look at it on this side of being gay, instead of on the other side.

To understand me, it is important to understand my relationship with God through His son Jesus Christ and the effects that relationship has on my life as a whole. And there's been so many effects. A lot of people call it inner-healing, healing of memories and things, and that's come as a direct result of, I feel, reading the Bible and finding out what the Bible says. Just the way that my walk with God affects my daily life, the changes that it's made; overall, I feel healthier emotionally than I did as a child. I also feel that my attitudes have changed. What Paul says in Galatians about the fruits of the spirit, I see those being manifested: the love, the joy, the peace. As long as I let God control my life and let Him run the show, then I notice His presence, and those changes become more and more evident in me. Sometimes it's really hard because there's still a lot of me that hasn't changed, and God pokes a finger on those areas and says, "Okay, we're going to work on this one now." Sometimes that's not easy. But my relationship with God has made me be realistic about who I am, my own limitations. I've been able to look at who I am and deal with me, the positives and the negatives, and I think had I not had the Lord with me, I don't know if I could have dealt with being gay. So I did it backwards. You're supposed to be gay and then get saved, and then the way they tell us we're supposed to do this, you'll become straight. I was saved, and then I found out I was gay. Looking back now, I can say, "Oh, yeah, I knew that all along." But once I reconciled those two aspects of my life, my Christianity, my walk with God, helped me to deal with all the rejection from family and friends. Hardly anybody in my hometown will even speak to me at this point. But I can look at my own character defects and stuff now and say, "Okay, I can let God take care of these." I know that there are times even now when I try to do it on my own and it just doesn't work. I'm going to be less boastful today, let's say. It doesn't work. But, God, you take care of this because I can't—that works. I was always shy, and I still am shy, but I never, ever thought I could get up and handle running a church. I idealized being a pastor. I thought it was this glamorous sort of job. Boy, was I wrong. But I've learned that as I listen to the Lord, like when I have to counsel people or put out fires, whatever's going on, He gives me the wisdom. I believe it comes through the Holy Spirit. I get the wisdom; I get the words, the way to say it so that the words mean something.

I know what it's like to go through suffering, and I can identify with the feeling of being isolated from God and separated. And it has helped when I've talked to people. I can say, "You know, it's okay." But people still question. Is it really okay to be gay and consider myself Christian at the same time? And probably my major gift is teaching, which is not always that compassionate of a gift. But because of what I've been through, I can temper what I teach with knowing that I've been there, too. It's not always an easy struggle. And I don't fault any of the people in church, even myself, for doubting because I've done it plenty of times. And I have to go back periodically and go over my own teachings to reassure myself at times. The doubts aren't very often, but of course they occur. If I make the mistake of watching channel 38, you know—well, he says this, so I've got to go back in the Bible and look it up and see where he yanks it out of context.

Ann: MCC or American Baptist?

Ann was born in Spain, where her parents were missionaries. At age five she and her family returned to the United States. Raised very conservatively in a Bible church, Ann's journey through her own years of college, mission work in Spain, and seminary has been a process of intensive questioning, study, and challenge. Now estranged from her father (her mother died of cancer several years ago), Ann is defining a new ministry that says, "In order to live up to our full potential, we must be honest with ourselves about who we are and learn to take pride in ourselves." For the time being, she works as an administrative assistant in an MCC church, but she is hoping to be ordained—either in the American Baptist denomination of her seminary training or in the Metropolitan Community Church.

In sharing her story, Ann describes an evolving process of asking difficult questions and moving in honest and integrated ways toward a deeper sense of herself as she answers the questions. There are, broadly speaking, four stages to that process that I would like to highlight. First, she received the inherited wisdom of her parents and her church. Second, moving away from home, she began to challenge some of those views as she prepared for, and unfolded, her work in Spain as a missionary teacher. The third stage was a time of intense scrutiny and introspection, when she was in an American Baptist seminary, which resulted in her beginning to come to terms with her homosexuality. Fourth, in recent months she has been weaving together this growing self-awareness with the threads of her theological development into an integrated self-understanding and sense of purpose as she forges her ministry and the direction for the years to come. Let's begin with her description of her intensely religious and committed family.

I was born in Barcelona, Spain, where my parents were serving as evangelical missionaries. I was the youngest of four children and the only girl. (Actually, my parents' second child was also a girl, but she drowned when she was two years old.) My parents were in Spain for ten years. They had intended to make missions in Spain their career, but they ended up returning to the States because of my mom's health problems. I was five years old at that time. My parents then bought a house in a Chicago suburb where Dad worked for the mission headquarters. Despite the fact that my parents eventually got very involved in ministry in the States, they never lost their love for Spain, and they passed that enthusiasm for missions on to us kids. I grew up with the dream of returning to Spain to "pick up where my parents had left off."

My parents believed that there was no higher ideal in life than to work hard to serve God as Lord and Savior. They had both worked very hard in Spain, where Protestant missionaries were not welcome. Their second term they started a church in a suburb of Barcelona where there was no evangelical witness. That church is still meeting today, and individuals there still lovingly remember my parents' ministry with them. After my parents returned to the States, they continued as "home missionaries" and lived on missionary salary, but they struggled to find a sense of fulfillment in their ministry here. Dad worked for awhile as the printer for the mission that had sent him to Spain, but eventually he moved into a ministry to alcoholics in a nearby rescue mission. He also worked as volunteer chaplain for the local county jail. My parents ministered together in a church for Hispanic people. Mom did a lot of speaking at missionary conferences and women's church retreats, where she shared her story of how God had worked in and through her life. Mom felt an intense sense of obligation to the churches and individuals who provided financial support to pay their missionary salary. Because of her insecurities, she never felt she had done enough to be worthy of the loving kindness and respect she so quickly earned from those to whom she ministered. Dad's ministry was mostly based on doing handiwork for others and witnessing while working alongside of them. Most of Dad's work was done behind the scenes, while Mom's ministry was more visible.

My parents struggled to fit their conservative theology into their more liberal lifestyle. Dad complained that he wasn't allowed to "wear the pants" in the family, and Mom was often in tears as she tried to be a submissive wife, yet felt the need to question Dad's decisions. They never resolved the conflict they felt between their lifestyle of equal partnership and their conservative, hierarchical theology. This fundamental incongruence together with their own insecurity created a great amount of tension between my parents.

Faith in God was always a part of my life. We had family devotions together almost every day while I was growing up. Mom tried to make it interesting for us children by either reading from a children's Bible storybook or reading a Christian novel to us. Dad would lead us in the formal time of prayer. Our parents also prayed with us as they tucked us into bed each night. I always preferred to have Mom tuck me in because she took the time to just sit and chat for a while, so that she really knew what was on my mind. Prayer time with Mom was a time to intimately connect with a loving mother and a caring God. On the other hand, prayer time with Dad was a formal religious event. Dad would get down on his knees next to our bed, use his "religious" voice, and speak to a holy God in "King James" English. Despite our parents' differing styles, they both taught us that our faith in God was not just our religion, but rather our driving force in life. All of life's decisions, from who to invite over for dinner to choosing a career, were considered questions of faith and opportunities to witness about God.

I attended a conservative Bible church with my family. At this church I was taught to be suspicious of the faith of anyone who was not a member of a conservative church. Sincerity without correct theology was not enough to lead to a "saving faith." Catholics and Pentecostals were definitely not heaven bound, nor were most Lutherans, Methodists, or even Southern Baptists!

The message about homosexuality was clear when I was a child—it was a sexual perversion. Though I don't remember a whole lot being said about it, the little I heard from friends, family, and church was very condemning. Despite the negative input, I always rather naively wondered what could possibly be so awful about two people of the same gender showing one another loving affection. It never made much sense to me, but being fearful of showing my ignorance, I never voiced my confusion on this issue.

In the second stage of her journey, Ann began defining her vocation of ministry by picking up where her parents had left off, that is, in Spain. This was a time when Ann began questioning the messages she had received as a child.

Having heard about Spain all my life, it just seemed natural for me to plan to return to pick up where my parents had left off. I suppose, since pleasing my parents was so important to me, I was hoping to be able to fulfill their dream for them. I studied Spanish in high school and then followed my brothers and parents in completing the three-year course of study at Moody Bible Institute. Then after doing a year-long internship at a Christian camp for low-income children, I completed my B.A. in Elementary Education. Whether doing ministry or studies, my goal was always missions in Spain. At age twenty-four I headed out to Madrid as a missionary teacher.

I loved my life and ministry in Spain, and I had every intention of spending my life there. I was confident, though, that my calling was to church ministry, not to teaching American children in a missionary school. My mission field council did not believe that I had the gifts necessary for church ministry in Spain, so when I pushed to move out of the school setting, they decided it would be best for me to head back to U.S. I had been in Spain just three years and probably could have stayed with another mission board, but somehow, despite my depression over leaving Spain, I knew it was time for me to go. My experiences during my time there had caused me to recognize my need for further theological study.

Although I lacked self confidence growing up as the "baby" of the family, and never initiated taking leadership roles like my brothers had done throughout high school and college, I did learn from them the importance of thinking for myself. My first act of "rebellion" against the accepted theology of my upbringing was to write a paper and give an oral report on the role of women in ministry. My brothers eagerly directed me to books written by people who considered themselves "biblical Feminists," which at my Bible school was considered an oxymoron. I happened to tell my piano teacher about the study I was doing, and she told me that her husband was a professor at a Baptist Seminary in the area that was supportive of women in leadership in the church. I filed that information away in my mind as I thought it might someday be of use to me.

It was during my second year at Bible school that my mother was diagnosed with bone cancer. At the time the cancer was discovered, it was already spread from head to foot. The doctors suggested that with chemotherapy Mom might have as much as two more years to live. She was in shock for the next few months and didn't do much of anything, but finally she decided that she wasn't going to sit around and wait to die. She would live life to its fullest and fight this disease with every weapon available to her. She kept up with the chemotherapy treatment, but also experimented with megavitamin therapy, vegetarian and juice diets, herbal teas, imaging white blood cell warfare, and faith healing. Mom's fight was not only physical and emotional, but it was also spiritual. Mom wrestled with God as she struggled to pray in faith believing that God would heal, yet at the same time seeking to have the faith to accept that healing might not be given to her. Mom's faith journey was a challenge to each of us in the family as well as to the many people with whom she shared her testimony. Mom never professed to be a great woman of faith; instead, she honestly confessed her fears and doubts and shared how God always held her close and walked with her. Mom lived an active life for five more years, and she counted each day a blessing and an opportunity! Unlike fundamentalist theology that professes to have clear-cut answers to all of life's questions, Mom's faith journey recognized that life is full of ambiguities. We aren't always given direct answers to our questions—we must simply step out in faith and trust God to bless each tentative step.

Not long after I graduated from Bible school, my brother informed the family that he and his wife (who he had met at Bible school) had separated. Their eventual divorce was a crisis of faith for our conservative family. Divorce couldn't possibly be within God's perfect will, could it? What about ministry after divorce? And remarriage?

Mom's fight with cancer had caused me to rethink my theology of prayer and healing. Now my brother's divorce was forcing me to rethink my theology of marriage, divorce, and church leadership. I couldn't see any way to dogmatically hold to traditional conservative thinking and still show loving respect for my mom and brother.

Mom was still alive and very active when I headed off to Madrid to fulfill my calling to missions in Spain. Surely here all of my training and biblical education would make sense! But again I found myself questioning. How could I condemn the faith of the sincere Catholic women I met there? Surely a God of love would not condemn them to hell just because their theology and religious practices were wrong! And who was I to say that they were wrong and I was right? Their moral principles were as high as mine. And their desire to seek God's guidance and give glory to God for answered prayer were also as high as mine. Who was I to stand in judgment of a faith that gave purpose and meaning to their lives?

It wasn't more than a month after I left for Spain that Mom's health started to go downhill quickly. I hurried back home just before Christmas, when her death seemed imminent. God allowed us to celebrate Christmas together, but by the New Year Mom was back in the hospital. Finally Mom gave up the fight and let God take her "home." I had lived to please my mother. Who was I without my mentor and best friend? Were the dreams I had inherited from my parents really mine? And what about my faith?

After Mom's death I returned to Spain. I loved my life there, but when my mission field council suggested it was time for me to head back to the States, I didn't really fight their decision. Despite the fact that leaving behind my dreams was painful, I knew that I needed to take time to find out who I really wanted to be and what I really wanted to believe in. So I said a tearful good-bye to my childhood dreams and enrolled in the seminary my Bible school piano teacher had told me about.

While attending an American Baptist seminary, I continued the painful process of letting go of my past while struggling to discover who I really wanted to be. At Bible school I had asked, "What do we believe about this?" Now at seminary I was determined to explore my options and remain open to the possibility that new information might change my perspective and thus my interpretation of who God is and how God responds. It wasn't easy to let go of the security of a dogmatic theology that gave clear-cut answers to all of life's questions. I cried a lot as I grieved the loss of the familiar. Just as it took a long time to heal from the pain of losing my mother, so it was a long, slow process to learn to enjoy the new sense of freedom I had as I let go of the confines of conservative theology.

Coming out was another step in the questioning that Ann had begun, a process that took hold while she was in seminary. This is the third stage of her spiritual journey.

I remember very clearly the first time I asked myself if I was "one of them." I was walking down the hall of my dormitory at Bible school. It was Sunday afternoon, and I was thinking about my special friend for the hundredth time that weekend. I was looking forward to Monday morning, when I would get to go to every class, plus meals with her. I thought to myself, "I'm in love!"—but then I thought, "Does that make me a homosexual?" Since I had been taught that homosexuals were perverts whose thoughts and actions were "an abomination unto God," I quickly denied this possibility. I was confident that my feelings were pure and not sinful in any way. Thus, despite the fact that over the next ten years after Bible school I often contemplated the question of my sexual orientation, I never voiced my concerns to anyone.

Finally at age twenty-nine, during my first year at seminary, I told my brother that someone had suggested that my feelings for another woman were homosexual. I expected him to assure me that I didn't need to worry about this accusation. I was sure he would tell me that whoever made that comment was obviously an insecure person who didn't understand that it is completely healthy for two people of the same gender to have a close, emotionally intimate relationship without the relationship being sexual. But instead of downplaying the accusation, he asked me, "So are you a lesbian?" I was shocked! How could my own brother suggest such a thing? Surely he knew that I was a good Christian girl! He went on to tell me that his wife had done a research paper in college about the topic of homosexuality, and that at that time both of them had come to the conclusion that homosexual relationships were not necessarily sinful. After those words of explanation he asked again, "So are you?" I told him to leave me alone. Although I didn't appreciate the way I felt my brother was pushing me to admit to something I didn't even understand, I was later able to thank him for giving me the permission I needed to begin to honestly consider the question.

Soon after this discussion with my brother, I decided to write a research paper for a pastoral counseling class on the subject of the "theology of homosexuality." I did a lot of reading and discussing with some good friends about what I was learning through my study. The question most pressing for me at that point was not, "Am I a lesbian?" Rather, I wanted to come to a conclusion about how I believed God felt about homosexuality. Through my study I began to understand that there are definitely people who are homosexually oriented. Our sexual orientation is not our choice, but, as with any sexual feelings, how we choose to respond to those desires is our choice. I concluded that a God of love would not allow people to be born with sexual desires and then not give them any moral options for positively acting on those desires.

The next quarter I took a class entitled "Human Sexuality in the Context of Pastoral Care." For this class I explored the theology of sexuality in general. As I studied, I began to understand that sex is not just the act of intercourse; rather, my sexuality and my level of comfort with who I am as a sexual being will greatly influence how I respond to many of life's everyday experiences. I concluded that sexual desires are a normal part of who God created humans to be. In fact, sexual desires are a gift from God that we should learn to appreciate, so that we can use these desires for our good and God's glory. Through my study for this class I began the process of letting go of the conservative religious teaching that sexual urges are a curse to be feared and denied.

Finally, that summer, after talking a lot more with my therapist, reading more books by lesbians and gay men, and finding myself again sexually attracted to a girlfriend of mine, I realized it was time for me to admit that I was—probably—homosexually oriented. I didn't feel completely comfortable with this conclusion, though, so I still held on to the remote possibility that maybe I was bisexual. Maybe if I met the "right" man, I could be attracted to men, too. I did visit a gay church in the area, but I just was not emotionally ready to accept what I knew intellectually was probably true. Also, I was not ready to give up all hope of being able to minister in a Baptist church.

When I was growing up, not much was said about the topic of homosexuality, but now in the '90s it had become the hot topic of political and religious discussion. Although I was not yet confident of my own sexuality, I was confident about my theology of homosexuality. I had no doubt that it was sinful for the church to stand in condemnation of men and women who were seeking moral ways to express their homosexual desires. I openly suggested in my seminary classes that my classmates should take the time to get to know Christian men and women who were gay before they dogmatically condemned them. I reminded my friends of the biblical story of Peter and Cornelius. Cornelius was a Gentile who was not a Jewish convert, yet the spirit of God came on him and the rest of the Gentile believers who were worshiping God in his home. When Peter saw these Gentiles speaking in tongues just as Jesus' disciples had done when they received the Holy Spirit, Peter led the Gentiles to the water of baptism. Despite the fact that he had grown up with the theology that all followers of Yahweh God must be circumcised, this experience caused Peter to recognize that God was blessing the faith of these Gentiles. "If, as you get to know gay men and lesbians, you discover that the Fruit of the Spirit is obviously present in their lives," I argued, "then you may find that you can no longer condemn these people who God has apparently chosen to bless." My willingness to speak up on this issue apparently won me the reputation as the resident gay woman on campus.

Eventually, as I began to feel that others had already decided that I was gay, I realized that I needed to get more comfortable with the label. I went back to Holy Covenant, the gay MCC church I had visited once before, and quickly became a regular attender there. I was very nervous at first, still uncertain that I really wanted to identify myself with "these people," but eventually I began to feel at home. It felt good to be accepted for who I was without having to defend myself.

At the same time as I was attending MCC, I was still very active in my American Baptist church. Worship and Sunday school met in the morning at First Baptist, while the worship service at the other church was Sunday evening. Even though I didn't tell anyone at the Baptist church about the other church I was attending, I still found that I was being asked to take a stand on the issue of homosexuality. Somehow the subject of sexual orientation came up in a discussion with my pastor, who admitted that he had not done much research on the topic. When he asked if I could help him to gain a better understanding, I offered to give him a copy of my paper on the theology of homosexuality. I later agreed that he could share my paper with a young woman he was attempting to counsel on the issue. At least six months later a couple of women in my young adult Sunday school class announced to me that they were engaged to one another. I was shocked! I had never imagined that their relationship was anything more than a friendship. What could I say? I tried to congratulate them, but I also wanted to be sure that they had really thought through the decision they had made. Eventually the mother of one of these women also realized that her daughter's relationship with this other woman was more than just a friendship. In an effort to help her mother to understand and not panic, the young woman in my class gave her mother a copy of my paper. The mother then went to the pastor to ask if he was aware of what this liberal seminary student was teaching the young people in our church. Rather than admit that he had been the first one to pass this paper out to one of these young women, he decided it was time to ask me to leave the church. His excuse was that "the church isn't ready to deal with the issue yet." Also, despite the fact that he had given me nothing but positive input and encouragement in the three years I had been attending there, now he claimed that I really didn't have the gifts for church ministry anyway!

I was devastated! I felt as though I had been excommunicated from and deserted by my church family. This was the church I had hoped would ordain me as an American Baptist minister. Now what? I had given up and grieved the loss of so much in the past five years since Mom's death; I didn't know if I could handle letting go of yet another dream for my future!

I was grateful that I already had a new church family to look to for consolation. Thankfully, the pastor at my gay church had also already begun to talk to me about taking more leadership at the church. My first sermon at Holy Covenant was a wonderfully healing experience for me. I shared with my new church family the pain I had experienced as I was asked to leave my other church family and as I faced the prejudice of homophobia. But I also told them how I was claiming God's promise to take all the painful experiences of life and transform them for our good and God's glory. It wasn't long after I preached this sermon that I began to build a relationship with the woman I would eventually marry.

Joanne claims that she knew from the first moment we met that I was the woman she would spend her life with. When she heard that I was a seminary student, though, she spent the next six months "running away" from me. Joanne had been raised Catholic, so when she thought of seminary, she assumed it must be like a convent with nuns and a lot of boring prayers and God talk. Then she heard me preach and began to realize that I had a life outside of the seminary. Finally she asked me out to a church-sponsored dance. I was excited about my first "dyke date," but I was also nervous since I still didn't really know Joanne at all. Well, the date turned out to be a flop because Joanne wasn't done running away yet, but at least it broke the ice for us. After that "date" we began chatting after church each week. Eventually Joanne decided to give me another chance and asked if I wanted to join her in a trip to the zoo. I accepted the invitation, and we had a wonderful day together! Within two weeks we had exchanged class rings and become "girlfriends." I guess it was our common love for animals that broke down the walls between us and allowed us to enjoy the fun-loving side of each other.

Dating Joanne was wonderfully exciting for me! I was finally having many of the experiences most people have as teenagers but that I had never had because I was so out of touch with my sexuality. I was thrilled to know that I was finally falling in love with a woman who wasn't afraid to love me back. Yet building a relationship with Joanne was also a horribly scary experience for me because I knew that now there was no turning back. I could never again deny my sexual orientation. I also knew that in order to live with integrity, I would have to be honest with others about my relationship with Joanne. Did this mean that if I was ever going to be the pastor of a church, it would have to be a gay church? I assumed it probably did, but I hoped against hope that it would not be my only option.

Ann's relation with Joanne grew, as did her own self-awareness, bringing her into the fourth stage.

Joanne and I were engaged just a few weeks after I completed my last seminary class. I graduated with my Master of Divinity in May and said my vows to Joanne the following February. Joanne's mom stood with her, and two of my brothers and their families stood with me to show their support of our commitment to one another. Friends from seminary, from Joanne's bowling league, and, of course, church friends also came to our Holy Union to help us celebrate our love for one another.

I never expected my dad to be present as I said my vows to another woman, but I had hoped that he would continue to be polite and welcoming toward Joanne. I was disappointed when I came out to him and found that he was completely unwilling to show any loving kindness toward my life partner. Joanne and I had been to visit in his home before he knew that we were a couple, but now that he knew that we were "living in sin," Joanne was not welcome. He said that he must show me "tough love" so as not to do anything that might encourage my "sinful lifestyle." He gathered all his friends to pray that his "prodigal daughter," who was living as a "lisbian" and consorting with a bunch of "homos," would come home as a repentant sinner. They prayed that God would do whatever it took to bring me to see the error of my ways, even if it took the death of Joanne! I suggested some books my dad and stepmother could read that would help them to understand my journey to come to terms with my sexuality, but they refused to read any liberal book that did not condemn "sin as sin." I talk with my father very seldom anymore because every time we talk, he feels the need to witness to me about my sinful ways. I have tried to show Dad that my faith in God is as real today as it was when I went to Spain as a missionary, but his theology will not allow him to believe that. He tells me that I am wrong to expect him to "compromise his faith."

Soon after I graduated from seminary, I began to work at my present full-time position as administrative assistant at Holy Covenant. Our copastors had just resigned and only had a few days to give me some basic "training" before they moved on to their new positions. The role I fill here is far more than just church secretary. I work closely with both the board of directors and the deacons. I help the board moderator to put together the agenda for board meetings, and I keep in contact with the chair of each committee to check on how projects are progressing. I also meet with the deacons each week to plan worship services and discuss pastoral care needs. I even preach once a month!

I think there's a good possibility that when we get a new pastor, I will sign up with our denomination as a student clergy. I know there would be plenty of opportunity for me to minister in this denomination, but I'm really not sure that I want to pastor a gay church. Most churches within the Metropolitan Community Church do not have much of a ministry to families because most gay couples don't have children. I miss ministry to a variety of ages—from infancy to elderly. I have never felt that my calling is to minister to the gay community but rather to help the "straight" community to understand and accept us. I'm also not sure that I am happy with the political structure of the MCC. I think I'm Baptist at heart. I know there isn't much opportunity for ministry for an openly gay woman in a Baptist church, but maybe I could work some other job to support myself and be involved in a Baptist church in a lay capacity.

I have no clear sense of direction right now as to "what I'm going to be when I grow up." Its kind of scary to be thirty something with school loans to pay and still have no career. I feel confident, though, that eventually it will become clear to me how I can use my gifts and abilities to adequately support myself while also being involved in some form of ministry. I just don't know if my job will also be my ministry.

"Coming to terms with my sexuality has transformed my life," Ann says, as she explains the most recent developments in her sense of self.

Coming to terms with my sexuality has transformed my life in many ways. Now that I am able to take pride in my sexuality, I am a much more confident, outgoing, and fun-loving person. I am also much more open-minded as I recognize that often new life experiences will change our point of reference and thus lead to a new set of conclusions. I no longer need clear-cut answers to all of life's questions; nor do I believe that if I have not won a battle, I must have lost it. Life's ambiguities take away some of our sense of security in knowing what to expect, but they also keep us on our toes, so that we do not become complacent or self-satisfied.

The placement director from the American Baptist denominational headquarters came to visit on campus at our seminary once a year. I met with her briefly each year. By my final year at seminary she had a good understanding of my struggle to live with integrity, yet find a place where I could use my gifts and abilities to serve the Lord. She didn't have any answers for me, but she was able to offer encouragement. She said that she was able to see a distinct difference in me from "who you were three years ago to who you are now." Then I was shy, obviously lacking in self-confidence, and very serious-minded (some might even say boring). Yet by my final year at seminary I was beginning to live as though I really believed that life is a gift from God that we are meant to enjoy. I had also begun to take pride in myself and appreciate the gifts and abilities God has given me.

Before seminary I had been taught to separate life into compartments and to accept certain parts of life as gifts to be enjoyed and others as curses to be controlled. Our spirituality and our intellect were gifts that we must nurture, while our emotions, our physical bodies, and our sexual desires were, generally speaking, curses that we must learn to control. Through my studies and through therapy I began to come to understand that all that we are—every desire that we have—is neither good nor bad. Our desires become sinful or blessed as we choose how to respond to those desires. We are even responsible for our response to those circumstances in life that we cannot control. A response of loving kindness, respect, and honestly will generally result in blessing. On the other hand, a hateful, judgmental, dishonest, or abusive response will generally become a curse.

I believe that in order to live up to our full potential, we must be honest with ourselves about who we are and learn to take pride in ourselves. As long as I denied my sexual desires, I was unable to take responsibility and decide what to do with them. Once I was honest with myself

Ann (right) *and Joanne: "The conclusion I eventually came to was that I would be better able to focus on serving God if my needs for intimacy were being met. I did not choose to be homosexually oriented, but I did choose to seek a morally responsible way to respond to it."*

and took the time to understand my desires, I was able to give them back to God and ask God to help me to use them "for God's glory and my good." It was also important at that point that I should give myself the freedom to consider my options and choose the one that I believed would be best for me. I had to weigh the possible negative and positive consequences of seeking a same-sex life partner versus the consequences of probably remaining single all my life. The conclusion I eventually came to was that I would be better able to focus on serving God if my needs for intimacy were being met. I did not choose to be homosexually oriented, but I did choose to seek a morally responsible way to respond to it.

As I have faced prejudice towards homosexuality, I have come to realize that our calling as Christians is not to convert the people we believe are sinners but rather to love all people. I have repeatedly asked my father, "Dad, why can't you just love me and trust the Holy Spirit with the outcome?" I know that my father believes that homosexuality is sinful, but our difference of opinion on this issue is not the wedge that separates us. Rather, the tension between my father and I is due to the fact that I feel judged and condemned by him. I am angry with my father for never taking the time to really listen to my "story" or to attempt to understand my journey. I am disgusted by his ignorance about what it means to be homosexually oriented and with his insensitivity in referring to his own daughter as a "homo." I am offended that he insists on assuming that I must somehow fit into his stereotypical ideas about the "homosexual lifestyle." Despite the fact that Dad regularly tells me that he loves me, I do not feel loved because he has made no effort to try to understand me. My spiritual journey has taught me the importance of showing love as we listen, watch, and wait. If we approach life with an open mind and give the Holy Spirit time to work, it is possible that we will discover that we are the ones who need to change.

Vincent: Being Rocked by God

Vincent, a native of Australia, grew up in a family—he had three sisters—he calls "rigorously Catholic," and he suffered physical and sexual abuse both as a child and later as a seminarian. In his vocation he has served in Australia, Japan, and now in the Chicago area.

Vincent is particularly honest and eloquent as he speaks of his journey. His pain, joys, and challenges are shared with equal frankness as he faces questions about his relationship to his community, the church, and God and what road is most healthy and has the most integrity for him. Ministry, for him, must reflect who he is as a fully human, gay man, and so he weaves together threads of self-acceptance, anger at the church, and his sense of calling to create a vision for his future vocation.

In this piece of Vincent's story, one can see three themes. In this first one, he describes a childhood in which the church and God were solace and comfort away from the abusive and lonely environment he found elsewhere. As his internal life deepened and matured, Vincent came to face his homosexuality and the dilemma of whether healing for him is found in relationship and intimacy or in community within the church. The evolving shape of his ministry and his relationship with God are the second and third themes that I have chosen to highlight here. Let's begin with Vincent's experience of God in the warm fog one day when he was a young child.

I remember when I was ten or eleven, I was outside playing in winter's evening, probably about four o'clock in the afternoon. And heavy fog used to come in, in that part of Australia in winter, and this came in so heavily that I couldn't see the garage or the kitchen on either side of me. The thing that was important for me was that I wasn't frightened because fear has always been a dominant emotion in my life. And I wasn't frightened. And I remember I was looking up into it and saying, "God is just like this; God is there, powerful and warm" 'cause the fog was warm, and then I remember giggling and going back and playing. I didn't make anything of it at the time. I didn't know then what I know now: that my home life was very strict and very punitive, and I think religion, for me, was the solace; it was a safe, comforting place.

I'd say my family was rigorously Catholic. Dad and Mum still go to church every morning; we had family prayer every evening; our family life was built around the church. In some ways I'm still curious about quite what that means. I guess in the postwar days in Australia, the Catholic church was starting to organize trade unionism and that sort of thing, and it was very much a working man's party or working man's religion. We have the Knights of the Southern Cross, who used to protect people who were getting fired because of religious reasons. And Dad was active in that. And that became a political party, and Dad was active in that in kind of a grassroots way, but he never went for politics. And then that got all mixed up with communism, you know, crazy thinking, so he pulled out, and that was that.

In my home there were strong messages about sexuality. I remember when I was about three, I had this little friend next door, a couple doors down, and we used to play with each other's bodies, genitals and that sort, and I was given one Christmas or birthday a little tent. I just got a vague memory of my being in this tent one day with Craig, and we were playing with each other, and the next minute the tent was just ripped out of the ground and burned. And there was nothing ever said. And looking back now, I think that's what that was all about.

And then later on when my eldest sister was developing, I saw her—I don't know how this happened—coming out of the bath, and her breasts were starting to develop, and I said, "Oh, look at her titties" or something like that. She was mortified and told Dad, and he really stuck into me. Worse than that, he took me into Mum and Dad's bedroom, where there

"And I remember I was looking up into [the fog] and saying, 'God is just like this; God is there, powerful and warm' 'cause the fog was warm, and then I remember giggling and going back and playing. I didn't make anything of it at the time. I didn't know then what I know now: that my home life was very strict and very punitive, and I think religion, for me, was the solace; it was a safe, comforting place."

was a little oratory and sat me down in front of it and told me how ashamed Mary and God and all the heavenly court would be because of what I'd done and I should not do that; and he never, never beat me on that occasion, which intrigues me. But he really frightened me, and so that area was taboo. I don't know why he didn't beat me that time. I don't. He's just a curious man. And my relationship is not resolved with him yet.

I was very severely physically abused all through my childhood. I would be beaten every day by Dad. He had a bad temper. He was also working, sometimes twelve hours a day. He would come home and Mum—I don't think she ever quite liked me—and she would tell Dad what I'd done wrong that day, and I would get beaten up for something that I had done. The words that sum it up for me now are that the only, *the only,* certainties I had yet about myself then were that I was going to be beaten. I didn't know where, and I didn't know what for, but I knew I'd be beaten. And I can see that God was the only constant there that was going to be comforting.

For Vincent, church was a "place where [he] was getting strokes," in sharp contrast to the rest of his world, that is, his home and his school.

I was an altar boy and served liturgies. It was taken for granted, I think. I'm not sure of this, but I think it was possibly more religiously religious for me than for my sisters. Dad pushed me into being an altar boy. In those days you had to learn Latin, which I used to spend lots of hours crying over 'cause I could never get the damn thing right. And I became very good at it. I enjoyed being up there; I think it was a place again where I was getting strokes, and I also felt it was in the area that I could truly do well. The messages at home were that I was an embarrassment to the family 'cause I was effeminate—I was very sensitive; I would cry very easily—whereas up there I used to train the others, so it was the area of competence that I liked.

High school was, for me, a very difficult and lonely time and place. I was at a Catholic boarding school, some three hundred miles from home. I was teased for being effeminate and "on good terms" with the priests who were teachers and dorm masters. I found it very easy and comforting to spend long periods in the chapel, where I had a sense of peace and acceptance. I feel this period developed a quiet "interiority" in me.

My nickname in high school, for five years, was "Queen," "Queen Dean." So I was different, I guess. I had not known I was gay at that point. I don't think I had much notion of being sexual, but I wasn't happy. I hated being at boarding school; I think it was a grace since it got me out of home, but it wasn't much of a trade, you know.

I think I was one of those kids who always wanted to be a priest. Actually, I think, looking back, I didn't want be a priest so much as I wanted to live in a religious environment. I always knew that; I always told everyone that; everyone knew that. I remember when we went away—the last year of high school, I think—on a trip to the local seminary and all the other guys in the class said, "Yeah, you will fit in here," and I thought, "Yes, I will fit in." I knew it was one of those givens—I am beginning to say now, "Let's have another look at all of this," but then it was a very smooth transition. My mother was against my going in so soon from school. She wasn't against my being a priest as much as not having time out. That always intrigued me. Dad never said a word. I think he was proud. And he told me that if ever I wanted to leave, that was fine by him and always to come home. He used to go to the seminary, and whenever my superiors came by, he would always get them aside and say, "How is it going?" I resented that a lot because I thought I'd left home now—leave me lead my own life. I think, for me, joining a religious community was a really smart way of leaving home. It was probably the only thing I could do that they wouldn't have been overinterfering with. And I knew they would be proud of me for doing it.

What stands out for me about seminary are the relationships I had with my peers, which was a wonderful experience, really. It was the first time, there, that I really felt at home; I'd never felt that anywhere before. I was with a group of guys—we were about twenty-five, and it was still before the place fell apart, so there were still twenty-four in my year—and I got on well with almost every one of them; they liked me and I liked them for the most part. I was given jobs that had responsibility, and I found I could do them. I was a leader, and I never knew I had those qualities before. People weren't calling me effeminate; they were just enjoying me, and that was a really lovely time, a real change from high school. And I found that I was quite intelligent, which I'd never known before either. By the time I got into the actual core theology course, which is usually a few years along the line, I was doing extremely well. And I realized I enjoyed doing this stuff. That was a wonderful experience.

Yet at the same time that intellectually I was thriving, I was emotionally dead. The last four years of my seminary were hell. I had a superior who used to be after me, literally, and he always said that I was hiding something. I never knew quite what he was after except that I knew it was something dark and dangerous. And I also knew that I was very attracted to other guys in the seminary, and if I had half a chance, I would wrestle with them, and I'd get aroused and get terrified by that. I had been sexually abused as a three-year-old as well. As I understand it now, I just shut off any sense of sexual feeling. I didn't know what I was doing; that wrestling was sexual, but really funny things kept on happening, and I was frightened of it. I knew that. Anyway, he finally said to me one night, "I think you're afraid of being homosexual." I nearly died, and it was some relief, after a day or so, that it was finally named and out. Then he took it on himself to say, "I don't think you are," and so he sexually abused me for four years. Masturbation, fondling me, getting me to do that to him: the last time he did it was the night before I left to go on my first appointment, which is amazing, really.

And it even surprises me that I know I split off part of myself to cope. I didn't know at the time, but my spiritual director told me a couple years after that he really thought I was going to have a breakdown the year after I left, and I think he's probably right.

In his first appointment as a parish priest in Australia, Vincent was "adopted" by a couple with a young family.

Now I think this family recognized there was something wrong. And I think they liked me as a person. And they welcomed me to their family. I told them about this guy, and they were a very dear couple, they had four boys, and they both said to me, "We trust you with our boys, and will you babysit for us?" And that was such an act of affirmation. I had no sexual feelings for the kids, but I was thinking everything bad about myself.

They, too, used to say, "We don't think you are homosexual, but it doesn't matter," so that helped. I think that was my first experience of being just loved. And I bloomed in that—I mean, it saved me from having a breakdown. It also stirred up some feelings—I find this still happens in me; when I get close to someone, I get in touch with a rage, and I just explode everywhere. As I got close to the wife, so also did my issue of being "swallowed up" by her grow. I eventually found this too much and withdrew from the relationship. I still have this issue, though I think I'm growing better at dealing with it. I see it now more clearly as a "fear of the feminine" more than being frightened of women.

As Vincent describes it, his coming-out process has spanned many years and continents. After being in parish communities in Australia, he was transferred to Japan.

I think I was unconsciously wrestling with my homosexuality at seminary; I don't think I consciously decided to wrestle with it until I went to Japan. In my coming-out history, the first point, I think, would be this guy saying, "I think you're afraid of being homosexual" and the relief I had around that. Then I think the abuse shut the lid on my sexual feelings, homo or hetero. Then my spiritual director when I left the seminary said to me, "So what if you're gay?" And I remember feeling tremendous relief that it wasn't going to be a big issue for him. It was for me. And I never talked about it with him after that. And then it wasn't until 1982 or 3 that I really knew I was gay, and I needed to talk about this with someone. And again, I had found an older man—forty years or something—who was a Presbyterian minister in Japan, and he was just wonderful. It wasn't a big deal with him. He had studied with people who were gay, and he was more interested in me than my being gay, and his acceptance of homosexuality helped me to accept it. The Lord was damn slow in giving me someone. [Laughs]

Up until that point I was not even masturbating. I was having a lot of wet dreams, but I wasn't masturbating. The other phase that is most important to me is when I came here to Chicago; I was still on the teeter-totter—maybe I am, maybe I'm not, I really think I am, but maybe I'm not. I knew that was one of the issues I needed to work on. And I think it's a delightful way that it worked out: as I started into the program, all the abuse started to come up, and I hadn't known that I had been abused. I knew the pieces, but I'd never put abuse onto it. I spent most of the year working through that through therapy and spiritual direction. And that's when I realized, as I was dealing with the abuse, that the orientation just stopped being an issue. I knew I was gay, I was feeling finer, finer, and finer about that as I worked with the abuse, and I still am working on the abuse issue. But the orientation, it's not even a question. It's a part of my identity, and also, it's part of my way of relating with God. I know God. The Vincent God knows is a gay man. And that feels really comfortable. For the Vatican or anyone else to tell me I'm bad, I know I'm not, and there's an anger behind it which feels really nice.

Vincent lives in Chicago now and works with religious and others who are studying to be spiritual directors. Even though he lives outside of his Australian religious community, he is still officially connected to it. As Vincent has matured in his sense of who he is as a gay man and a priest, he has been exploring whether his vocation includes remaining in community or not. At the center of this discernment process is the question of whether celibacy or an intimate relationship is more healing for him. What follows are his reflections about these questions.

The support of a religious community was very important in my earlier years, but it is very insignificant at this stage of my life. And that's a cause of concern 'cause I'm not too sure where my future lies. Through my appointments I got weaned from that anyway. In the seminary I was in a community of about fifty people for eight years. And then I was in Australia for five years in parish areas; communities of three and four, I think, were the biggest size. And then I went to Japan for eight years after that, and I was in communities of two and then on my own. So now I have very little emotional sense of these people being important to me, and there's something going on there which I haven't quite figured out yet.

Where I'm at right now is I have to see whether I am actually living that before I've made the decision. I think the pattern of what happens to me is that my wisdom seems to be ahead of my words. I find myself doing what I need to do before I realize it. And that first intrigued me this last year or so: I'm actually living it now, without having taken any legal steps to separate from my community. Am I doing that, or am I having a break from it? I'm not sure yet. I made that the focus of my retreat over the summer. And the message was very clear: it's not yet. Other issues came up, you know, kind of left field, that I wasn't expecting, and I came away none the wiser for my future, but with a real peace that it's not yet, and I think I'll be able to look at that when it is time. I'll be just fine until then.

That's the truth; I am discovering I am quite fine with all that. My family is not, and my community is certainly not. But I am. I find that it's a fine place to be. It's mystery, and it's uncertain, and I'm not going to rush into anything that I don't know. My community is not pestering me. This July will be the end of my contract with my community and my organization. That's why I made it the focus of the retreat.

I have a new superior. And the man who was elected, who took over January 1st, was not a man I was very comfortable with. And then about late March I got this letter to say that he was coming through in two weeks' time. So that really panicked me. As I told you, my original arrangement back in Australia was to leave the States at the end of July. Now I decided I wasn't going to do that, so with his arrival I let all of that from July back up to March, back up to two weeks' time. I really struggled with how much I am comfortable telling him. I'm angry with him from a lot of past stuff, so I really don't think he deserves to know any of it. And the other part of the struggle was, the more I would tell him, the more he's going to understand and be able to say, "Do what you need to do." So that was a dilemma. I worked around that and eventually decided I needed to do what was only best for me. And I came to a lot of peace about that. When he came, I sat down and told him my whole story, including that I wasn't going back to Australia. It would be a foolish thing for me to leave just to be in another place. And I said, for me, the issue at the moment is my health. And I was prepared to take a leave of absence if it came to that. He said he did not think that needed to be the case. He had no idea of my history. Of course, he zeroed in immediately on the sexual abuse from the seminary days. That caught his attention. And we talked a lot about that. And eventually, he was kind of okay and kind of not okay about my being gay. He was making statements like,

"Are you celibate?" and "Isn't it nice when gay men can be celibate in the community?" And I was thinking, "Hey, you know, there's a lot of heterosexual men who I've wondered about," but the focus stayed where I needed it to stay. And eventually he said, "Do what you need to do"—which was really nice. And that's where I am now. I have to write a formal letter to his council saying what I want. Just last night I said in the letter that for me, the focus in what I'm discerning is what style of life now is going to be health promoting and healing for me. I don't know the answer to that. But I do know that I need to be faithful to where I've found God. And that's through coming to grips with my orientation and through developing a lifestyle and relationships where there's healing taking place. I don't know whether I will choose celibacy. And I'm not in a relationship, so it's hard; I feel a need to have more experience in a relationship before I can decide. That was the fruit of my retreat this year.

That's at the heart of it, for me, in the struggles: community or not community, religious community or relationship. Where am I going to be growing as a person more? Is it going to be in a one-on-one relationship, or is it going to be as a member of this religious community? If I go back to community, then what happens to a partner? I don't have much difficulty with poverty, but where does realistic sexual behavior fit in there? What with my woundedness in that precise area, I'm not all that sure that healing is in celibacy for me. I know my sexual relationship with Norman, and those other guys, have been really important. Right now, it's not a guilt thing. It just makes too much sense, what I'm doing. But if I decide to go back, I feel a need to really look at that. I don't know the answer to that. I really think someday I will. I sure as hell hope to.

This lady who was my director on the retreat really stretched my boundaries—I'm rather black and white; I think that's the legacy of a lot of abused people—and she kept on saying, "Are you sure it's as simple as that?" Now that's new thinking for me. She says the either/or nature of this choice is a very male-stereotypical way of thinking about religions, about souls. And I just don't know about that. In some ways there is an either/or, I think, for married people or for a person in a relationship; an open relationship doesn't quite do it for me. And I don't feel threatened by her comment, but I really feel there's something that intrigues me. She was positing a new model of religious life, which maybe is what I'm seeking. I don't know.

Vincent had been in a significant relationship with another man, Norman, when we first met, but that had ended by the time we came back together a few months later. Through this relationship he learned a great deal about himself and God. He says, "As I have risked intimacy, I have come to know an intimate God."

I terminated my relationship about the end of October, which was pretty painful. Intimacy is a difficult, challenging, painful, and wonder-filled road for me to walk along, and I feel I have miles to travel yet. And at the same time, I know that as I have risked intimacy, I have come to know an intimate God, who is within me and who, at the same time, is much bigger than I am.

I've learned lots about myself in the relationships I've had. I learned how lonely I am. I've learned what a tender heart I've got. I think I've learned how terribly frightened I am of getting close to someone and being rejected. Not of them saying, "I'm going to leave you." I don't have an abandonment issue, as such; I think I've been abandoned for most of my life. I'm frightened I'm going to be found out as being bad inside, again. That's very painful—when people get angry with me now, it hurts, somewhere in here. It's taken me a long time to name the wound there, where I've been told by Dad for so long how bad I am. So there's a fear around that. I'm also afraid of committing, of really giving my whole heart to another person, because what if I see someone else that I like, that kind of fickleness. I think I'm learning that I can be vulnerable with someone that I really like, and I can be very challenging to them. I'm not satisfied with having it always being a one-way street. I really go after the other person. That was an issue with my former lover. It was really nice; I really liked the way we worked it through on one particular occasion. I remember challenging him on not sharing a couple things with me, and he said to me: "It's not that I don't want to tell you; it's just that I get frightened after I've told you. I don't know what's going on inside of you." And I really knew what he meant, and I knew that doesn't stop me anymore. It used to, but it doesn't stop me anymore. I'm not frightened that

that's going to break me up. And I celebrate in that 'cause that's real growth for me. It's taken a long time to get to that point, not to be frightened of how I feel.

Spirituality and sexuality are intricately intertwined for Vincent.

For me, I am talking about my spirituality all the time, you know. I don't understand this, but for me sexuality and spirituality are like that: when I'm talking about one of them, I'm really talking about the other, too. That's my inner experience also; it's not either/or. When I'm explaining them, I put them out. We're doing orientation here at the moment, and last week I told my story to the people here, and that's what I told them about. I said, "I want to talk to you about my secrets and my gifts, and that's God and sexuality." Both secret and gift, both of them are.

Let me start with Norman. One of the real ways Norman gifted me was in being able to argue and get angry and letting him get angry with me. I just knew I was much more comfortable with him than other human beings, and that certainly affects the way I am here. I know people who are sitting in that chair now, who I see in my work as a spiritual director, don't pour as much shit on me as people in past years would. I call them on that, and his tenderness helped me be much more gentle to people when I say, "This is your issue, you know." So it's this kind of a strengthening inside me that I sense has made me a more whole person, I think.

In terms of God, well, let me tell you an incident from my retreat. I went out there with the focus of Vincent's future, but God gave me all these abuse issues, and I really was pissed off about that. I remember saying to my director: "This is not fair. I've spent five years working on this, and I wanted something different." And she was neat; she said: "Well, I don't blame you. How about focusing a little bit for two hours tomorrow on the abuse issues and then see where it goes from there?" So we spent the rest of the week on it, but toward the end of the week I remember getting angry again, and I said to God: "I really do think this was unfair. You still haven't given me any clarity about my future." And while I was in that kind of prayer time, I remembered this scene from *Fried Green Tomatoes,* when Ruth dies. Izzy's sitting on the bed crying, and the old black woman comes up to Izzy and grabs her from behind and rocks her. And I had a real sense that that's what God was doing with me. The words that came were, "No, it's not fair, and Vincent, this is your story; this is who you are." I feel that's where God and I are at the moment, that God's rocking me and also holding me quite firmly. This is where you are. And that's okay; I can wrestle with that. And at times I can sink into being rocked, so there's an act of passive tension going on with God all the time. And see, that's why I think it's a bit like that fog experience: that it's there, it's overwhelming, and yet at the time it's also very tangible. But I can't control it; I can't grasp it.

I guess I'm playing around in my mind with things like, Has my acceptance of my orientation changed, and how has that changed my self-understanding and my understanding of God? I don't know. That's wandering around inside of me; it's important to me right now, I think. There's a richness in there that I suspect is in not only every gay person, but probably in every person who's in a minority group and comes to grips with that. I don't know; I just have a sense in my own life that the more comfortable I get with my orientation, two things seem to happen: I become more angry and determined not to be put down, and the other thing is I have a sense of the expansiveness of God along with that. These really are human prejudices; this is not how God sees things at all. I don't know; it's something which I hesitate to say, it touches on arrogance, really, but I just have a sense that that kind of understanding of God and how God sees us is one of the fruits of the struggle of being a minority. And I guess coming to grips with my orientation continually stretches me to become bigger minded, broader minded. I think I have a greater acceptance and understanding of some of the things I hear on the telephone line; I caught myself off-guard the other night—I can't even remember what this person's particular persuasion was—but I remember at the end thinking, "Most Catholic priests wouldn't feel okay about that. That's not what we're trained to feel about." I like that part of me that could put the details aside and really try to live with the person, and I thought, "I haven't learned that; that's a gift that's come to me, trying to be open with my own self, too." I really am on the fringes of the church. And I'm teaching here, working here, which is on the fringes of most church places. And my community is Dignity, which is not exactly at the heart of mother church. I feel quite okay there. I'm filled with joy being there, you know. But yesterday I had to speak down here at the local parish church about spiritual direction, and I thought, "You are lovely people, but you're not my community." The pastor—he's a great man, I think he's gay, and I don't know that he knows that—he's got this $10,000 project at the moment fixing up his front porch or something, and I was thinking, "I used to get into that, but no more; that's not the way life is for me anymore."

My prayer is, "Accept my sexual feeling." What I'm thinking of goes back to what I was sharing with you just a minute ago. I find my prayer, at the moment, is, "Help me to accept my sexual feelings and my lonely feelings as not being something bad, but something that You are in, and I need Your help to find someone to love." So I am struggling. Even that prayer tells me that there is still a lot of homophobia in me happily at work, that I'm not comfortable with the feelings that I've got, the desires, the longings. I think a big part of me is not yet "there"; I'm still working on it. And I find myself wanting the grace to say, "Vincent, they are as good as any other feelings I've got." I struggle with that. And so I think part of that struggle is of a God who's really very nonjudgmental. Who simply is part of everything that's going on. It's not this is the good, and that's the bad, and you've got to get rid of this. It's a strange dichotomy that I don't have any trouble holding all this. Until I tell someone else, then I think, whoa. But my image of God and my experience of God is of some energy, some life force, who is very, very broad. And at the same time, the more I accept that, the more I feel an intimacy with God down here. The broader that gets, the more focused it gets in here. It's curious that that would be true of my experience. And it's not subjective; it's not personal. I'm finding the more I honor that experience—and this is a new experience—I really am moved, and I feel a real sadness. It's not simply, "This is wrong; this is unjust" (that's part of it), but I want to cry when I see that sitting out there. Like I just went for a walk along the lake this morning, and there was this guy—I don't know how old he is; I can't tell anymore; their lifestyle changes—he had all his belongings in about four garbage bags, and I just had to stop and think, "I don't know how I'd be if that was me."

I had another thought as we were talking, in terms of my own self-acceptance versus community. I was talking with a guy last night on the phone, and he said one of his goals in life is to get married—he's a gay man—to get married and have children. And I said to him, "Are you talking about marrying a woman or a man?" And he laughed, and he said, "It would be sinful for me to marry a man." And it really struck me. The simplicity in the way he said that. I think one of the devils I struggle with at the moment, in the loneliness especially, is a desire not to choose celibacy because I'm frightened of my sexuality. I lived that for forty years. I can see it now. I think when I'm sick of looking for someone: "I've tried the bars; that doesn't work. I've tried The [Lesbian and Gay Community] Center; that hasn't worked. I've tried Dignity; that hasn't worked. I've tried Frontrunners [a group of runners and walkers in the gay and lesbian community]; that hasn't worked. I think I'll just go back to community; I'm sick of looking." So, I think, for me, and I think, especially for gay men who have been sexually abused, the sexuality-spirituality lines get muddled. I have to really be aware that my fear of sexuality, that's been my wound—that I don't run away from that by going back to community, by being celibate again. I really have a strong sense—and I don't think I can say this very publicly because I feel very frightened to say that—but I think I have to: healing for me is going into the wound and being sexual. And not in celibacy. But the question is, For how long? Is that a lifestyle, or is that a phase of my journey? Yes. And I need someone to do that with. I can't do it alone. That's probably the simplest I could put it. Whenever I get close to someone, that part comes up, and I find myself telling myself all the bad things about this person, and it's usually because I'm frightened.

It just occurred to me that I somehow suspect that the more I enjoy being gay, the more reason I can let go of that official stuff. It's almost as if the more I enjoy being gay and accept that, it puts me a long way from the center of things. So the "duty" thing is not as heavy as it was. And that's really significant for me because I was for very many years at the heart of all that. I've got a lot of embarrassment, more embarrassment than guilt, around some of the things I did as a pastor. I was perfectly correct. But I know I wouldn't do it now. And I think accepting my own truth has been a big part of that.

Vincent's evolving sense of himself and God has clearly had an impact on where he sees himself going in his ministry—including possibly working with the gay or HIV communities. For the last several years he has been volunteering at a local gay and lesbian community service agency, The Center. He has also been worshiping with Dignity, a group of lesbian and gay Catholics.

I see myself continuing in some form of ministry. Making big bucks doesn't draw me. I want financial security, but going and working in the corporate world is not part of my self-understanding. I think I really am discovering a giftedness in this area, in the work I'm doing here. That's not only self-discovery; that's being told to me. I'm slowly learning that from different people every year, so there's truth there, you know. So it's in this kind of area that I'd want to stay in; now I don't know whether it's going to be always with these type of people, people on sabbatical, the spiritual directors.

I was just chatting briefly with a leader at The Center the other night. I said to him then that I've been at The Center four years now, and when I went to The Center, I went for me. I knew I had no knowledge of this gay world, and I was curious. I wanted to meet other guys; I was hungry. And I worked for a good three years on administration, and now this past year I've been on the AIDS hotline, and I had to do that to gain experience and to expand my boundaries and meet my fear of my homophobia. And I just had the sense now that I'm starting to turn a corner, I can give something to The Center now, too. I have no idea what that's going to be, but I just think that I'm not going now so much for me as I'm going for them. I can do something for them, you know, which is a little different from Dignity. I'm going to Dignity for me at the moment. I have no taste at all for any involvement in ministry. I hate saying mass, and their group seems a really comfortable place to meet. I know that I've got no desire to minister, that I need to be ministered to, and they're comfortable in a way most church groups wouldn't be with an actual priest. But for The Center, it's different. I feel comfortable in the gay community generally. And it's interesting, for me, anyway, the more comfortable I feel, the less I seem to go up to the North Side now just to go to the bars. The first three or four years I would go up every week, Friday / Saturday nights, with a couple of friends. Now, Norman didn't like going to the bars, and I felt okay with that.

The other piece I want to mention is that on the hotline, especially, I'm noticing that whenever I do a shift, I come away from that feeling really energized, really thinking, "I could be with those people, whether it was someone who was afraid of going through a test or someone who's found out that they have AIDS." I had one last week who's HIV positive and is terrified of passing it on to their grandchildren because they sleep in the same bed. I'm just intrigued by that area and the energy it has for me. I don't know that I want to move into AIDS ministry, and yet there's something about that that's saying: "There's something here for you. That doesn't have to be Chicago; that can be anywhere." I'm wondering if serving gay people is part of that, if that's what God's got in mind. I've gone from hiding in fear to openness, and now I'm comfortable knowing that I've got something which these people could use.

I wonder whether it's the gay community, some part of the gay community, which is going to challenge my hiddenness about being gay again. I admire the full-time staff people at The Center. Everyone must know they're gay, whereas everyone here knows my orientation, but people back home necessarily don't know. But that could be one more step. Most people in my community don't know. But I've come out to my superiors. I've told them that's why I'm here, that's one of the areas I'm working on, and they have different degrees of being comfortable with it. I've had a lot of understanding, I think, more than I did before.

Things happen every now and again, and it's usually like a comment someone on the hotline will feedback to me, when I think, "I am moving more and more into this area of working with gay people and those with HIV." And I don't know concretely; it's more like psychologically I'm moving into it more than I am actually physically changing a lifestyle. I'm very energized by doing that sort of work, by being with those people. I think of examples: one lady on the hotline was sharing some really sad stuff with me about her HIV status, and we talked for thirty, forty minutes, which is long, and at the end, she said to me, "I'm really grateful that you could be with me through all this." She said, "I could never tell a priest what I told you." And I thought, "That's saying something to me about my presence," and I didn't say, "Well, honey, guess what." But it really was a gift to me; it affirmed something.

I think being gay has made me and continues to make me a more human person. I have this kind of sense, every now and again, when I sit down quietly and I get in touch with a softness inside of me that I really like, that it's a very sacred place. And I know when I'm sitting one on one with somebody, when I can find that place and just be there, that really sacred things happen both in me and in that other person. I feel uncomfortable saying, "Because I've chosen to walk this journey, I've become a better minister." I hope good ministers are such because they're honest human beings. To me, that's the important part. It's really important for me to find God's choice and desire for me is to be the human person that God made me, and everything else is quite secondary.

Conclusion

THESE twelve men and women, and the other fourteen who were also part of this study, are my teachers. In fact, I believe they have a great deal to offer *all* of us, whether we are academics studying spiritual development, clerics trying to foster spiritual growth, or others intensely on our own spiritual journeys. Their lessons are about reclaiming a spirituality that was denied, forgotten, or hidden; about reflected and evolving faith; about the pain of being excluded and the grace, power, and growth that emerge from the deepest sorrow and struggle; and about anger and reconciliation. Their stories are poignantly honest, and they reflect, cumulatively, an enormous amount of work "breaking the frame" that has been constructed in our society around a prescribed picture of what it means to be spiritual.

I have been fortunate in that I have lived with these life stories—and the compelling questions they raise—for four years. In the course of doing this research, I have spent hours listening to these individuals in person and then relistening to the tapes; I have had the opportunity to read the transcripts of each individual interview over and over again. Each time I come back to them—as a social psychologist, a gay man, and someone on a spiritual journey himself—I am left with the same messages: we need to write our own stories, *particularly* when they challenge our society's dominant understandings of how the world works. We need to tell our stories, to share their uniqueness and particularities as well as those elements that are more common and make us human. And we need to listen to and honor each other's stories, to know that there is more than one way to be spiritual.

This trilogy of writing, telling, and listening works together to forge our lives and our spirituality within a larger society that is going through its own transformations. We live at a time when many are bringing into question the norms and values we, as a culture, have taken for granted for a very long time. David Nicoll (1984, 4) writes:

> The heart of the matter is this. We are in mid-stride between an old and new era, but we have not yet found our way. We know the old no longer works; the new is not yet formed clearly enough to be believed. As many Indian tribes have suggested, it is all a question of story. Our story—the account of how the world came to be and how and why we fit into it—has been around a long time. It has shaped our emotional attitudes, stimulated our actions, and provided us with perspectives on life's problems. It has consecrated our suffering, integrated our knowledge, and offered us hope. Most of all it has provided us with a context in which our lives could function in a meaningful fashion. We . . . could awake in the morning and know where we are. We could answer the questions of our children, we could identify crime and punish criminals, everything was taken care of because the story was there. But now, between stories, we are confused. We are developing a new story and, in the process, altering much of what we think, feel, and do. What our grandchildren will accept as fact, we are in the process of discovering and creating. In this context, it is important for us to recognize we are facing a change that matters.

These transformations take on an added dimension when an individual doesn't fit into society's mainstream, for even in more static times they challenge "basic" cultural values. As Sandra says in her interview, gay and lesbian people present just such a challenge—just by being themselves. Then, on top of this, they dare to claim a spirituality that has been denied them. The breaking with these dominant fictions is poignant and courageous, indeed.

If we—gay, lesbian, bisexual, or heterosexual—blindly accept the worldview we are handed, fluid as it may be in these turbulent times, we will never know ourselves. As the men and women in this book show us, breaking away is frightening. It generally takes us through a time of incoherence when no explanation or answer seems quite right. But as we detach more deeply from the patterns we were given, we come into touch with who we really are—we listen to our inner voices instead of those outside of us. As Elaine Pagels (1979, 126) has translated the gnostic Gospel of Thomas, "If you bring forth what is within you, what you bring forth will save you. If you do not bring forth what is within you, what you do not bring forth will destroy you."

These twelve men and women offer us a rich composite portrait of this very human process of struggling with society's mythology about what it means to be gay (or lesbian or transsexual), spiritual, and religious. They show us the fiction that the accepted understanding is for them and the importance of transforming the story of their lives from someone else's biography into their own authentic autobiography. Here are twelve individuals who, to reach points of self-reconciliation, have had to confront and tear apart the myths and stories they inherited about who they were and who they would become, about the way the world works and who is good and who is bad, about how they fit into our religions and spiritual traditions. I think of Rachel, who made a sharp break from her family in terms of her values about difference (especially, Latinos and homosexuals); of Mary, who had to experience a dark night of the soul as a result of her disengagement from a conservative upbringing that could no longer sustain her; and of Gerald, who had to disconnect from a faith that had harmed him greatly until he could reconstruct and reclaim who he was.

Choosing to leave behind these predictable and stable myths and to opt for the unknown was a courageous leap of faith for these people, who knew only that there was no other choice. They rarely knew who or what, other than their own emerging sense of self, would sustain them in this time of beginning again. These men and women were fortunate in finding, sooner rather than later (in most cases), companions and communities that could help point them in an affirming direction.

Characteristics of the Dominant Fiction

Not every one of these individuals experienced exactly the same version of the culture's dominant fiction. What Vincent encountered in his rigorously Catholic home in Australia was significantly different from the values of Gerald's rural Indiana Methodist family, and both of these varied notably from the conservative missionary upbringing that Ann and Mary experienced in their households. The religion-as-life-insurance orientation of Harry's Old World parents, the rather traditional midwestern experience that Mark describes, and Rachel's eclectically Jewish home all seem to differ sharply from one another. Yet when we dig beneath the surfaces of these worldviews, we can uncover some of the most basic elements of a generalized dominant fiction. Sometimes the difference between two apparently dissimilar understandings is only one of degree.

Clearly, this composite story was not true for everyone, at least in its starkest forms. Different constellations of these beliefs and values could be found in the twelve households. But this overall philosophy was common enough to be more than an occasional occurrence or a drawn-out stereotype. In some situations the value might not have been explicitly expressed, whereas in the more conservative circumstances there were very clear statements of right and wrong, of what to believe, of who God was. These were often tempered in those families with a less fundamental understanding of the role of religion in their lives. Even when the actual content was softened, the tone of the message might have been very similar. In Harry's, Sandra's, and Denise's homes and communities, the emphatic clarity of a particular perspective (*This* is the way the world is) strikes analogous notes, even while the specific substance of their views differs strongly.

I would like to highlight four of the most pronounced aspects of the mythology that many of the families and communities adopted:

- "There are clear rules"—perhaps one right way—about how to come to God, to Christ, and, ultimately, to salvation. Sometimes this message did not come out explicitly until someone broke the rules (Vincent's innocent comment about his sister) or questioned the faith (Denise's coming out, at least from the perspective of her mother and sister). Ultimately, these individuals' lives were seen, at core, as a challenge to the homophobic claim upon which the next element of the dominant fiction is based.
- "Homosexuality is bad and certainly not part of the true way." Ann's father and Gerald's ex-wife are close and intimate family members who

painfully challenged their loved ones' self-acceptance of their sexual orientation. Perhaps Dan's situation is the only one of the twelve in which this was not a significant experience, eclipsed as reactions to his sexual orientation were by concerns about his health.

- "To be a good boy or girl, you have to believe; if you don't, you're bad. God will judge and punish you if you are bad (or act in a way that is contrary to this one right way)." Approval comes from following the given path. This, of course, is a corollary to the first two tenets, yet its judgmental quality is worth underscoring. If there were no penalty or cost to misbehaving with respect to the core theology, then the weight of the oppressiveness would be much less. The actions of Rafael's and Vincent's fathers are obvious examples.
- "Above all, keep up appearances. The neighbors should not see inside the family closet. If you don't believe, act is if you do." Consider Denise's fashion show church, Sandra's reflections on the hypocrisy of a church that could honor a man who was abusing his children, and Gerald's and Harry's descriptions of their families.

It is important to note that the dominant fictions were not always or wholly painful or damaging. Even the children of the most conservative families can point to the love and closeness that were shared by the family reading the Bible together and discussing and building beliefs. I am reminded of Mary's and Rafael's descriptions of families that were strongly connected through their times of sharing, homes where, as Rafael says, the Bible was "lived out." Indeed, if the picture thus created had been completely negative, the challenges these individuals faced in breaking from the faith would probably have been lessened. That something significant and fulfilling was keeping them connected to and wrestling with both the negative and positive aspects of their childhood traditions heightened the struggle.

Taking the Steps to Greater Integrity and Wholeness

In giving up the received "wisdom" of family and community, participants in this study evolved new models of identity and spirituality. These value and belief systems did not just appear; they were constructed over time and through profound introspection—and they continue to evolve. On the surface, they appear to be quite varied, as different as New Age Goddess worship, twelve-step philosophy, and Protestant Christianity. Yet none is either stereotypical or orthodox. In reflecting on the varieties of religious and spiritual expression that these twelve men and women have adopted, one can identify some underlying tenets and values that appear broadly (if not somewhat uniformly). As will quickly become obvious, the values overlap. I have chosen to include them even so because each statement represents a slightly different facet of the whole.

Gay men and lesbian women can have rich spiritual lives. Indeed, they can even be ministers, lay leaders, and priests within relatively mainstream traditions. They are not limited, however, by more orthodox approaches to spirituality, and wherever their paths have taken them, they may have come to view their spirituality as a crucial element, if not the cornerstone, of their lives. Every piece of this book underscores the truth of this assertion.

The spiritual journey is just that—a journey. It continues to have confusing and compelling turns, moments of illuminating growth, and level times of stagnation and calm. The snapshot nature of the previous chapters may inadvertently suggest that the participants have arrived at a spiritual endpoint, but that clearly is not so. New questions continue to arise, and old ones return with new facets. And these individuals, by and large, have found all of it to be valuable: resting in the calm of momentary clarity, boredom, or certainty as well as growing from new insights. One indication of the dynamic nature of their journey is that many, if not most, of these men and women find themselves in different places now than they were when interviewed. Vincent is no longer working in the organization in which he was training spiritual directors. Rachel feels much more settled than she was when she shared her story, having reached a point where much of the turmoil has subsided and the pieces have come together; Ann has left MCC and is active in a local American Baptist church, though not without some controversy. Mark writes, "I am much more quiet inside. I have so much serenity, but also so much more 'knowing' or wisdom about who I am and why I am here. It's funny being in this place." And, sadly, Dan has succumbed to AIDS.

There is great benefit in "living in and loving the questions," as Rafael expresses the matter so eloquently. Ambiguity has opened great doors for these individuals. It has fostered a creativity that allows them to seek new answers to old questions. They have found that living in a black-and-white world may simplify their lives, but it can also render them stultifying and psychically dead. Rafael is not the only one who has had that experience, of course; Vincent speaks of the time it is taking him to resolve major questions regarding whether it is healthier for him to live celibately in community or to be in a loving and committed relationship with another man. Both of these men are asking quite different questions now than they were years ago—and yet they are still asking questions. The mysteries do not stop as one matures spiritually. Deep questioning has been a notable element of the journey for others as well. Denise and Mary have wrestled with the issue of whether they can call themselves Christian. And Dan dealt with some very profound questions, perhaps ones that we all have at one time or another but that were more pressing to him as he confronted his own dying: Is there a God? Why does He allow AIDS? And what will happen after I die?

Movement into and out of certainty, faith, and questioning is natural. There are times of clarity *and* confusion, and these come and go naturally with life's ebbs and flows. Denise and Dan demonstrate some of this movement in the ways their questions changed between the first and second interviews—Denise to a more solid claiming of her Christian faith and Dan to a greater acceptance of his health situation. Mark has moved away from a more visible and dogmatic embracing of the teachings of Gurumayi and finds himself at a more naturally integrative place in which the various pieces flow together. And Sheila and Vincent, in particular, describe the wisdom that comes some time before their consciousness of important life changes.

The struggle itself is valuable. Not only are the questions important, but also there is significant learning that comes from going through the pain, angst, or sorrow and coming out the other side. John, whose story is not shared here, describes this kind of growth as "grace through brokenness." Sandra speaks of how rough the trip is, but that it is "definitely worth it." A few years before the interviews, Harry was on the verge of taking his own life, yet that deep bottoming out propelled him into a new stage of growth.

Several of the individuals who shared their stories in these pages wondered aloud about how their journeys might have been different had they not been gay or lesbian. Often they speculated on how the challenges of coming out and reconciling their spiritual and sexual lives presented them with opportunities they might otherwise not have had.

The understanding of a higher power, of God(dess), changes as one addresses the challenging life issues of integrating sexuality and spirituality. In most cases the language used suggests a bigger, more expansive or accepting God. Ann, Vincent, Gerald, and Rafael—all "professionally religious"—speak of this kind of metamorphosis through their own religious study and life experience; Vincent is particularly eloquent as he casts his thinking about God's love for him as a gay man: "It's really important for me to find God's choice and desire for me is to be the human person that God made me, and everything else is quite secondary." Harry and Rachel both allude to an evolution in their concepts of God that came largely through their twelve-step work. Rachel describes this movement away from the more defined conceptions of childhood through her "lava lamp" metaphor, whereas Harry makes the statement that "you can make a lampshade God . . . if that's what works for you."

The individual is an actor in her or his spiritual life. Instead of passively receiving the traditions of a religion or the teachings of a professional cleric, these men and women forged their own spirituality by *letting go* of their need to have all the answers or to control such as Rachel or Harry) and by *engaging proactively* in study (Ann, for example), experience (Mark), choice (Sandra), and reflection (Vincent).

Sharing and Listening to the Stories

As I ponder these lives, I am reminded of Alan Poe, whose story was the epilogue in George Vaillant's classic *Adaptation to Life* (1977). After having put forth a model of human development, Vaillant lifted up the story of someone in his cohort who, being gay, did not fit. This was someone whose story needed to be told—precisely because it was different from the others—but almost wasn't, again because it didn't fit. The men and women you have met in this book don't fit either, in this case society's image of what it means to be religious or spiritual.

Frequently, individual participants told me how pleased or honored they were at being asked to share their life story with me, and they thanked *me* for my time. Similarly, when I sent drafts of transcripts and chapters out, more often than not the recipient said something to me about how honored he or she felt in seeing the story in print. Some said they had never told another person in such a complete fashion about their spiritual journeys; others, who had been to spiritual directors or therapists, said that the nontherapeutic dimension of our meeting was helpful in letting them explore. The offering of one's spiritual story is an important and all too rare experience.

As a way of coming full circle, I want to return to my own story in concluding this book. In the beginning of this chapter, I suggested that my spiritual journey has been enhanced by my engagement with the lives of these folks. They have caused me to explore, challenge, and reflect on my own values and experience. They have deepened my own process of breaking with the dominant fictions that formed my conception of religion. And like many of the participants, I have become more reflective and calm at the same time that I continue to push myself gently toward new awareness.

What I have learned most intimately is the need to trust my own story and to allow it to unfold. Yet the very experience of working on this book has shown me that I cannot do that alone; I am greatly enriched by listening to the experience of others. Just as we need to trust our inner wisdom to find ourselves, we also need to learn from each other. We cannot live in the absence of each other.

I am reminded of a children's book, *The Other Way to Listen* (Baylor and Parnal 1978). In that story a young child is learning from an older man how to listen to the trees, rocks, and other parts of our natural environment. The mentor in this tale offers many reasons for our common inability to listen: we don't take enough time; we feel better than the rock, or whatever it is we are trying to listen to; we are too occupied with other distractions. Those lessons apply to our human encounters as well.

Indeed, it rarely happens that we *really* listen to others. It is so uncommon that we have to pay professionals to do that for us.

But this kind of deep and empathic listening does not come easily. We live in a world that is, by and large, deaf to our stories, especially if they do not fit the dominant fiction. We live in a world where there are some stories that are more acceptable than others: the most honored stories are white and male and heterosexual and middle or upper class. I think about what I learned in my history class: who (male) conquered whom, who discovered what, generally in Europe and postencounter America. I didn't learn much about the women who created what great ideas and writings and nurtured these men, about the fact that Plato and Michelangelo were probably gay, or, except in a passing comment, about the gifts of Africans and Asians.

The stories of others—both those that are similar to mine and those that are different—can enrich and heal me. Familiar ones help me to understand that I am not alone, a feeling that nearly every gay or lesbian child, in this study and others, has reported. They lessen my fear, support my sense of self, and affirm me as a legitimate part of the extraordinary diversity of human experience. Stories of lives that are different from my own help me to develop and expand my understanding of the world, enabling me to see that not everyone shares the values and perspectives that I take, too quickly, for granted. These stories provide me with a fuller understanding of the world and support me in becoming more empathetic and less judgmental.

On one level, these stories are about the spiritual lives of twelve gay, lesbian, and transgendered individuals. Yet on another, the book addresses the value of honoring the whole of human experience without privileging one experience above others. As those who have spoken through these chapters have said so eloquently, life is a journey that we must embrace in all its facets, colors, and tones.

APPENDIX: METHODOLOGY

FOR those who are interested in more detail about the methodology of this study, I provide this summary. The goal of this study was to understand the way coparticipants—gay men and lesbian women—describe their spiritual journeys, beginning with their own definitions of spirituality. Methodologically, this perspective led to a design in the tradition of "new paradigm research" (Reason and Rowan, 1981), "naturalistic inquiry" (Guba and Lincoln, 1981, 1982; Lincoln and Guba, 1985), and "narrative studies" (Mishler 1979, 1990). At the heart of this methodological approach was the intent to understand these individuals as they understand themselves within their life contexts. That is, I hoped to discover how the events and experience of each person's life helped shape how he or she makes sense of his or her spiritual journey. This, of course, leads to an important qualification: the findings are not systematically generalizable (in the way more traditional ones are); rather, they are *suggestive* of issues and trends that gay and lesbian people *may* experience. Indeed, it is virtually impossible to have a meaningful generalizable study when the key participants are gay men and lesbians. Facing the homophobia of society, as well as what they have internalized themselves, gay men and lesbian women are often reluctant to volunteer for studies that require them to disclose, particularly if they are not yet comfortable with their homosexuality. This reluctance means that those who do take part are more open than the average and hence not completely representative of the gay and lesbian population as a whole.

I designed and distributed surveys as a way of identifying individual participants for in-depth interviews and beginning to uncover broad movements in their spiritual journeys. These were sent to networks and organizations in the Chicago area, particularly those associations that defined themselves as religious or spiritual (such as gay and lesbian Jewish, Christian, twelve-step, and pagan groups). The questionnaires were generally made available to members through announcements at meetings and other functions. In addition, I placed two ads in Chicago gay and lesbian newspapers; interested respondents called me, and I sent surveys to them. Approximately three hundred were distributed, along with brief letters of explanation; seventy-five were completed and returned. The form asked for the respondent's definition of spirituality, the importance he or she placed on spirituality in his or her life, and the identification and brief explanation of key moments of spiritual import. When completing the survey, the participant could, if interested in being interviewed, write down his or her name and phone number; otherwise the questionnaire was anonymous.

Fifty-five individuals offered to be interviewed; in the end I selected twenty-six, seventeen men and nine women, to participate further. These people came from a variety of traditions and had come to very different places on their spiritual journeys. They were chosen for the interviews largely because of the *variety*—in age, religious affiliation, gender, life experience, and spiritual journey—and the *shared* value they placed on spirituality in their lives, as represented in the surveys. This last commonality allowed me to focus on that group of people within the gay and lesbian communities who to some degree had chosen to integrate spirituality into their lives to a significant degree. The study does not reflect how those who find spirituality less important incorporate (or not) spiritual considerations into the ways in which they make meaning for themselves.

As a group, the ages of the respondents at the time of the interviews ranged from twenty-nine to sixty-one for the men and twenty-five to fifty-one for the women. The majority (twenty-three) of respondents were white; two were Hispanic, and one was African American. Three men openly identified themselves as HIV positive. The majority of interview participants lived in the greater Chicago area, though most had grown up in other communities both within the Midwest and elsewhere. As children, all report some religious affiliation, but the sense of connection to the tradition varied widely, from merely nominal to intensely committed. The religious identification of their families of origin included a wide range of Christian denominations (including Southern Baptist, Lutheran, Roman Catholic, Methodist, Christian Scientist, Anglican, and Disciples of Christ); in addition, two individuals came from Jewish families with a strong tradition, if not current practice. At the time of the interviews, all described a significant spiritual identity. Asked about the importance of spirituality to them on a scale of 1 to 10, 35 percent of respondents said 10, 61 percent responded 6 to 9, and one individual (4 percent) answered 5. Their adult religious affiliations were quite varied (including Taoism, Siddha Yoga, Unity, Metropolitan Community Church, Goddess worship, and gay-positive Christian groups); a commitment to their original childhood religions continued for only six participants (and even these persons found gay-supportive groups within their denominations that may not be representative of the institutions as a whole). In addition, many identified twelve-step programs as the primary source of their spiritual grounding. It was a deliberate research strategy to select individuals from a broad range of possible religions so as to be able to explore a panorama of spiritual journeys and not to be bound to a single religious group. Although it is difficult to untangle the participants' deep spiritual feelings and the fluidity of their journeys, the overall movement was from more traditional childhood religions to ones that allowed them to express themselves and not hide their sexual identities.

I interviewed the respondents in their homes or, in the case of two, their offices. The interviews were open-ended, in many cases lasting up to five hours over two sessions. Common to all of the interviews were some time spent discussing the broader context of the participants' lives (family background and personal life résumé) and then a much deeper exploration of their spiritual experiences based on the events they had identified in the questionnaire. Transcripts of the interviews were coded to identify individual spiritual passages and trends as well as to allow comparisons.

The messages in the life stories collected through the surveys and interviews were substantiated in other ways as well: through (1) interviews with spiritual directors who work with gay men and lesbian women, (2) facilitation of workshops on gay spiritual journeys at conferences and training programs, (3) participation in retreats for gay men and lesbian women who are interested in deepening their spirituality, and (4) "member checking" (Guba and Lincoln, 1981), or verification of transcripts and my understanding of their interpretations of life events with research participants.

BIBLIOGRAPHY

Abalos, D. 1993. "The Sacred and Political Grounding of Multicultural and Gender-fair Education: The Creation of a New Transformative Story." Symposium conducted at DePaul University, Chicago, Illinois.

Balka, C., and A. Rose (eds.). 1989. *Twice Blessed: On Being Lesbian or Gay and Jewish.* Boston: Beacon Press.

Baylor, B., and P. Parnal. 1978. *The Other Way to Listen.* New York: Scribner's.

Benner, J. S. 1941. *The Impersonal Life.* Marina del Rey, Calif.: DeVorss.

Boswell, J. 1980. *Christianity, Social Tolerance, and Homosexuality.* Chicago: University of Chicago Press.

Boyd, M. 1986. *Gay Priest.* New York: St. Martin's Press.

———. 1991. *Amazing Grace: Stories of Gay and Lesbian Faith.* Freedom, Calif.: Crossing Press.

Cass, V. C. 1979. "Homosexual Identity Formation: A Theoretical Model." *Journal of Homosexuality* 4 (3): 219–235.

———. 1984. "Homosexual Identity: A Concept in Need of Definition." *Journal of Homosexuality* 9 (2–3): 105–126.

Coleman, E. 1982. "Developmental Stages of the Coming-out Process." *Journal of Homosexuality* 7 (2–3): 31–43.

Curb, R., and N. Monahan (eds.). 1985. *Lesbian Nuns: Breaking Silence.* Tallahassee, Fla.: Naiad Press.

Fein, S. B., and E. M. Nuehring. 1981. "Intrapsychic Effects of Stigma: A Process of Breakdown and Reconstruction of Social Reality." *Journal of Homosexuality* 7 (1): 3–13.

Fortunato, J. 1982. *Embracing the Exile.* New York: Seabury Press.

Fowler, J. 1981. *Stages of Faith.* San Francisco: Harper and Row.

———. 1984. *Becoming Adult, Becoming Christian: Adult Development and Christian Faith.* San Francisco: Harper and Row.

Fox, M. 1983. "The Spiritual Journey of the Homosexual—and Just About Everyone Else." In Robert Nugent (ed.), *A Challenge to Love: Gay and Lesbian Catholics in the Church,* 189–204. New York: Crossroad.

Glaser, C. 1988. *Uncommon Calling: A Gay Man's Struggle to Serve the Church.* San Francisco: Harper and Row.

Goffman, E. 1963. *Stigma: Notes on the Management of Spoiled Identity.* Englewood Cliffs, N.J: Prentice-Hall.

Guba, E. G., and Y. S. Lincoln. 1981. *Effective Evaluation.* San Francisco: Jossey-Bass.

———. 1982. "Epistemological and Methodological Bases of Naturalistic Inquiry." *Educational Communication and Technology Journal* 30: 233–252.

Heyward, C. 1989a. *Speaking of Christ: A Lesbian Feminist Voice.* New York: Pilgrim Press.

———. 1989b. *Touching Our Strength: The Erotic as Power and the Love of God.* San Francisco: Harper and Row.

Hunt, M. E. 1991. *Fierce Tenderness: A Feminist Theology of Friendship.* New York: Crossroad.

Lee, J. A. 1977. "Going Public: A Study in the Sociology of Homosexual Liberation." *Journal of Homosexuality* 3 (3): 49–78.

L'Engle, M. 1993. *The Rock That Is Higher: Story as Truth.* Wheaton, Ill.: Harold Shaw.

Lincoln, Y., and E. G. Guba. 1985. *Naturalistic Inquiry.* Beverly Hills, Calif.: Sage.

McNeill, J. 1987. "Homosexuality: Challenging the Church to Grow." *Christian Century* 104: 242–246.

———. 1988. *The Church and the Homosexual.* Rev. ed. Boston: Beacon Press.

———. 1995. *Freedom, Glorious Freedom.* Boston: Beacon Press.

Mead, G. H. 1962. *Mind, Self, and Society.* Chicago: University of Chicago Press.

Mishler, E. 1979. "Meaning in Context: Is There Any Other Kind?" *Harvard Educational Review* 49 (1): 1–19.

———. 1990. "Validation and Inquiry-guided Research: The Role of Exemplars in Narrative Studies." *Harvard Educational Review* 60 (4): 415–442.

Mollenkott, V. R. 1992. *Sensuous Spirituality.* New York: Crossroad.

Nelson, J. B. 1978. *Embodiment: An Approach to Sexuality and Christian Theology.* Minneapolis: Augsburg.

Nicoll, D. 1984. "Grace Beyond the Rules." In James Adams (ed.), *Transforming Work,* 3–16. Alexandria, Va.: Miles River Press.

Nugent, R. (ed.). 1983. *A Challenge to Love: Gay and Lesbian Catholics in the Church.* New York: Crossroad.

Pagels, E. 1979. *The Gnostic Gospels.* New York: Random House.

Perry, T. 1972. *The Lord Is My Shepherd and He Knows I'm Gay.* Austin, Tex.: Liberty Press.

Reason, P., and J. Rowan (eds.). 1981. *Human Inquiry: A Source Book of New Paradigm Research.* Chichester, U.K.: Wiley.

Reinharz, S. 1984. *On Becoming a Social Scientist.* New Brunswick, N.J.: Transaction Books.

Ritter, K., and C. O'Neill. 1989. "Moving Through Loss: The Spiritual Journey of Gay Men and Lesbian Women." *Journal of Counseling and Development* 68: 9–15.

———. 1992. *Coming Out Within.* San Francisco: HarperSanFrancisco.

Roberts, J. 1970. *The Seth Material.* Englewood Cliffs, N.J.: Prentice-Hall.

Roof, W. C. 1993. *A Generation of Seekers: The Spiritual Journeys of the Baby Boom Generation.* San Francisco: HarperCollins.

Rosaldo, R. 1993. *Culture and Truth: The Remaking of Social Analysis.* Rev. ed. Boston: Beacon Press.

Scanzoni, L., and V. R. Mollenkott. 1978. *Is the Homosexual My Neighbor?* San Francisco: Harper and Row.

Struzzo, J. A. 1989. "Pastoral Counseling and Homosexuality." *Journal of Homosexuality* 18 (3–4): 195–222.

Troiden, R. R. 1979. "Becoming Homosexual: A Model of Gay Identity Acquisition." *Psychiatry* 42: 363–373.

———. 1984. "Self, Self-concept, Identity, and Homosexual Identity: Constructs in Need of Definition and Differentiation." *Journal of Homosexuality* 10 (3–4): 97–110.

Vaillant, G. E. 1977. Adaptation to Life: How the Best and Brightest Came of Age. Boston: Little, Brown.

White, M. 1994. *Stranger at the Gate.* New York: Plume.

Whitehead, E. E., and J. D. Whitehead. 1982. *Christian Life Patterns.* Garden City, N.Y.: Doubleday Image.

———. 1984. *Seasons of Strength: New Visions of Adult Christian Maturing.* Garden City, N.Y.: Doubleday Image.

Williams, R. 1992. *Just as I Am: A Practical Guide to Being Out, Proud, and Christian.* New York: Crown.

Zullo, J. R., and J. D. Whitehead. 1983. "The Christian Body and Homosexual Maturing," In Robert Nugent (ed.), *A Challenge to Love: Gay and Lesbian Catholics in the Church,* 20–37. New York: Crossroad.

ABOUT THE AUTHOR

David Shallenberger is an associate professor in the School for New Learning at DePaul University. He specializes in his teaching and scholarship in issues of personal, organizational, and social transformation, especially with relationship to how we understand those who are "other." His publications have focused on the experience of gay men and lesbian women at work, at play, and in their spiritual lives and in the role of dialogue in bridging differences. He shares a home with his life partner, Harvey, and their dog Josh, cat Lucie, iguana Ilo, and rabbits Cosmo and Madeleine.